JAMES HOWARD KUNSTLER

Home from Nowhere

REMAKING OUR

EVERYDAY WORLD FOR

THE TWENTY-FIRST CENTURY

Simon & Schuster

SIMON & SCHUSTER
ROCKEFELLER CENTER
1230 AVENUE OF THE AMERICAS
NEW YORK, NY 10020

COPYRIGHT © 1996 BY JAMES HOWARD KUNSTLER
ALL RIGHTS RESERVED,
INCLUDING THE RIGHT OF REPRODUCTION
IN WHOLE OR IN PART IN ANY FORM.

SIMON & SCHUSTER AND COLOPHON ARE REGISTERED TRADEMARKS
OF SIMON & SCHUSTER INC.

DESIGNED BY KAROLINA HARRIS

MANUFACTURED IN THE UNITED STATES OF AMERICA

1   3   5   7   9   10   8   6   4   2

LIBRARY OF CONGRESS CATALOGING-IN-PUBLICATION DATA

KUNSTLER, JAMES HOWARD.
HOME FROM NOWHERE : REMAKING OUR EVERYDAY WORLD FOR THE
TWENTY-FIRST CENTURY / JAMES HOWARD KUNSTLER.
P.   CM.
INCLUDES INDEX.
1. CITY PLANNING—UNITED STATES.   2. URBAN BEAUTIFICATION—
UNITED STATES.   3. ARCHITECTURE—UNITED STATES.
4. ARCHITECTURE AND SOCIETY—UNITED STATES.   5. QUALITY
OF LIFE—UNITED STATES.   I. TITLE.
HT167.K85 1996
307.1'2—DC20   96-28066
                                                    CIP
ISBN 0-684-81196-0

For Jennifer,
my beloved ideal companion

ACKNOWLEDGMENTS

I'M very grateful to Catherine Johnson for furnishing the drawings in Chapter 5 that illustrate so gracefully the central principles of this book. Peter Katz has been a most valued colleague and sounding board through its composition. Steve Gilman graciously let me into his green world for half a year. Dan Cary endured many hours of interviews and showed me around the maw of south Florida. Andres Duany and Lizz Plater-Zyberk gave me the run of their office in Miami. Doug Kelbaugh put me up in his bright art-filled house way up on a hill in Seattle. Peter Calthorpe has been, by turns, illuminating and hilarious. Dan Solomon sets the standard for civility in principle and practice.

I'm grateful to my editor, Dominick Anfuso, his tireless assistant, Cassie Jones, and to my literary agent, Russell Galen, and his tireless assistant, Jill Grinberg, for walking this book through the labyrinth of publication.

Salutes to my colleagues in the Congress for the New Urbanism: Jonathan Barnett, Alisa Block, Kevin Borsay, Stephanie Bothwell, Catherine Brown, Charles Buki, Buff Chace, Julie Cofer, Rick Chellman, Robert Davis, Bill Dennis, Hank Dittmar, Victor Dover, Douglas Duany, Ellen Dunham-Jones, Raul Garcia, Bobby Gibbs, Buzz Goss, Tom, Vince, and Geoff Graham, Robert Gray, Elizabeth Guyton, Tony Hiss, Alan Hoffman, Xavier Iglesias, Randall Imai, Grantland Johnson, Mary Jukuri, Ken Kay, Fred Kent, Joe Kohl, Walter Kulash, Phil Langdon, Bill Lennertz, Marianna Leuschel, Bill Lieberman, Gianni Longo, Tom Low, John Massengale, Lisa McDonald, Rich McLaughlin, David Mohney, Bill Morrish, Ron Morgan, Liz Moule, Susan Mudd, Paul Murrain, Jim Musbach, Mark Nickita, John Norquist, Tony Nelessen, Neal Peirce, Steph Polyzoides, Shelly Poticha, Connie Pulcipher, Bill Rawn, Jonathan Rose, Joel Russell,

Robert Russell, Christine Saum, Mark Schimmenti, Joel Schwartz, David Sellers, Kennedy Lawson Smith, Jeff Speck, Doug Storrs, David Sucher, Anne Tate, Ramon Trias, Mike Watkins, Bill Westfall, Roger Wood, and Todd Zimmerman.

I'm indebted to Jonathan Hale, E. Michael Jones, Daniel Kemmis, and Fred Turner, for their own wonderfully insightful books.

Paul and Martha Lawrence, Robert Liberty, Elise Johnson-Schmidt, Jack Lucks, Milt Hayes, Mike Houck, Henry Turley, and Charles and Janet Whitehouse were most accommodating out there in the heartland where the rubber meets the road.

Bill Batt and Al Hartheimer of the Shalkenbach Foundation helped this particular math moron through the maze of tables and figures that define the world of property taxation.

Cheers to Tom Lewis, John Muse, and Jeff Olson here on the home front.

Thanks to Tom Toles for the excellent editorial cartoons.

A *shaynem dank* to the brotha-man, Peter Golden, for our daily telephone colloquy.

"Life in the U.S.A. gizzard had changed. Only a clown
could fail to notice.
So then, failing to notice would be a possibility."

—THOMAS MCGUANE

CONTENTS

(PETER KATZ)

PROLOGUE:

THE VICTORY DISEASE

O N E dangerously sunny morning in April 1994, six guys were sitting around the attic porch of a house in the Florida panhandle swapping theories as to why the everyday world in America had become such an abysmal mess. All of them were architects except me. It was the day after the annual Seaside Prize had been awarded and some of us were still a little woozy from the festivities. The prize recipient, Christopher Alexander, author of *A Pattern Language* and other influential books, was there. So was Andres Duany, one of the designers of Seaside, the town we were in; Witold Rybczynski, the writer of graceful books about cities and buildings; Peter Calthorpe, the California architect and planner; and Paul Murrain, a young British landscape architect. The house was one designed by Leon Krier, the architectural theorist and, it is probably accurate to say, godfather of the movement to repair the damage done to our world by Modernism. Krier was present only in the spirit of the house, but his was a palpable presence.

Calthorpe had the floor. Lean and urbane, Calthorpe, forty-five, was in a humorously expansive mood. He proposed two theories. The first was The Stroke Theory. World War Two, he said, was so traumatic that it had caused the same kind of damage to western civilization that a cerebral hemorrhage can wreak on a human mind. It had made the advanced nations of the world lose some of their most important abilities, to forget their own history and culture, as a stroke victim loses his powers of speech, his memories, the particulars of his education. All the ghastly office buildings, banal dwellings, crappy commercial structures, and other common architectural garbage of our everyday world, Calthorpe proposed, were like the inchoate squawkings and bleatings of a stroke victim who had lost the ability to express himself. This theory met with such general approbation that Calthrope went on to propose a second.

This was The Stupor Theory. World War Two, he said, was the high tide of our fathers' generation. All these American men in the full bloom of youth had marched off to a terrible war against manifest evil and won a decisive victory for democracy and decency. In the process, many of them had the adventures of a lifetime—moments of heroism, romances with grateful foreign girls, days and nights enjoying the spoils of liberated castles, profound friendships with army buddies, and, finally, the worshipful reception of the folks back home, with a sweet package of emoluments upon return to civilian life, including free college tuition and low-interest home mortgage loans.

These young men, Calthorpe went on, were immediately absorbed into postwar corporate life, fitting well into large hierarchical organizations. Corporate life was familiarly regimented like the army, where so many of them had lately enjoyed their heroic exploits. They knew how to give and follow orders, and patiently await promotion.

The downside was that their greatest adventures were over, that life on the commuter platform with hundreds of other guys in gray flannel suits was in some elemental way an awful comedown. What was there to look forward to? Selling ten million units a month of Oaties breakfast cereal for decades to come? How did this compare to drinking seventy-year-old cognac in an Alsatian castle with a pistol strapped to your leg and a seventeen-year-old French cutie in your lap, having spent the day slaughtering Nazis? Of course, there would be the compensations of family life, a nice house in those new suburbs, a shiny new car, the fabulous panoply of washers, driers, Mixmasters, TVs, hi-fi's, and power mowers, autumn days teaching Skippy to throw a football, winter nights at the school auditorium watching Princess dance in her toe shoes, summer evenings presiding over the backyard barbecue, and . . . wait . . . was that all? Is that where it ended? Flipping hamburgers and wieners in a joke-bedizened apron and a clownish chef's hat?

Well, yes, for a lot of them. This was what life had to offer after the stupendous adventure of World War Two. A whole generation of heroes slipped into a permanent semicoma, soothing their boredom and anomie with heavy doses of hard liquor—their beloved martinis—and living out the rest of their days in an alcoholic fog. This, Calthrope said, explained why the world they built for us—the suburban sprawl universe—was so incoherent, brutal, ugly, and depressing: *they didn't care about what they were building. They were drunk most of the time, in a stupor.* (This also, he added with wicked parenthetical glee, explained feminism: a whole generation of daughters raised by emotionally remote, perpetually plastered fathers.)

These theories admittedly veer into burlesque, but there is still much to admire in them. The Stupor Theory especially comports with the phenomenon known among historians as The Victory Disease, the condition in which a nation's military triumph carries within it the demoralizing seeds of its own later destruction. In *The Geography of Nowhere* I argued that the building of suburbia as a replacement for towns and cities in the United States was just such a self-destructive act. I attempted to describe the tragic process. I argued that the living arrangement Americans now think of as *normal* is bankrupting us economically, socially, ecologically, and spiritually. I identified the physical setting itself—the cartoon landscape of car-clogged highways, strip malls, tract houses, franchise fry pits, parking lots, junked cities, and ravaged countryside—as not merely the symptom of a troubled culture but in many ways a primary cause of our troubles. I stated that all reasonable indications suggest we will not be able to continue this pattern of living, whether we like suburbia or not, and I sketched some of the remedies that were then just beginning to present themselves.

I wrote *The Geography of Nowhere* as a layman attempting to make sense of a national condition that seems at best complicated and at worst incomprehensible. My approach was that of a citizen-observer, not of a design professional. It seemed to me that the country was full of normal people, including plenty of intelligent ones, who were distressed by their surroundings but unable to articulate their feelings. My intention was to give shape to those feelings, to turn inchoate emotion into coherent thought. Since then I've come to understand one of the chief impediments preventing us from comprehending the tragedy of our everyday environment: American culture is very abstract. Suburbia fails us in large part because it is so abstract. It's an idea of a place rather than a place. The way you can tell is because so many places in this country seem like no place in particular, and a lack of particularity is the earmark of abstraction.

Our knowledge of cities is increasingly abstract, too. Fewer and fewer Americans have any experience living in good ones, or in any city at all— good, bad, or mediocre. Historically, American cities at their best have left much to be desired, an issue of great significance which I will discuss further. In any case, few American cities today even function in any normal sense and many are virtually empty shells.* What Americans know about city life these days often turns out to be secondhand or worse. We read in the newspapers and magazines about urban war zones we would never dare to visit. Our images of the city come from cop shows and rap videos on MTV or old Warner Brothers gangster movies. It happens that I grew up in Manhattan, in one of the few fully functioning cities in America, so this book includes a discussion of that singular place (Chapter 11) and its meaning vis-a-vis the rest of America.

Because our notions about place have become so abstract, our remedies for the problems of place have tended to be equally abstract. The "urban renewal" schemes of the previous generation stand as disastrous abstract fantasies that managed to rebuke nearly everything known about human behavior and embedded in civic design up to that period. On the more ordinary level, we have today's remedies for the depressing banality of the suburbs: a fake fanlight window in a tract house is the supposed solution for the problem of a house designed and built without affection for nobody in particular. A Victorian street light is the supposed cure for overly wide, arbitrarily curvy streets that are poorly defined by tract houses. This book seeks to identify those failures, and it necessarily contains a good measure of ridicule, which is the inescapable fate of the ridiculous.

But it also attempts to investigate the nature of successful design. I believe that certain physical relationships work well because they are consistent with human psychological needs that are probably universal and haven't changed over time. A consideration of these issues leads ineluctably to the condition we call beauty, which for too long has been dismissed as an insoluble mystery of "taste," or worse, relegated by the academic avant-garde to the dumpster of irrelevance. When intellectuals take the position that beauty is a subject beneath discussion, it seems to me

---

*A noontime stroll I took on a regular weekday in downtown Des Moines in April 1995 comes to mind, the streets unpopulated, the desolation complete. It made an Edward Hopper painting look like Mardi Gras.

that a culture is in real trouble. I wish to readmit the discussion of beauty to intellectual respectability, and in Chapter 4 I will attempt to do so in the context of what used to be called civic art.

I wrote *The Geography of Nowhere* without any formal training in architecture and town planning, which should not be taken as an apology or an excuse but as a plain statement of fact. In the period since then, I have had the chance to move around the United States, to see more places, and to consort with many architects, planners, and designers who very graciously undertook to fill the holes in my education—a process hardly completed. I still write as a citizen-observer, but a better informed one than the last time around. For instance, I can now state with more precision the historical and cultural origin of the suburban house, and why it is such a problem for us. If I seem to retread some ground in this book, it is either to furnish a coherent historical bridge between points of discussion, or to bring a fresh angle to a subject touched on in *The Geography of Nowhere* and inadequately treated there. The heart of this book is an argument for raising our standards in respect to our ordinary surroundings, along with some very explicit technical suggestions for accomplishing it.

Many of the people I have met between these two books are working to design a human habitat of much better character and quality than the mess we're actually stuck with. They even incorporated themselves into an architectural reform movement called the Congress for the New Urbanism (CNU) and held a series of meetings around the nation.* The New Urbanism aims to reinstate the primacy of the public realm in American life. In the chapters ahead I will discuss the nature and the meaning of the public realm in detail. The physical form that the New Urbanists envision is at once deeply familiar and revolutionary: the mixed-use neighborhood in increments of villages, towns, and cities. It is familiar because it is the way America built itself through most of our history, really until the end of World War Two. It is a physical form that complies exactly with many Americans' most cherished notions about our nation at its best. And yet the New Urbanism is revolutionary because it starkly contradicts the world of suburban sprawl that has become the real setting for our national

*See *The New Urbanism: Toward an Architecture of Community*, by Peter Katz (New York: McGraw-Hill, 1994), a fine book illustrating the movement's principles and an array of projects by its proponents.

life, and the source of so many of our woes. In doing so, the New Urbanism contradicts most established rules and methods for building things,
particularly our zoning laws.

This movement, in my view, is one of the most hopeful developments
on the national scene. I share the belief of its members that if we can repair the physical fabric of our everyday world, many of the damaged and
abandoned institutions of our civic life may follow into restoration. If
nothing else, I think we stand to regain places to live and work that are
worthy of our affection. And since a great many good things proceed from
affection, I believe some of our desired social aims might naturally follow.

This book is not a technical manual, however. The fields of architecture
and town planning have their own professional associations, including the
CNU, and contain plenty of agitators working for technical reform within
them. My aim is the popular consensus, the bond of agreement between
ordinary citizens about what is good or bad, acceptable or unacceptable.
The old towns and old buildings that we cherish are great not necessarily
because architects were so much better trained in 1848 or 1908—though
it may be so—but because a consensus demanded better work, and especially work more respectful of the public realm. This book seeks to restore
those standards at the popular level. Our great-grandfathers didn't have to
argue about the basic need to embellish buildings in order to nourish the
human spirit. The need to do so was assumed, agreed upon on a broad popular basis. In terms of the larger cycles of history, I believe we are ready to
revive standards of work and orders of design that might be described as
classical—as in coherent principles based on what is already known about
human needs, in distinction to the despotic experiments conducted by
heroic-genius-artist-revolutionaries on human guinea pigs that have characterized the architecture and planning of our age. Every age considers itself modern. It is the special ignominious fate of Modernism to have
chosen a name for itself so inanely inhospitable to the judgment of history.

Finally, we arrive at the recognition that civilization needs an honorable
dwelling place, and that the conditions of making that place ought to depend on what is most honorable in our nature: on love, hope, generosity,
and aspiration.

WHO WE ARE

"It's morning in America!"
—POLITICAL ADVERTISEMENT

H I S T O R Y doesn't believe anybody's advertising. History doesn't care whether nations rise or fall. History is merciless and life is tragic. Human consciousness begins with the notion that there is a beginning, a middle, and an end to all things. This unhappy consciousness attends all human endeavor, and it has at least one consolation, as the playwright Samuel Beckett once observed: "Nothing is funnier than unhappiness."

The United States is the wealthiest nation in the history of the world, yet its inhabitants are strikingly unhappy. Accordingly, we present to the rest of mankind, on a planet rife with suffering and tragedy, the spectacle of a clown civilization. Sustained on a clown diet rich in sugar and fat, we have developed a clown physiognomy. We dress like clowns. We move about a landscape filled with cartoon buildings in clownmobiles, absorbed in clownish activities. We fill our idle hours enjoying the canned antics of professional clowns. We perceive God to be an elderly comedian. Death, when we acknowledge it, is just another pratfall on the boob tube. *Bang! You're dead!*

Unhappiness is manifest at every level of the national scene. From big city to the remotest rural trailer court, our civic life is tattered and frayed. Unspeakable crimes occur in the most ordinary places. Government can't fulfill its most basic role in guaranteeing the public safety. Our schools, in many cases, barely function. The consensus of what constitutes decent behavior fractured with the social revolutions of the 1960s and has not been restored. Anything goes.

Community, as it once existed in the form of places worth caring about, supported by local economies, has been extirpated by an insidious corporate colonialism that doesn't care about the places from which it extracts its profits or the people subject to its operations. Without the underpinning of genuine community and its institutions, family life has predictably disintegrated, because the family alone cannot bear all the burdens and perform all the functions of itself and the community. Spouses cannot fulfill each other's every need and marriages implode under the presumption that they ought to be able to. Children cannot acquire social skills unless they circulate in a real community among a variety of honorably occupied adults, not necessarily their parents, and are subject to the teachings and restraints of all such adults.

We have used our unprecedented wealth and technical ability to construct a massive edifice designed to deny and confute life's essentially tragic nature, and this has made us ridiculous. That is why, for example, this sign ☺ is now recognized as the most inane cultural symbol ever produced by a supposedly great civilization. We're struck by the boldness and simplicity of its utterly false message.

Everything we love and care about in this world is subject to the tragedy of eventually being lost to us, including our very selves. The easy response to this terrible condition is to create a world full of things that are not worth caring about. That is precisely what we have done in the United States. This is why the suburban housing subdivisions are so sickening in their endless, banal replication. They deny and confute the tragic nature of life because they are places not worth caring about. When a hurricane blows away sixty condo clusters along the Florida Coast, nobody outside Dade County sheds a tear for what is lost, and not because other Americans are heartless, but because people of even modest intelligence can tell whether places are worth caring about, though perhaps they can't say why. In the heartland, mobile home parks are commonly referred to as "tornado bait." Nobody could say that about an Italian hill town and get a laugh, not even an American.

It is the effort that human beings make to put the marks of skill and love on the artifacts they leave behind that ennobles us in the face of life's tragic nature, and lifts us close to the domain of angels. To behold a beautiful building, or a beautiful painting, or a beautiful garden made by someone now dissolved into time, and to be moved by these things, is to experience a residue of skill and love expended in the face of certain destruction, and this once again speaks to the tragic nature of the human predicament.

It is not an accident that the entertainment industry is the one major enterprise at which no other country has been able to overtake us. No other civilized country is so preoccupied minute by minute with make-believe, with pretending, with fantasy. We demand fantasy in order to distract ourselves from the reality of life's tragic nature, and since reality tends to be insistent, we must keep the TVs turned on at all waking hours and at very high volume. Yet fantasy is ultimately less satisfying than reality, and only deepens our hunger for the authentic.

We use the term *theme park* as a common pejorative because we understand that theme parks' stock-in-trade is the substitution of the fake for the authentic, and many of us find this degrading. We look at a highway strip mall designed to look like a bunch of nineteenth century barns linked together and we say disdainfully that it has that "theme park look." Nobody's fooling us. A tract of houses tarted up with Victorian gingerbread has that "theme park look" because the decoration doesn't do a thing to make the development an authentic town. It still doesn't have public gathering places, stores, offices, workshops, residences for people of different income, or any of the other necessary ingredients. They're all zoned out.

When the Disney Corporation proposes to build an American history theme park amidst the Civil War battlefields of northern Virginia, it seems a sort of obscenity. Theme park, after all, is an updated term for what used to be known as an amusement park. Battlefields have traditionally been perceived as sacred places, to be regarded with a certain awe and solemnity in memory of the tragic deeds that occured on them. Disney, therefore, proposes to sever the distinction between the sacred and the amusing. So we envisage a depiction of the battle of Bull Run, where 20,000 Americans lost their lives, in the spirit of "Pirates of the Caribbean" and the stomach begins to quiver.

We long for enchantment in life, for the moments when we can feel close to the angels, but such enchantment need not derive wholly and exclusively from illusion. That is the tragic falsehood of Hollywood, which has infected every layer of our culture. It is particularly false respecting the issues of place, of the everyday environments where we live and work, seek love, raise our children, struggle to accomplish things, commune with our friends, grow old, and pass away. The sort of enchantment I speak of is the feeling of being in love with the world we inhabit, akin, I think, to what Saul Bellow meant when he said that love was *gratitude for being*. These are the feelings that derive from what is best in our natures, in their interaction with nature in general—for instance, the way we feel when twilight softly settles on an American small town on a summer night. Watching a movie of this only approximates the real thing, as watching a soap opera day in and day out only approximates having real relationships with real people.

So it is with the places where we spend our days on earth. An approximation of a neighborhood or a town is not enough—and, tragically, that is what every American *housing subdivision* is. We long for the real thing, but we have lost the means to provide it for ourselves. An office park is not a park, and we know it. What's more, we feel cheated knowing it, and going to the office park day after day chips away at our dignity until after a few years have gone by, our sensibilities are too worn down to register the discomfort of this loss as something more than a vague itch.

All our efforts to nullify life's tragic nature have paradoxically led us into deeper unhappiness. What we have done to the physical fabric of our country finally is not an illusion at all but a genuine tragedy. We have come close to making civilized life impossible in the United States.

A REASONABLE HATRED OF CITIES

You needn't look much further than our national character to understand why we created suburbia. The anti-urban bias in our history is real, and for pretty good reasons. Nearly everything about the rise of cities in America was a kind of industrial nightmare. Places like Chicago, Detroit, Cleveland, St. Louis were the creatures of industrial expansion in the period 1830 to 1930. They had no prior existence (and in some cases not much of a subsequent existence). There is no medieval Cleveland underlying the present city. When the Renaissance was in full swing, Detroit was a bosky dell resounding with birdsong and the cries of the Potawatomi. Our cities arose out of wilderness practically overnight. Chicago grew like an algae bloom from a frontier outpost of a few thousand souls to a colossus of nearly two million in fifty years. You could leave town for a month and not recognize your neighborhood on return. These cities were laid out strictly for the convenience of real estate speculators with hardly a thought to civic art. They were then built, and the pieces assembled within them, to accommodate industry of increasingly large scale, and large-scale industry was not a pretty thing. It invariably defeated the human scale, and in doing so, it degraded the human spirit. In the popular imagination, it always carried connotations of hell on earth. Americans' historical experience of city life has been of a bleak, relentless, noisy, squalid, smoky, smelly, explosively expanding, socially unstable, dehumanizing sinkhole of industrial foulness congested with ragtag hordes of gabbling foreigners.

When thinking about these things, we ought to remember that industrialism was (and still is) a historical experiment whose outcome is as yet unknown, that it is laden with unanticipated consequences, and that it is not necessarily synonymous with all that is implied by the word civilization. The recognition that new technology did not guarantee human moral progress would prove to be one of the major disillusionments of the twentieth century. Much of what makes European cities tolerable are remnants of the pre-industrial ages, particularly the public spaces associated with history—the ancient civic plazas, the market and cathedral squares, the military parade grounds, the palaces and playgrounds of the aristocracy—and the agreeable human scale of all these old things. The streets of these cities often have the intimacy and meandering character of ancient cowpaths, which many once were. Where heroic redevelopment has since intervened, such as Haussmann's redesign of Paris in the 1860s, even the new monumental boulevards were detailed to accommodate human spiritual needs as well as vehicular traffic. Special attention was paid to the proportioning of buildings, visual focal points, tree planting, the creation of parks, and other devices of civic art.

Within each nation or city-state, Europeans enjoyed a level of cultural agreement lacking in America. Many issues concerning how to build things were settled matters of tradition, and traditions, by definition, didn't have to be continually reinvented or debated. The Dutch had one way of making a roof and the Sienese another, lending visual harmony and cultural distinctiveness to their towns, and both methods were time-tested. The same was true for building materials, colors, and decorative features. In America, the main point of cultural agreement was that cities should serve industry, and our approach to problem solving in other departments of town planning has often been improvisational, even where excellent solutions already existed. For instance, Europeans have known for centuries how to treat a riverfront so that it equitably serves both commerce and public enjoyment. In America, urban riverfronts almost never included any provision for public amenity and still don't. The river-bank is commonly the site of a freeway, leaving our cities cut off from their rivers.

As late as the third quarter of the nineteenth century, continental Europe had barely begun to industrialize by American standards. France, Germany, Italy, and Austria were still nations of small-scale artisans, merchants, and peasant farmers. Europeans had a memory of city life antecedent to industrialism, and they associated it in their imaginations with many of the best things that life had to offer. To them, the city was synonymous with civilization. Europe's one true industrial behemoth of the nineteenth century, England, made a disgusting mess out of her cities, but consoled herself with the romance of operating a colorful, far-flung empire, much as America compensated for its urban squalor with the romance of a vast, beckoning frontier.

There came a brief, anomalous period between 1893 and 1918 when Americans consciously decided to make something better of their cities and towns. A generation of architects led by Daniel Burnham, Charles McKim, and Richard Morris Hunt, turning back to Europe for ideas, rediscovered the notion of civic space and the principles of civic art, and stood dazzled before them as though they'd found the missing ingredient in American life—which, to an extent, they had. The result was the City Beautiful movement, dated precisely from 1893 because that was the year of the Columbian Exposition at Chicago. Through the device of the Exposition this group of architects and planners alerted ordinary Americans to the strange and exhilarating idea that public space was something other than the scraps left over from private development, that it could be deliberately shaped, artfully decorated, and put to spiritually nourishing use.*

The City Beautiful movement, therefore, represented an important shift in the broad popular consensus about what city life meant. And that consensus furnished the political support for action to make our cities better than they had been. For twenty-five years America indulged in the great public building spree of the City Beautiful movement, anticipating a coming golden century of national glory, racing to create an architecture worthy of that vision. Almost all of America's great public places and finest public structures date from this optimistic era, among them the New York Public Library, the San Francisco City Center, many state capitols, most of our great museums, and Burnham's redesign of the Great Mall in Washington, D.C. These efforts coincided with the heyday of the electric streetcar, a device that liberated the poor and middle classes from the insularity of their own neighborhoods, giving them access to all parts of the city, and particularly to its symbolic and economic heart: downtown. It was a time of the American city's greatest centrality.

The reality of the twentieth century, as we now sadly know, did not jibe with that shimmering, hopeful vision of a golden age. In fact, it got off to a very rocky start with World War One. If we accept World War Two in Calthorpe's metaphor as a sort of international cerebral hemorrhage, then World War One might be viewed as western civilization's first suicide attempt. It scared the hell out of Europe and spawned a generation of political maniacs there. Since none of the carnage of World War One took place on our soil, the war seemed to make America merely very cynical. With its end in 1918, the idealistic attempt to create spatial unity and public amenity in American cities ceased. The idealistic City Beautiful movement rolled over and died.

In its place commenced an effort to impose the automobile and its needs on urban space. Henry Ford had introduced his Model T in 1907 and by the end of World War One he had perfected the assembly line method of

---

*That is, in forms other than as a large, romantically landscaped park—which served a quite different purpose as a symbolic rural preserve within the growing enormity of the urban fabric. (The origin and significance of Olmsted's Central Park will be found in Chapter 11.)

production to the degree that his car was now affordable to the mass of Americans, including even his own factory workers. Unlike railways and electric streetcars, which had promoted the centrality of the city, the automobile, with its awkward need for parking space and tendency to clog streets, promoted the opposite: a centrifugal flinging outward away from the center. And when the program for imposing cars on the city proved problematical, a new consensus was quickly reached to give up on cities altogether and erect a substitute for them in the hinterlands.

THE AMERICAN DREAM

A constant counterpoint in American history to the reasonable hatred of industrial cities has been the notion of its antidote: the individual dwelling place in the natural landscape. The image had such potency because it was more than an idle wish, it was always a real option. In Europe, all rural land had long been divided up, often in the form of enormous private domains, with ultimate title held by monarchs or the church. Ordinary people not already in possession of land as yeomen had little hope of acquiring a scrap of their own. In America, a seemingly endless supply of undeveloped land in newly incorporated territories belonged to both nobody and everybody, and the federal government organized a rational scheme for distributing ownership to all comers as quickly as possible for next to nothing in payment. The lone settlement in the woods was not a myth but an established fact, reenacted a million times by real people. One can hardly conceive of a system more conducive to an extreme form of individualism and less supportive of any notion of the common good. Yet it remained the popular alternative to the problems posed by the industrial city. The larger factories grew, and the grimmer cities became, the more romantic and desirable a dwelling in the natural landscape seemed.

We are not necessarily who we think we are as a people. American democracy contains strange illusions and paradoxes. The motive force behind it is not a drive for equality but rather a mechanism enabling some citizens to excel while enabling others to fail, that is, a drive toward *in*equality. The saving grace of the process is that most citizens fall somewhere in between, because life is full of surprises, dilemmas, hazards, pitfalls, misfortunes, afflictions, vicissitudes, calamities, and amazing reversals—the equipment of tragedy—and nobody gets out of this world alive.

The great leveler turns out to be not the U.S. Constitution but the grim reaper.

Rather than being a classless society, we are very much a class-conscious society, perhaps class-obsessed. It is probably in the nature of human intelligence that we tend to divide ourselves into social categories. The more complex our societies, the more criteria we bring to bear on the question and the more increments of status we perceive. The late Soviet system, for instance, supposedly based on the abolition of class, probably had more subtle distinctions of bureaucratic rank and privilege than the British peerage at the height of empire. American democracy has hardly vanquished the human tendency to make social distinctions. No people on earth brag so much about their equality and no people spend so much time and energy trying to prove that they are better than the next guy.

We like to think that democracy is the glue that holds our society together. Paradoxically, it may act more as a centrifugal force flinging us away from the center and driving us apart, much the same way that the automobile operated on the city—so it is easy to understand why the automobile suits the American spirit so perfectly. In our current national folklore, democracy exists supposedly as a system solely devoted to promoting individual liberty, the right to be left alone to pursue happiness in one's own way, to do whatever we please *as* we please. Any connection to some idea of the public interest is now severed. This is the position of today's "property rights" extremists, who wish to abolish all attempts to regulate land use. It seems to me that such an extraordinary view of democracy is essentially absurd and cannot sustain communities. Rather, it undermines communities and the institutions they contain, since democracy only has meaning as an organizing principle for the group, not as a shibboleth for individuals living in a vacuum. The current popular conception of democracy, therefore, finds physical expression not in neighborhoods, towns, or cities but only in individual homesteads. This is the meaning behind the other monster of our reigning zeitgeist: the American Dream, the antidote to the industrial city.

There are really two distinct models for the homestead in the natural landscape—though they have become increasingly muddled in the popular imagination. The first model is the lone settlement in the wilderness, the pioneer and his family living in a stump-filled clearing. For the sake of simplicity, let's call it the *little cabin in the woods*. The second model is the English manor house in the park.* Both models came to America early in our history and both of them have enjoyed a long run of active service in the ever-mutating national mythology.

The pilgrim settlers of Massachusetts lived in replica medieval villages.† It was not until the pressures of population growth combined with the Stuart restoration's overthrow of the Puritan oligarchy in the late 1600s that scattered settlement became possible, and then it quickly became the predominate mode. The log cabin is said to have originated in Delaware with a settlement of Swedes. It was the logical method for erecting a temporary house in places where trees were abundant and sawmills not yet established. So when land west of the Appalachians opened to settlement after the Revolutionary War, the log cabin became the universal artifact of the frontier. (The annals of the Ohio Valley mention log courthouses, too.) The *little cabin in the woods* became a staple of popular culture in its then rudimentary forms: the comic stage plays and wildly successful published exploits of Davy Crockett, the winning presidential campaign of William Henry Harrison (born in a log cabin), the images of Thomas Cole and his fellow landscape painters, and the hagiography of Abe Lincoln.

The southern plantation house is the English manor in a park with a few minor alterations. Some southern pioneers skipped the log cabin phase of settlement altogether and set directly to raising a manor out of stark wilderness, bringing the whole kit of tools necessary with them, as well as the labor pool. William Faulkner depicts such a scene vividly in his novel *Absalom, Absalom!* A mysterious stranger named Sutpen rides into the Mississippi hamlet of Jefferson one summer morning in 1833. He buys a 100-square-mile tract of land outside of town, vanishes, and returns two months later in a covered wagon with a French architect at his side and twenty African slaves fresh off the boat. They set up a brick kiln, a saw, and

---

*The English manor in a park is merely the Anglo-Saxon version of the country villa, which has existed in some form since biblical times. The Romans really refined the idea as a more-or-less permanent mode of life. The English manor contains elements derived from the medieval castle.

†For a more complete overview of the composition of the Puritan village, and a closer look at the Puritans' theological preoccupations and confused notions about the wilderness, see *The Geography of Nowhere*.

a planer, and go to work. The locals sometimes pack lunch and ride out to "Sutpen's Hundred" on horseback to

"watch his mansion rise, carried plank by plank and brick by brick out of the swamp where the clay and timber waited. . . . [They] worked together, plastered over with mud against the mosquitoes and . . . distinguishable one from another by [Sutpen's] beard and eyes alone and only the architect resembling a human creature because of the French clothes which he wore with a sort of invincible fatality until the day after the house was completed. . . . Unpainted and unfurnished, without a pane of glass or a doorknob or a hinge in it, twelve miles from town and almost that far from any neighbor, it stood for three years more surrounded by its formal gardens and promenades, its slave quarters and stables and smokehouses; wild turkey ranged within a mile of the house and deer came light and colored like smoke and left delicate prints in the formal beds where there would be no flowers for four years yet."

The fetish of the southern plantation house was further adumbrated in movies like *Gone With the Wind*, and half-baked versions of Scarlett O'Hara's Tara now stand replicated in countless suburban subdivisions around the United states.

When, around the mid-1800s, it first became desirable and possible to build large-scale suburbs outside of the increasingly disgusting industrial cities, these two models—the manor in a park and the cabin in the woods—emerged as the basic building units. They soon metamorphosed into a sort of amalgam, neither one nor the other, or sometimes a confused inversion—the log cabin in a park, or the manor in the wilderness. (An especially weird permutation took shape in W. W. Durant's "great camps" of the Adirondacks. Built for plutocrats like William Henry Vanderbilt and J. P. Morgan, and sited at the center of vast and remote forest estates of several thousand acres, these houses were virtually log castles. It was the fashion to carry the wilderness theme to the hilt inside, with "rustic" furniture made of peeled logs, twigs, and birch bark, and whole herds of stuffed beasts looming on the walls.) As Americans began the experiment of attempting to create whole communities out of individual country villas, the earliest planned suburbs such as Llewellyn Park, in West Orange, New Jersey (1853), and Riverside, outside Chicago (1869), express the difficulty of trying to reconcile these two contradictory ideas. The fetish of the lone dwelling would prove to have strange and enduring consequences for American society into our time.

Llewellyn Park and Riverside can be described as *romantic* suburbs because they were designed to project the allure of the wilderness without its wildness. The houses were deployed on large lots landscaped to simulate little clearings in the woods. Yet the houses themselves were mansions by today's standards, not rude cabins, and the "wilderness" was an artificial park. Each house was intended to stand in splendid isolation, without relation to the others. Besides houses, these suburbs contained little of the usual components of a real town—shops, workplaces, hotels, restaurants, theaters, or housing for tradespeople. This equipment remained in the city.

The railroad was the enabling mechanism. Both Llewellyn Park and Riverside were made possible by commuter links to New York and Chicago. In time, small commercial nodes formed around the commuter depots of railroad suburbs like these, though in the years before World War Two major retail and everything else remained centralized in the city, supported by an elaborate delivery network of railway express agencies. From its inception the chief characteristic of the American suburb was not of an organically real town, nor a civic place, but a place of fantasy and escape. The notion of life it expressed had the further psychological repercussion of enabling those who lived in such suburbs to believe that they could conduct their industrial activities without suffering any of the unpleasant consequences these activities typically entailed. Along with the suburb itself as a physical artifact, this notion of freedom from the consequences of one's social behavior has also persisted in the mental life of Americans. If anything, it has only become more gross and elaborate over time, so that today millions of Americans are employed in all sorts of destructive enterprises—killing other people's local economies, wrecking towns and cities with inappropriate "development," paving over rural landscapes, ruining ecosystems—without the dimmest sense of remorse or responsibility, returning at night to their homesteads in an artificial wilderness, and the blue light of an electronic hearth with its diverting and reassuring imagery.

As time went on, and ever-larger classes of Americans evacuated the cities, the basic suburban pattern of residential enclaves without the other equipment of civic life persisted and multiplied. The addition of the automobile to the suburban program aggravated its imbalances, ultimately to a grotesque degree. (More about that later.) It is interesting to note, though, how the concept of the American Dream mutated from a set of ideas about liberty to the more explicit notion of a suburban house as the material reward for sacrifice and honest toil. That mutation occurred in the years after World War Two, spurred by our sudden stupendous affluence and egged on by the advertising industry, especially by its operatives in televised political campaigning. Precisely when the suburban equation finally began to fail in the 1980s, when the average price of the suburban house began to exceed the ability of the average family to buy one, this notion of the American Dream mutated once again from a reward into an *entitlement*, something that the American Way of Life owed to the average citizen as a kind of birthright.

I began this chapter by saying that history is merciless. It is also perverse and ironic. History's first rule is that everything changes. Human beings, on the other hand, like to believe that good things should last forever. When they discover the truth, they often feel cheated, like children who discover there is no Santa Claus. This is the case with the extraordinary postwar economy that boomed and boomed and allowed Americans to build the hugely expensive drive-in fantasy world that is the mature auto suburb. That economy is now fading into history. Perversely, as soon as its demise became manifest, Americans began to insist that they were entitled to it and all its goodies forever, because . . . well, because *we're number one!* As a result, we now find a strong undercurrent of political grievance among those who once were termed middle class and who suddenly realize that the American Dream in the form of a suburban house with two cars has been denied to them. This sense of grievance is apt to build and grow uglier as suburbia and its trappings become increasingly unaffordable to an ever-broader class of Americans.

The idea of a modest dwelling all our own, isolated from the problems of other people, has been our reigning metaphor of *the good life* for a long time. It must now be seen for what it really is: an antisocial view of human existence. I don't believe we can afford to keep pretending that life is a never-ending episode of *Little House on the Prairie.* We are going to have to develop a different notion of the good life and create a physical form that accommodates it.

Fortunately, history can instruct us. Many of the forms we shall need for our continued existence were invented in past ages and are still used in other advanced societies—for instance, authentic, fully equipped towns and cities. The knowledge needed to re-create these things can be retrieved from the cultural garbage barge where we tossed it a few decades ago. Many of these forms have their recognizable American prototypes, so that the process will not be a matter of imposing weird foreign patterns on American life. A few lucky Americans still live in real, fully equipped neighborhoods and towns—though they tend to be very expensive places because under our present rules for new construction they cannot be replicated, and the law of supply and demand is still in force.

The knowledge needed to build coherent neighborhoods and towns is waiting to be put to use as a replacement for the continuing spread of suburbia. The movement is already under way to accomplish this transformation. Like any challenge to the status quo, it is meeting lots of resistance. Much of this resistance is mindless and some of it is sinister. We have the ability to restore the dwelling place of our civilization. The more difficult question is: do we have the will to be civilized?

2

THE PUBLIC REALM AND THE COMMON GOOD

I T is easier to understand why Walt Disney's Magic Kingdom is such a big hit in America after visiting the latest version of it outside Paris, France, where the enterprise is a gigantic flop (over $1 billion in losses the first two years of operation). Americans love Disney World back home because the everyday places where they live and go about their business are so dismal that Disney World seems splendid in comparison.

American cities are dismal. The majority of American small towns have become dismal. Of course, those two types of places represent America as it developed before World War Two, and their current state must be understood as one of abandonment and dereliction. The newer suburban subdivisions are dismal, too, in their own unique way, as are the commercial highway strips, the malls, the office parks, and the rest of the auto-centric equipment of the human habitat. Their architectural shortcomings aside, these places are dismal because the public realm that binds them together is degraded, incoherent, ugly and meaningless. In case the term *pub-*

lic realm seems vague or mystifying, I shall attempt to define it with some precision.

The public realm is the connective tissue of our everyday world. It is made of those pieces of terrain left between the private holdings. It exists in the form of streets, highways, town squares, parks, and even parking lots. It includes rural or wilderness landscape: stretches of the seacoast, national forests, most lakes and rivers, and even the sky (though "air rights" are sometimes bought and sold in the cities). The public realm exists mainly outdoors because most buildings belong to private individuals or corporations. Exceptions to this are public institutions such as libraries, museums, zoos, and town halls, which are closed some hours of the day, and airports and train stations, which may be open around the clock. Some places, while technically private, function as quasi-public realm—for instance, college campuses, ballparks, restaurants, theaters, nightclubs, and, yes, shopping malls, at least the corridors between the private shops. Their owners retain the right to regulate behavior within, particularly the terms of access, and so the distinction must be made that they are only nominally public. The true public realm then, for the sake of this argument, is that portion of our everyday world which belongs to everybody and to which everybody ought to have equal access most of the time. The public realm is therefore a set of real places possessing physical form.

The public realm in America became so atrocious in the postwar decades that the Disney Corporation was able to create an artificial substitute for it and successfully sell it as a commodity. That's what Disney World is really about. In France, where the public realm possesses a pretty high standard of design quality and is carefully maintained as well, there is much less need for artificial substitutes, so few people feel compelled to go to EuroDisney. The design quality of everything at EuroDisney is about five notches *beneath* that of the most mediocre French street corner. The quality of the park benches and street lamps in EuroDisney is recognizably inferior to the park benches and street lamps in ordinary French towns. Even the flower beds lack finesse. They look like berms designed for corporate parking lots. There are more interesting things to eat along nine linear yards of the Rue Buci on the Left Bank than in all the magic kingdoms of EuroDisney.

The design quality of Disney World in Orlando, on the other hand, is about 1.5 notches better than the average American suburban shopping mall or housing subdivision—so Americans love it. Forget about how cheap-looking the benches and lampposts might be—we don't even have sidewalks in most of suburbia (and besides, nobody walks there anyway)—so *any* benches and lampposts seem swell. Americans love Disney World, above all, because it is uncontaminated by cars, except for a few antique vehicles kept around as stage props. By and large, they do not know that this is the reason they love Disney World. Americans are amazingly unconscious of how destructive the automobile has been to their everyday world.

Main Street USA is America's obsolete model for development—we stopped assembling towns this way after 1945. The pattern of Main Street is pretty simple: mixed use, mixed income, apartments and offices over the stores, moderate density, scaled to pedestrians, vehicles permitted but not allowed to dominate, buildings detailed with care, and built to last (though we still trashed it). Altogether it was a pretty good development pattern. It produced places that people loved deeply. That is the reason Main Street persists in our cultural memory. Many people still alive remember the years before World War Two and what it felt like to live in integral towns modeled on this pattern. Physical remnants of the pattern still stand in parts of the country for people to see, though the majority of Americans have moved into the new model habitat called Suburban Sprawl.

For all its apparent success, Suburban Sprawl sorely lacks many things that make life worth living, particularly civic amenities, which Main Street offered in spades. Deep down, many Americans are dissatisfied with suburbia—though they have trouble understanding what's missing—which explains their nostalgia for the earlier model. Their dissatisfaction is literally a *dis-ease*. They feel vaguely and generally un-well where they are. Nostalgia in its original sense means homesickness. Americans essay to cure their homesickness with costly visits to Disney World. The crude, ineffective palliatives they get there in the form of brass bands and choo-choo train rides leave them more homesick and more baffled as to the nature of their disease than when they arrived—like selling chocolate bars to someone suffering from scurvy—and pathetically, of course, they must return afterward to the very places that induce the disease of homesickness.

Historically Americans have a low regard for the public realm, and this is very unfortunate because the public realm is the physical manifestation of the common good. When you degrade the public realm, as we have, you degrade the common good.

The public realm is furnished with some nonphysical equipment in the form of laws, beliefs, social agreements, and preeminently language, which enables all these other mechanisms to operate. One might call language the *basic operating system* of the public realm, without which all the other *applications* needed to run human society would not function. When you degrade this equipment, this language, as we have in our time, then you impair the ability of a group of people incorporated as a republic to think about the common good.

Civic life is what goes on in the public realm. Civic life refers to our relations with our fellow human beings—in short, our roles as citizens. Sometime in the past forty years we ceased to speak of ourselves as citizens and labeled ourselves consumers. That's what we are today in the language of the evening news—*consumers*—in the language of the Sunday panel discussion shows—*consumers*—in the blizzard of statistics that blows out of the U.S. Department of Commerce every month. Consumers, unlike citizens, have no implicit responsibilities, obligations, or duties to anything larger than their own needs and desires, certainly not to anything like the common good. How can this be construed as anything but an infantile state of existence? In degrading the language of our public discussion this way—labeling ourselves consumers—have we not degraded our sense of who we are? And is it any wonder that we cannot solve any of our social problems, which are problems of the public realm and the common good?

CIVIC LIFE AND CIVIC ART

It is significant that the word *communicate* shares the same root with the word *community*, which is the Latin *communicare*, "to put in common," for we are suffering a crisis of community in this country and it expresses itself physically in the poor connections between the furnishings of our everyday world, especially in our disregard for the public realm, which forms the tissue of connection, and its consequent impoverishment.

The term civic life has an analog in the term civic art. Civic art refers to the effort we make to honor and embellish the public realm with architecture and design, in order to make civic life possible. This implies that the decoration of buildings and their arrangement in the landscape in order to define public space is not a frivolous matter. Relinquishing such attention to detail actually damages civic life on several counts. When buildings fail to define public space at a scale congenial to humans—as along any commercial highway strip—people cannot *be* there in safety and comfort. They will not walk there. They will not pause and mingle there with other people. They will not *communicate* there (or put anything in common). They will not contribute to a social organism that is larger than themselves. One inhabits the commercial highway strip isolated within the steel walls of a motor vehicle, cut off from other people. Such places are therefore profoundly uncivil. They impoverish and diminish us socially, and the *community* pays an enormous price for this incivility in terms of social dysfunction, ruined institutions, and misbehavior. Civilization becomes impossible under these conditions.

The decoration of buildings affects us similarly. The symbolism of architecture imparts very clear messages to individuals. The blank brick wall—a very common feature in American towns—conveys many messages. It says, *The street has no meaning, and you, Mr. Pedestrian, are a meaningless cipher.* It says, *The public realm has no significance and what goes on there doesn't matter.* It says, *We don't care what goes on outside our building. The outside might as well not exist.* The Modernist movement in architecture provided an ideological basis for this sort of attitude. Its promoters assumed that buildings only made egotistical statements about their owners at the expense of lesser folk—and that therefore we ought to abolish the decoration of buildings altogether. No more fancy windows, big doors, pointy roofs, slanty roofs, curvy roofs, balustrades, friezes, pilasters, pediments, modillions, festoons, swags, lunettes, dados, trefoils, spandrels, corbels, finials, quoins, and all the other "filthy" and "oppressive" claptrap of architectural history. To speak of this as an ideological error barely hints at the damage it did to public life in our time.

In reality, the decoration of buildings works two ways. Pennsylvania Station, with its mighty columns and soaring glass arcades, might have aggrandized the major stockholders of Pennsylvania Railroad, but it also honored the street where the building stood, the people who walked in that street, and, by extension, the city and its populace as a whole. It said, *This is the grand entrance to a great city and it belongs to you.* It made the act of arrival a civic celebration for everyone who stepped through its doors. It has been replaced today by a station that is little more than a hole in the ground, and which is reflected in the abysmal quality of the public railroad that it serves.

Beyond symbolism, the decoration of buildings has a crucial bearing on how well or how poorly buildings connect their own activities with the public realm, so that public and private activities can interact and flow gracefully, permitting us to move easily from one activity to the next: from the private office to the domain of the street to the hotel lobby to the restaurant and back out to the street again. Buildings properly designed and embellished minimize the friction between these transitions, so that we don't have to waste time repeatedly solving and re-solving the same old problem—like how to get in and out of a place—but rather can get on with more important things: our lives.

I went to a conference at the University of Texas in 1994. The campus, in Austin, is a pretty good ensemble of buildings dating from the Beaux Arts period. The open spaces and quads between the buildings are comfortable in scale and nicely embellished with fountains, benches, and orderly rows of trees. The building where the symposium was held, however, was a 1960s-vintage monstrosity dropped onto the campus like a refrigerator on a croquet court. From the visitor's standpoint, it seemed to lack any apparent entrance. A ten-minute reconnaissance around the thing was necessary to locate the door, because the entire first floor consisted of identical glass wall panels. This has a number of negative consequences. It makes you feel unwelcome, in an official way, as though the institution itself doesn't want you there. It compromises a person's dignity. It probably even elevates your blood pressure. A problem solved long ago by human ingenuity—how to signify the entrance to a building—has been made into a problem unnecessarily all over again.

What started out in Europe as an avant-garde political reaction to the horrors of industrialism—Modernism—degenerated, upon reaching America, into dogma and style. The result, visible all over America today, is a public realm almost entirely devoid of buildings that honor or embellish it, and a crippled civic life in which citizens are made to feel worthless. It matters that the junior high school looks like a fertilizer factory, and that the town hall looks like a wholesale beverage warehouse, and that the library looks like a shipping container, and that a hotel looks like a medium security prison because these buildings dishonor the public realm as they dishonor their institutional roles in our lives, and in their design they make civic life impossible.

AN UNCIVIL REPUBLIC

There is an old antagonistic relationship in our culture between city and country which transposes into the opposition between the individual and the group. The European city and its *civitas* represented everything from which people fled to America: stifling class restrictions, occupational barriers, ethnic friction, religious intolerance, and overbearing government. America and its great open spaces promised, above all, the ability to be left alone, to minimize one's relations with a larger community and any of its bothersome agencies. This argument between city and country reached a formal apogee in the United States Constitution and the tentative early years of a republic groping to define itself.

The Federalists, led by Alexander Hamilton, imagined a city-based commercial republic that defined the common good as a matter of competing interests mediated by Adam Smith's "invisible hand." Citizens of such a republic were not required to seek after anything higher than their individual interests. The invisible hand of market laws would mitigate all defects of human nature as expressed in political economy. The "strong" federal government they advocated was nothing like the monster we have today. Its role would be limited to a few specific tasks such as protecting the coastlines, supporting a banking system with a stable national currency, and putting down insurrections like the Whiskey Rebellion of 1794—the grisly excesses of the Revolution in France being very much on the Federalists' minds.

The Jeffersonian Anti-Federalists (later Democratic-Republicans, and finally Democrats), in contrast, proposed a looser confederation of vested landholders who were able, by dint of classical education, to rise above their selfish interests and empathetically imagine a higher public virtue.

In hindsight it is paradoxical that Hamilton's "individualistic" view arose out of the city context while Jefferson's communal "higher public virtue" view arose out of the rural context, because in reality it *worked* just the other way around: country life on isolated farms allowed individuals to withdraw from participation in society, while the inhabitants of towns and cities had to learn to get along with each other, meaning they had to create institutions to define the public interest, which they invariably did in terms of some appeal to higher public virtue. In short, it was the country people who (contrary to Jefferson) preferred not to be responsible for others, and the city people who (contrary to Hamilton) couldn't avoid their responsibility to others. This paradox ended up expressing itself some seventy-five years later in the form of the Civil War, because the city people of the urban commercial North finally could not avoid taking responsibility for the enslaved Africans of the rural agricultural South.*

It was James Madison's genius at the time of the constitutional convention to postpone this conflict by conceiving a practical republic that mediated the Hamiltonian and Jeffersonian models while it rationalized a basis for everyone's freedom from the needs of the group. In Madison's view human nature was inherently lacking in sufficient virtue to overcome self-interest. Individuals tended to fall into categories or classes motivated by similar self-interest, which were then called *factions*, e.g., farmers and merchants. Therefore, central government was necessary in order to *balance* and *control* the competing interests of factions. This freed all individuals from obeisance to abstract notions of virtue or to a common good based on altruism or empathy. In the Madisonian republic the worst instincts of the city dwellers and the country dwellers were to be merely managed by playing interests off against one another in a theater of governmental checks and balances. Whatever greater good emerged from this experiment in political mechanics would be understood as an artifice—the logical outcome of a Cartesian worldview that modeled the operation of the universe on clockwork rather than a moral position. Finally, in Madison's model there was the safety valve of a vast frontier. Obdurate individualists who absolutely refused to play the game of balanced factions could escape to wild places where they would be left alone. The safety valve of the frontier operated until the end of the nineteenth century. A national folklore of heroic individualism and thrilling violence grew out of it. It was a great spectacle of incivility. Its demise was fittingly sudden and dramatic.

The extraordinary year 1893, highlighted by the Columbian Exposition at Chicago, included some other remarkable events. At that year's meeting of the American Historical Association, also held in Chicago, Frederick Jackson Turner read a now-famous paper officially declaring the American frontier closed. An obscure figure at the time, the thirty-two-year-old Turner had only recently completed his Ph.D. at Johns Hopkins. What he said was not on the order of a policy statement by a political leader. But his

*I maintain that slavery was the principal cause of the Civil War.

address, regarded in the years since as "brilliant," signaled the end of an epoch in American history and the beginning of something new, thrilling, and as yet mysterious. Turner went on to a distinguished career on the Harvard faculty. His declaration about the close of the frontier thundered through the national psyche for decades. (It was required reading in my freshman American history survey course in college, 1966.) In summary, I think it's fair to say that Turner's speech articulated a widespread recognition already taking shape in the intellectual mainstream. The import of it was this: Americans were now compelled to settle down and learn how to be civilized. The safety valve of escape to the frontier for those with deeply antisocial tendencies was no longer a realistic option.

The close of the frontier and the Columbian Exposition were an amazing nexus of historical forces. Turner defined the problem and the Exposition posed the solution. The problem was nowhere left to run off and be uncivil. The solution was an explicit attempt to bring civility to the design of American cities using the language of classical Roman architecture and French city planning.

A third momentous phenomenon of that year was less a tangible event than an ongoing development: Henry Ford doggedly toiled over a series of prototype horseless carriages in a back street workshop in Detroit. Few people noticed, and those who did differed widely on the potential value of such a frightful contraption. But Ford persevered and as the century turned, his automobile emerged as the dominant element in the shaping of our everyday world.

What happened during the crucial twenty-five years spanning 1893 to 1918, it seems to me, is clear: Americans, given the choice between civilizing their cities through public works, and using the car to escape the demands of civility, chose the car. All the money that had gone into the great public building projects of the City Beautiful prior to World War One was afterward channeled into refitting the city to accommodate cars, and building highways in and between cities, to enable the construction of new automobile suburbs outside the city. The addition of cars in huge numbers to American cities by the 1920s made them more noisy, frightful, and disgusting than they had ever been before, and gave Americans even more reason to hate them.

By the 1920s the stage was set for the wholesale abandonment of the cities, the adoption of a view that lead ultimately to the extreme separation of uses and the perversities of contemporary zoning laws, and the establishment of the anti-city known as suburbia. It was a view of the city as a place fit only for work and vice, and of the suburb as the exclusive realm of the home—and a particular kind of home at that: the *little cabin in the woods* (and its mutant varietals), a recapitulation of the frontier experience, a way to avoid the burdens of civility.

PLACE, RACE, AND POLITICS

One unanticipated consequence of the abandonment of cities and the rise of this suburban utopia is a host of social problems that have baffled the nation's political resolve for more than a generation. The problems of crime, drug abuse, gang warfare, out-of-wedlock births, incompetent parenting, idleness, and other incivilities are now identified with an "underclass" left in the otherwise abandoned central cities. I hope I have made it clear that the repudiation of city life was woven into our national experience at the very start, and reenacted over the past 200 years. The current situation is just another act in the drama.

Because I will be speaking here specifically about the black underclass of the big cities, I am probably at some hazard of offending someone on racial grounds. That is not my intention. Certainly social pathologies are distributed among other races, ethnic groups, classes, and geographic sectors of the nation, including suburbia, but I don't think there is any need to debate the proposition that these pathologies exist in exaggerated form in the black urban ghetto. Since the future of American cities is now so entwined with the recent history and present troubles of this group, I feel that it would be cowardly to pretend that there is no such thing as a black urban underclass today and to avoid discussing it.

The original sin of American political life was slavery, and though the institution was officially abolished in 1863, the nation has yet to stop suffering the consequences of it. It was the greatest incivility of our history, and it produced the Civil War, an event at once monstrous and ennobling. Possibly we will recover from slavery and its reverberations and move on to become a civilized country; possibly we will not recover from it, but instead will plunge into deeper national tragedy.

Black Americans were present in small numbers in American cities at the nation's founding both as free individuals and slaves. Differences in culture and economic organization between the North and South were significant. Slavery might not have persisted in the South as long as it did without the invention of the cotton gin (1793), which gave a renewed impetus to the plantation system and the way it organized labor. The cotton gin itself was an early industrial tool and the same forces that spawned it spurred an urban industrial boom in the North, including the large-scale production of fabrics made out of cotton. One by one the northern states abolished chattel slavery in the early 1800s. Meanwhile, northern industry organized its workers into a new system that might be described as voluntary factory-wage slavery.

While blacks did not enjoy equal protection under the law anywhere in the United States, their opportunities for economic advancement were better in the urban North than in the rural South. After the Civil War, former slaves migrated from the rural South to big cities in several waves. At first, their numbers remained modest and their presence was subsumed in the numerically more momentous arrival of the Irish, Italians, Jews, and other Europeans.

Booker T. Washington, born a slave, embodied a strategic solution to the predicament of blacks in the post–Civil War period. His popular rhetoric held that honest effort, education, and good will would be rewarded with economic advancement, and that whether the white majority accepted blacks as social equals or not, blacks would eventually prosper as free citizens in America. Washington's beliefs were consistent with ideas about the value of work, literacy and decent conduct in mainstream American culture at that time. Washington believed that blacks should concentrate their energy on vocational training and the accumulation of capital. He strongly disfavored political agitation, believing economic achievement to be self-evidently empowering.

Since racial discrimination was institutionalized in this period, blacks were prompted to set up in professions and businesses to serve their own people. This should not necessarily be viewed as negative because in the late nineteenth century it quickly led to the formation of a black middle class, and therefore to real economic improvements for individuals and families who had lately been treated as little better than living farm implements.

Washington's idea that blacks should submit passively on the issue of full political equality was forcefully rebuked by the figure who came to succeed him as the leading spokesman for black Americans in the early twentieth century. W. E. B. DuBois, a Massachusetts native and Harvard graduate (Ph.D., 1895), would become director of publications for the NAACP and editor of its magazine, *Crisis*. His 1903 book, *The Souls of Black Folk*, urged an end to the official hypocrisy of "separate but equal" and set the agenda for the civil rights struggles of mid-century. As a practical matter, however, until after World War Two these debates affected a minority of a minority. Many more American blacks remained in a condition of quasi-slavery as sharecroppers in the rural South, stoically enduring as unwanted strangers in what was now their native land, demoralized by a long bondage, and stripped of their ancestral cultural heritage.

After World War Two, the invention of the mechanical cotton picker put the entire Southern black sharecropper class out of business at one stroke, stimulating a numerically massive migration of poor rural blacks to cities. Companies like Ford actively recruited rural blacks, in some cases sending buses down south to get them. It was an era when foreign immigration was much more restricted, labor was in high demand as the postwar economy boomed, and factory wages were rising to unprecedented high levels. This time the arrival of blacks in northern cities was viewed by whites with alarm. The evacuation of the cities for the suburbs by whites was already under way, but the postwar black migration accelerated the process. The neighborhoods that greeted these rural newcomers had already been through several cycles of physical deterioration—first by the effects of big industry, next by the imposition of cars, then by neglect during two decades of depression and war. They were slums. Government-sponsored housing projects meant to replace slums in many cities were so badly designed that in remarkably short order they became arguably worse environments than the old urban fabric.

There may be many contexts for discussing the problems of the inner cities today, but I have to argue that above all they are problems of behavior, and therefore of culture, which is behavior transmitted over time. How do we account for behavior that seems practically suicidal on such a vast scale? It is probably fair to say that slavery undermined the black family—the degree and nature of the damage is currently under debate by historians. Emancipation was as much an ordeal as a jubilee. It was attended by years of dislocation, social disorder, raised expectations, and dashed hopes. Nicholas Lemann makes the point that under slavery's successor system, sharecropping, a distinct set of social behaviors emerged in the form of casual attitudes about marriage, childbearing, parental responsibility, as well as violence, drug and alcohol abuse, and illiteracy.* Slavery and share-cropping both had thwarted individual initiative and promoted passive at-titudes to a paternalistic economic system. The ex-sharecroppers who migrated north after World War Two brought with them family arrange-ments and forms of behavior that were apt to prove self-defeating in the urban setting.

Within a generation the well-paid factory jobs that had drawn many poor Southern blacks to the cities began to evaporate. After 1973, manufacturing jobs declined steadily in New York, Boston, Baltimore, Pittsburgh, Cleveland, Detroit, St. Louis, and Chicago. Under these con-ditions, old cultural attitudes reasserted themselves with devastating re-sults. People who had only begun to experience economic advancement were now left in idleness and dependency.

The civil rights struggle was played out against the background of this migration and of America's presumed position of political and moral lead-ership in a postwar world. However, it was a drama played out at first in the small-town South, where racial bias was more clearly and formally institu-tionalized in Jim Crow laws, not in big cities, where the problems of race, culture, and economics were becoming less easy to understand. In fact, the changing dynamics of the civil rights movement itself would exacerbate the problems of the cities.

The civil rights movement passed through several stages. The first stage of nonviolent protest, led by Martin Luther King, Jr., was an appeal for the nation to live up to its own professed moral standards and democratic prin-ciples. It culminated in the Civil Rights Act of 1964 and the Voting Rights

---

*The Promised Land: The Great Black Migration and How It Changed America, by Nicho-las Lemann (New York: Knopf, 1991). Lemann synthesizes the research of Gunnar Myrdal, Charles S. Johnson, Hortense Powdermaker, John Dollard, and Arthur Raper conducted among black Southern sharecroppers during the 1930s and 1940s. Their conclusions about social behavior are strikingly consistent. "All these writers reject wholeheartedly the idea of black inferiority," Lemann says, "but they agreed that family life among sharecroppers was different from the ordinary family life of the rest of the country" (p. 29). "It was clear," Lemann continues, "that whatever the cause of its differentness, black sharecropper society on the eve of the introduction of the mechanical cotton picker was the equivalent of big-city ghetto society today in many ways" (p. 31).

Act of 1965, which finally put into precise federal statute what the Thirteenth, Fourteenth, and Fifteenth Amendments had failed to spell out one hundred years earlier in respect to citizenship and equal protection under the law.

These acts were quickly followed by President Lyndon Johnson's Great Society, which sought to make restitution for past injury and inequality with a complex menu of compensatory programs. About the same time these programs got under way, and especially after the murder of Martin Luther King, Jr. in 1968, the civil rights movement veered into its Black Power phase, an agenda that was militantly separatist and anti-assimilationist. It was as though all the previous victories of the movement in removing legal barriers to equal opportunity, combined with the recent political violence of assassination and the Vietnam War, had aroused an anxiety in blacks that could only be expressed in political rage. The Great Society now combined with the Black Power movement to produce some extremely unfavorable consequences. The former promoted a psychology of entitlement to special treatment (the opposite of equal protection under the law), while the latter advanced the idea that blacks should not join mainstream American culture—indeed, that to do so was a traitorous act.

The vicious combination of entitlement and alienation has been in force ever since with the following results. Affirmative action and related programs of preferential treatment have paradoxically reinforced notions of inferiority, particularly among the supposed beneficiaries, with profoundly demoralizing effects. Separatism, "black nationalism," and their philosophical offshoots have reinforced the hobbling notion among many blacks that it is basically impossible to join the American mainstream, and that any attempt to try—for instance, speaking standard English—is a betrayal of black culture. There is more institutional segregation on college campuses today than in the 1960s because black students, perhaps out of anxiety, demand their own separate facilities and are preferentially granted them by college officials who, above all, want to avoid embarrassing conflict. Separatism also insists that for the purpose of promoting educational and economic advancement people be treated strictly as members of groups, depriving them of their individuality, the most powerful means for true advancement, indeed the only means for achieving personhood.

The social engineering side of the equation by way of legislated social programs and government bureaucracy has been similarly problematical.

By subsidizing the setting up of one-parent households, cash payments to unwed and teenage mothers have enabled out-of-wedlock births and arguably increased them as a percentage of total births. Under the terms of those subsidies—for instance, the "man-in-the-house" rule—the government has sanctioned the absence of fathers, marginalized the role of men in poor communities, and discouraged family formation, which in turn has lead to entrenched poverty for single-parent families headed by women. Children raised in that setting are prone to grow up clinically depressed, with all the behavior that it implies. In the era of crack cocaine, and the wild irresponsibility it produces in adults, some children are raised by virtually nobody. These horrendous conditions yield children who are without hope, unsocialized, doomed to reenact the scripts of failure, inclined to self-medication (ie., drugs), unable to empathize with others, and willing to commit violent acts against them. Boys raised without fathers tend to be very anxious in general and specifically resentful toward women, leading to further devaluation and abuse of women.

This tragic sequence of outcomes might not have been possible without the misguided and good intentions of whites seeking redemption for the sins of slavery, bigotry, and racial discrimination. But as Shelby Steele points out, "the concept of historic reparation grows out of man's need to impose a degree of justice on the world that simply doesn't exist. Suffering can be endured and overcome, it cannot be repaid. Blacks cannot be repaid for the injustice done to the race, but we can be corrupted by society's guilty gestures of repayment. . . . The hardest thing for any sufferer to accept is that his suffering excuses him from very little and never has enough currency to restore him. To think otherwise is to prolong suffering."*

The corruption that Steele speaks of is manifest today in America's cities, where the demoralized underclass dwells in what must be incontestably called war zones. It is hard to imagine a more uncivil version of the city. The American city has finally enacted the nation's enduring cultural script, becoming, at last, uninhabitable and therefore justifying the mainstream's complete and final rejection of it.

It seems to me that the public interest demands a new approach to these conditions of urban squalor, despair, and inertia; that it requires above all

*The Content of Our Character, by Shelby Steele (New York: Harper Perennial, 1991, p. 119).

the political reinstatement of the value of the individual within the frame-work of a civil society. It implies the end of mechanisms for hedging or fudging equality before the law, in particular preferential treatment based on race. And it implies a single standard of decent behavior for all citizens. I believe social conditions would improve significantly if the cash pay-ments of the welfare system were replaced as much as possible by civic in-stitutions whose main business would be the actual caretaking of people by other live human beings. For instance, we desperately need orphanages for the uncared-for children of incompetent parents, or a kind of combined orphanage and group home in which incompetent parents might live with their children under supervision while they learn the skills of parenting.

The call for orphanages has provoked loud objections, based apparently on the sentimental idea that children must be kept with their parents at all costs. Under the present system an irresponsible single mother can retain custody of her child at the cost of the child's future. In the event that a child is removed from a toxic household by the courts and social agencies, there are not enough decent foster homes to receive these mistreated chil-dren, and we apparently lack the will as a society to establish the kinds of civic facilities that would care for them, namely orphanages.

The standard image offered as a counter-argument is of Oliver Twist in the workhouse and his miserable bowl of gruel. This position seems espe-cially unworthy of those who might call themselves politically progressive. If that *is* the only way we can conceive of an institution to nurture un-wanted children, then we really are in trouble as a society. We seem quite willing to build prisons with up-to-date amenities and comforts: gymnasi-ums, sanitary eating halls, warm sleeping quarters, hot showers, recreation rooms with cable TV. If we put a fraction of the effort, money, and will into building decent orphanages, where children would receive regular hot meals, some basic social instruction, some personal attention and encour-agement, and perhaps even a hug at bedtime, we probably wouldn't need so many state-of-the-art prisons to take care of adults who were once un-wanted, uncared-for children. Addressing why many inner city teenage gang members seem not to mind going to jail, the Reverend Jesse Jackson explains that it is often the first time that adults have ever taken an inter-est in their behavior.

We need civic institutions to care for other kinds of troubled people, too: mental hospitals for the mentally ill, poorhouses for the indigent, homes for the disabled, settlement houses where immigrants can go to learn the language and customs of the country they have chosen to enter. We had these institutions in the past when we were a much less wealthy nation. The state of New York emptied its regional mental hospitals beginning in the 1970s on the grounds that the patients were a politically oppressed minority group and that keeping them hospitalized was therefore unjust. It is more likely that the gigantic, unmanageable scale of these hospitals, each housing thousands of patients, was the problem, not hospitalization per se. Rather than redesign them on a humane and workable scale, we chose to scrap altogether the idea of sheltering and looking after the mentally ill. The patients were released under the assumption that new psychotropic drugs would permit them to function more or less normally on the outside. Somehow, public health officials overlooked the fact that the first thing many released psychiatric patients do is stop taking their medication. Today, in the face of overwhelming evidence that this is so, and with the freezing streets of our cities teeming with psychotic homeless people off their meds—some of them quite dangerous—we still maintain the public pretense that mental hospitals are less humane than the streets. What is more, in our effort to sort out the rights and entitlements of psychotic homeless people, we forget to consider the effect of their uncivil behavior on the public realm and the common good.

It must be obvious that we need facilities to take care of people who cannot or will not take care of themselves. Being morally offended by terms such as orphanage, poorhouse, or mental hospital seems a poor excuse for doing nothing. If it helps, we can come up with new names. Prep schools. Social service academies. Rehab centers. It doesn't matter in the long run, because euphemisms have a way of automatically assuming the power to cast shame. The term *mental health unit* replaced *sanitarium*, which replaced *insane asylum*, which replaced *madhouse* without any loss of stigmatizing power along the way. What could be milder in syntax than *reform school*, and think of the connotation. Shame may be an unavoidable feature of the human condition that will not be abolished by euphemism.

Indeed, there is a potent argument that shame plays an indispensable role in our ability to be civilized. A fourteen-year-old girl ought to be ashamed of becoming pregnant. It is an event that is more than likely to ruin her life and her child's life. An idle, improvident, but otherwise ablebodied person ought to be ashamed of having nothing useful to do. Those who would like to hand out self-esteem to the urban poor as though it were some kind of elixir seem to have lost sight of the fact that the only enduring source of self-esteem derives from individual effort and achievement.* Otherwise, we might as well hand out cocaine, which makes people feel wonderful without accomplishing anything of importance to themselves or to those who depend upon them.

The grave problems of the urban underclass and the resulting disintegration of city life in our time can be viewed reasonably as the failure of a particular species of political idealism. It is the failure of the well-meaning impulse to make up for the tragedy of the past, or to make up for the stark fact that life really is difficult, at best, for practically everybody, and often brutally unfair. In the hopeful years after World War Two, this brand of politics joined hands with a gigantism of enterprise, both corporate and governmental, that all but destroyed local economies and wrecked local communities—WalMart and the U.S. Department of Housing operate at the same scale. And since the community level is perhaps the best place to resolve issues of rights and responsibilities, postwar idealism's greatest folly was to destroy the civic context itself.

CAN AMERICA BECOME CIVILIZED?

I don't know if we will be able to reinstate a social contract that recognizes both rights and responsibilities within a civic context. It will certainly not be possible unless we restore that context, and I mean in bricks and mortar. I began this chapter by arguing that there is a vital relationship between the character of our surroundings and the common good, that rights and responsibilities need a civic setting in which to dwell, and that such a setting is identical with the physical setting of our lives, an actual place that must be worth caring about.

It is easy to be discouraged. The general political attitude among the suburban well-off is that they have been willing to try almost any expensive social experiment *except* returning to live in towns and cities. In the face of this shunning, the will to behave constructively has been rather conspicuously absent among the urban poor themselves. But the poor nevertheless have responsibilities and obligations too, beginning with civil be-

---

*I attended a symposium on *The Future of the American City* at Yale in January 1994, at which dispensing self-esteem to the urban poor was a primary theme.

havior and extending to useful work. One of the unfortunate side effects of the psychology of entitlement is the notion both among the poor and government officials that jobs must be *given* to idle people, and that they must be *good* jobs—which I take to mean something like professional careers. Nothing could be further from the way the world really operates.

In reality, people search for some way to make themselves useful and are rewarded with pay. The will to make oneself useful must precede the finding of a rewarding situation. And such situations are rarely tendered to the unwilling. It would be nice to live in a world where everybody could be a brain surgeon, a movie star, or a starting player in the NFL. But those positions are in short supply, and most of us must seek other avenues of usefulness. This seeking usually entails much trial and error, which forms the basis of our experience and, in theory, improves our character. And so we make our ways in the world, commonly upward from some lower situation to increasingly better ones.

Under the present political psychology none of this is considered necessary. The government is supposed to promote the supply of a commodity called *jobs* and also the training for these *jobs*, which is somehow extrinsic both to the institution that goes under the name of regular schooling, and the personal will of each individual to be useful. In reality, the leap from functional illiteracy and chronic idleness to a position as even a sales clerk seems implausible. To expect private employers to happily hire multiple-conviction felons is also probably asking too much. A troubling aspect of the problem is that menial labor is now beneath *all* Americans, including those who have the skills or ambitions to do nothing else. Much of what is called menial labor really involves the caretaking of things, places, and persons, and it is especially sad that there is so much to take care of in this country with nobody willing to do it.

It may strike some readers as an unbelievable effrontery to state that the poor ought to work in menial jobs. I am not arguing that they ought to live in violence and squalor—just the opposite. Before World War Two this was a nation full of menial employments, and many people so employed lived more decently than today's poor do, particularly in the cities where, for all the cities' historic shortcomings, the poor at least had easy access to a great deal of cultural and civic equipment. Poor people may have lived in cramped tenements in 1911, but they had access to well-maintained parks, low-cost public transit, safe streets, free public schools, excellent public libraries, museums, baths, and infirmaries. Most important, this civic equipment was shared by everybody. People of all stations in life went to parks, museums, and libraries. The poor *saw* the middle class and the wealthy every day in the public realm of the streets. They observed their behavior, and were constrained in their own behavior by seeing them. The poor saw where the rich lived. A boy from Hell's Kitchen could walk ten minutes across town and stand within a few yards of William H. Vanderbilt's front door on Fifty-ninth Street and Fifth Avenue with no fear of being hassled by private security guards. In short, the poor lived in a civic context that included the entire range of social classes, so that many of the problems of the poor in the cities were also the problems of the middle class and the rich.

Today the poor in most American cities live only in the context of the poor. The only place they see the other America is on television, and then through a wildly distorting lens that stimulates the most narcissistic, nihilistic consumer fantasies. Since the poor, by definition, can't participate fully in consumer culture, the predictable result is rage at what appears to be a cruel tease, and this rage is commonly expressed in crime. What may be equally damaging is that the poor see very little in the way of ordinary polite conduct, very little civil behavior. They do not see people routinely going about honorable occupations. What they do see all around is mayhem, squalor, and disorder, and almost no evidence that it is possible to live a happy life without being a sports hero, a gangster, or a television star.

The problems of the cities are not going to be relieved unless the middle class and the wealthy return to live there. For the moment these classes are off in suburbia, inhabiting those *little cabins in the woods* grouped together in the subdivisions as a symbolic antidote to the city. They will not return to the cities unless a couple of conditions obtain. One is the economic failure of the suburban equation, a likely event. A second condition is whether the cities themselves can be made habitable.

I believe the first condition will come to pass within the next twenty-five years. All the evidence (discussed in Chapter 3) demonstrates clearly that suburbia is becoming unaffordable and unsustainable, and its denizens seem to dimly apprehend this, like people hearing distant thunder on a still summer's day. The economy makes them nervous. Companies are shedding employees. They feel anxious, trapped. For the first time in

American history, there is nowhere else left to go, no place to escape to. What will they do?

I'm afraid they may misunderstand the crisis of the suburbs, particularly as it manifests in the personal catastrophes of lost jobs, declining incomes, falling property values, family breakups, and misbehavior. Poor people are not the only Americans afflicted by the psychology of entitlement. Middle-class suburbanites really believe that they are owed a package of goodies called *the American Dream*, and when they are suddenly deprived of it, they may get very angry and vote for political maniacs.

The Republicans are now in charge of things at many levels of government, and though they have been shouting the loudest about the crisis of "family values," they are also the chief boosters of suburbia, which is to say, of a profoundly uncivil living arrangement. Their chosen way of life, therefore, is at odds with their most cherished wishes for a civil society, and so it is unlikely that they are going to be able to solve any of the social problems they deplore—even the problems of their own children's behavior.

Suburban moms and dads wonder why their fifteen-year-old children seem so alienated. These kids are physically disconnected from the civic life of their towns. They have no access to the civic equipment. They have to be chauffeured absolutely everywhere—to football practice, to piano lessons, to their friends' houses, to the library, and, of course, to the mall. All they live for is the day that they can obtain a driver's license and use their environment. Except then, of course, another slight problem arises: they need several thousand dollars to buy a used car and pay for insurance, which is usually exorbitant for teens, often more than the price of their cars. Is it really any wonder that these kids view their situation as some kind of swindle?

Americans are convinced that suburbia is great for kids. The truth is, kids older than seven need more from their environment than a safe place to ride their bikes. They need at least the same things adults need. Dignified places to hang out. Shops. Eating establishments. Libraries, museums, and theaters. They need a public realm worthy of respect. All of which they need access to on their own, without our assistance—which only keeps them in an infantile state of dependency. In suburbia, as things presently stand, children have access only to television. That's their public realm. It's really a wonder that more American children are not completely psychotic.

In order to make American towns and cities habitable again, we will have to take the greater portion of public money now spent on subsidizing car use and redirect it into replacing the civic equipment of the cities that we allowed to be trashed over the past several decades. The cost of doing these things is, fortunately, apt to be less than the cost of continuing to subsidize the suburban automobile infrastructure. For instance, a single new freeway interchange can cost $600,000,000, which is the same cost as building and equipping an entire twenty-mile-long electric trolley line.*

If there is any frontier left in America today, it probably exists in the vast amounts of underutilized, reclaimable real estate of our towns and cities. While the underclass occupies certain urban neighborhoods, other enormous districts stand virtually abandoned. Great swaths of inner Detroit, Cleveland, and St. Louis consist of empty, rubble-strewn lots, with hardly a building standing for scores of acres around. While the water and sewer lines may need updating, the infrastructure of streets and building lots already exists, and in a physical form that is much more emphatically civic than suburbia. These vacant wards beg redevelopment and present tremendous business opportunities. It may be hard to imagine suburbanites abandoning the leafy cul-de-sac subdivisions for the inner city, but these urban neighborhoods could become as beautiful and functional as we have the nerve to imagine. There is no reason why Cleveland, Detroit, and Harlem could not become as finely functional and spiritually gratifying as Paris.

Where does the underclass go if the cities are reoccupied by the well off? The underclass ceases to be an underclass and becomes something else: a working class of honorably occupied people who make less money. They share the city with other classes, as was always the case in history until our era. They observe the same standard of public conduct as everybody else. They live on less desirable streets in less desirable buildings, but they need not live either in material or spiritual squalor. They can share the aspirations of the mainstream and they can exercise their will to move upward in society by the traditional means of education, diligence, and respectful behavior.

Making our cities habitable again will take a rededication to forms of building that were largely abandoned in America after World War Two. It

*Author's interview with Milwaukee Mayor John O. Norquist, June 1995.

will call for devices of civic art that *never* really caught on here, but have always existed in older parts of the world—for instance, waterfronts that are integral with the rest of the city. The human scale will have to prevail over the needs of motor vehicles. There will have to be ample provision for green space of different kinds—neighborhood squares, wildlife corridors, parks—because people truly crave regular contact with nature, especially pockets of repose and tranquillity, and having many well cared-for parcels of it distributed equitably around town improves civic life tremendously.

The transformation I propose will not be possible unless Americans recognize the benefits of a well-designed public realm, and the civic life that comes with it, over the uncivil, politically toxic, socially impoverished, hyper-privatized realm of suburbia, however magnificent the kitchens and bathrooms may be there. I don't believe that we can be an advanced society without cities. Tragically, American cities have become unworthy of the American republic. Our task is to make them worthy, to reconstruct them in a physical form that is worth caring about, and to reinhabit them. It is unfortunate that people who consider themselves politically progressive sneer at the idea of urban "gentrification" as a supposed affront to the poor. This attitude logically leads to a position that the middle class and the wealthy have no business reinhabiting the cities, and it has led to many misguided efforts to defeat attempts at urban redevelopment (see Chapter 6). This attitude must change. Otherwise, the middle class and wealthy will have to consider themselves morally restricted to life in the suburbs—an untenable proposition.

The common good demands a public realm in which to dwell. It can't sustain itself merely in our hearts or memories. This is, finally, the sentimental fallacy of the suburban patriot: that hanging a cast-iron eagle over the garage door proves you care about your country.

CHAPTER 3

CAR CRAZY

ANYBODY who thinks we're going to be using cars twenty-five years from now the way we've *been* accustomed to using them in the recent past ought to have his head examined. That phase of our national history is over.

We characterize this period as the Auto Age not just because driving machines came into existence—they will continue to exist—but because some quirks of history and economics made the mass ownership of cars temporarily feasible in America, and in so doing imposed an unprecedented, technologically tyrannical regime on every particular of our daily lives. By the mid-twentieth century, owning a car had become a prerequisite for first-class citizenship in the United States. It was assumed that every adult would own a car and use it constantly for the most mundane tasks—to go to work, get lunch, buy aspirin—and even for some sacred activities like attending church and making love. The everyday environ-

ment that America constructed after World War Two to accommodate
this regime was a radical departure from the traditions of civic design, with
all it implies about the painful trial-and-error process of what works and
what doesn't over eons of history, which we call acquired culture. That was
all thrown in the garbage. The new environment was designed primarily
for the convenience of motorists, secondarily to assist corporations in
moving vast volumes of merchandise via cars, tertiarily, for ease of maintenance, quatrarily for protection against lawsuits, and leastly, for the spiritual fulfillment of people. The news is that we can no longer afford that
living arrangement. The car-centered, car-*dominated*, human habitat can
now be viewed—like Leninist economics—as an experiment that has
failed.

The car itself should not be viewed as a failure, only the use we made of
it in the first century of its existence. Henry Ford's great accomplishment
was not "inventing" the car—other men experimenting in oily workshops
developed similar machines about the same time—but in rationalizing the
mass production of cars so that any gainfully employed American could
own one. In the minds of his countrymen, Ford made the car an instrument of democracy and hence of human progress. But what goes on in the
collective consciousness of a nation is not always consistent with the way
things really work. For instance, we are keen on the pleasurable psychology of the car and rather blind to its baneful effects on society.

Consider our confusion over geographic mobility and social mobility.
The first entails getting from point A to point B physically; the second entails bettering one's position in the esteem of other men. In America the
distinction is a blur. Historically, Americans have accomplished the latter
by way of the former. The place of origin is not supposed to count either
for or against anybody—a social premise would appear to militate *against*
the love of place as a basic value. An eighteen-year-old leaves East Jesus
for the State U., invents something like a vacuum spray valve as a young
engineering graduate, drives all over the United States selling the little
plastic widget to every paint, oven cleaner, and underarm deodorant man-
ufacturer in the land, makes $50 million, gains admission to what passes
for high society, and ends up in a 10,000-square-foot villa on Biscayne Bay
with a heart condition, too far gone to even use the Stairmaster in his mag-
nificently equipped home gym. He remains vaguely ashamed of his origins

as a native of East Jesus, and tells interviewers from the TV networks only that he "hails from the Midwest." The automobile embodies this mixed metaphor of social and physical mobility, and the confusion that arises from it is embedded in our national character. During the most desperate years of the Great Depression, people gave up their ancestral farms before their cars, because the car represented at least a chance to start over somewhere else. In America one goes somewhere in order to become something. Motion becomes an end in itself, and the mass of equipment needed to support this motion—highways, freeways, fast food huts, lube joints, tract housing—makes every place so bleak that we hate where we came from, hate where we end up, and don't want to pay much attention to what we're passing through. Even now, when car dependence is causing so much aggregate misery and tearing apart the physical fabric of the society in which individuals hope to rise, the car is still viewed as both a magical means and a miraculous end. For the most visible big "winners" among us, the young movie and sports heroes out of adolescence only in the glandular sense, a hugely expensive custom-made car is still the highest trophy of success, of *having arrived*. (From where? Who cares where?)

Our car culture also reflects much confusion over the ideas of democracy and freedom. Freedom, as comprehended by the founders, stood for the management of affairs at an appropriate hierarchy of scale, meaning there are certain decisions best left to individuals, families, corporations, communities, counties, states, and nations in that order, and that human happiness depended on the proper match. Their main objection to conditions prevailing in 1776 was to the inappropriateness in scale of the British Crown attempting to regulate the day-to-day affairs of people 3,000 miles away spread across a region many times larger than England itself. The founders were not against hierarchy or authority in general. They were not cultural relativists.

Today, both hierarchy and authority are strictly taboo, and basic institutions such as the criminal justice system stand in disrepute as ineffectual or lacking the will of enforcement. Democracy in our popular culture includes the ideas that all opinions, like votes, have equal value, that all values are relative, and that nobody is better than anybody else. College professors are especially tenacious on these points lately, which is a curious intellectual position for those who are supposed to transmit standards of excellence. The devaluation of standards supports some collateral notions, for instance, that there are no social prerequisites to parenthood, that property ownership carries no obligations to the common good, and that the marketplace is the sole arbiter of what makes life worth living. Paradoxically, under this kind of democracy citizens spend inordinate amounts of time, money, and energy trying to prove that they *are* better than others by accumulating costly totem objects. There is an obvious relation, by the way, between our present unbalanced notions of property rights vis-a-vis the vestigial common good and our mania for accumulating status totems such as cars: it is the behavior of people who literally don't know their place in the world.

Freedom, in this culture, means that whatever makes you happy is okay. This is the freedom of a fourteen-year-old child. Freedom to eat a whole box of donuts at one sitting. Freedom to make a mess, to be loud and obnoxious, to blow things up, to inflict injury for the thrill of it, to conceive babies without care or thought for the consequences. Mostly, it is freedom from authority, particularly parental authority which, when it exists at all now, often functions at a level qualitatively no higher than a child's. Under this version of freedom, there is no legitimate claim for any authority to regulate human desires—not even the personal conscience—nor any appropriate scale of management, and all supposed authorities are viewed as corrupt, mendacious, and irrelevant. This view of freedom is not what Hamilton, Jefferson, Madison, and the other founders had in mind. It is not a coincidence that the appeal of cars in our time derives from these crude emotional states masquerading as ideas about democracy and freedom.

BEFORE CARS—AND AFTER

Historically, the sheer vastness of this nation underlies our fascination with innovative transport per se. Prior to the invention of railroads and the enormous task of building rail lines, the frontier was barely habitable. Anyone living some distance from a navigable waterway might as well have settled on another planet. On the western side of the Appalachians, even good waterways presented problems. Farmers of the Ohio River Valley in the early 1800s could only ship grain in one direction: downstream to the Mississippi, and ultimately to New Orleans. It was a very long trip, so these settlers of what was then the frontier were inclined to convert their grain into whiskey, a value-added product in our parlance, which could be shipped and stored indefinitely without spoilage problems (unlike raw wheat, whiskey improved with age). Yet, this rational practice infected their culture to the extent that drunkenness became endemic and public violence commonplace. The court annals of early Louisville and Cincinnati read like bulletins from a poorly run detox center.

The railroad made civilization possible on the American frontier, speedily transforming it into something other than a frontier in the process. Railroads by nature had strong centralizing tendencies. They promoted compact urban development for the obvious reason that they couldn't go absolutely everywhere. They relied on central terminals for passengers and freight. In the days when all railroads were privately owned, many cities had more than one large terminal serving different lines. Boston had North and South Stations, New York had Penn and Grand Central, and so on. Nineteenth century businessmen and manufacturers wanted to be as close to the center as possible.

Where previously undeveloped land was concerned, railroads tended to produce nodes of settlement at regular intervals along a linear path. This linear pattern did not produce corridor development as we know it today, because steam-powered trains could not efficiently stop and restart every quarter mile. So, each separate node grew into a compact town or city, with miles of countryside in between. It wasn't until the 1890s, when electric motors made it possible for trolleys to stop and resume speed easily, that linear "streetcar suburbs" began to radiate out of the central city. However, automobiles became commercially available a mere ten years after the introduction of electric streetcar systems, and soon put them out of business in the United States. So we really have to look to Europe to see the longterm effect of the electric streetcar on cities, and their experience supports the view that streetcars do not destroy central cities.

Besides, until the early twentieth century there was no precedent in human culture for cities that were *not* compact and centralized, so the railroad and streetcar only reinforced age-old cultural habits. If anything, they increased the scale of centralization by an order of magnitude, so that cities became larger and denser than ever before—to a point of unpleasantness. Certainly the scale of factories increased fantastically in the years between 1865 and 1915, requiring ever larger buildings, and more workers, who required, in turn, evermore cheap housing. These workers arrived off farms, which were increasingly subject to mechanized operations needing fewer human hands, and off boats from Europe, where they might have become an increasingly volatile and politically dangerous "surplus population." Workers' housing in places like New York City took the form of instant slums.

Railroads brought up American towns and cities to world scale and then surpassed that scale practically overnight. Chicago rose from a muddy trading post to a city as large as Paris in half a century. Every American town of consequence suffered in some way from hyper-rapid development. Few formal design constraints were allowed to interfere with the primary goal of filling platted blocks with buildings. It was all the authorities could do to make provision for the most rudimentary of civic embellishments: courthouse squares, a few parks. Still, there was strong informal agreement, or public consensus, about the acceptable way to build things that individuals didn't dare violate. Modernism had not yet lowered the standards of architectural expression, and individual property owners took personal pride in the decoration of their buildings. This helped in creating interesting and imaginative street-walls. Walk the Lower East Side of Manhattan today, where many buildings from the late nineteenth century still stand, and you will see that even tenements were decorated more elaborately than schools and libraries are in our time. Since everybody, rich and poor, spent some time walking in the streets, the salient point of agreement was that the feelings of pedestrians mattered. The street had to be worth walking down. Otherwise, the only formal artistic principle brought to bear as a matter of explicit code was the discipline of the grid, itself fraught with the limitation of monotony.

Like all technological wonders, railroads had unanticipated consequences. In Mumford's phrase, railroads brought the ambience of the coal mine straight into towns and cities. The amount of noise and soot they generated shocked people who remembered cities before railroads. The marshaling yards took up valuable civic space, overwhelming waterfronts in particular. The rail corridor itself created a zone of squalor wherever it ran through an urban neighborhood—though nothing compared to the squalor imposed by cars, which diminishes *all* neighborhoods and *all* civic spaces.

Outside of towns and cities, the farmers, who comprised over half the U.S. population after the Civil War, lived in relative isolation, and the gulf between city and rural culture widened as the twentieth century approached, with many political complications. The great national issues of the period 1870 to 1920 increasingly reflected this gulf, and the farmers universally blamed their problems on the railroads (with their city-dwelling, top-hat-wearing, opera-going, millionaire owners). The Granger movement was largely an organized opposition to railroad freight-pricing policies. Aspects of Populism, particularly the "free silver" debate, were country-versus-city issues. The anti-saloon movement was part of the culture war between city and country life. Ironically, its highest achievement, the national prohibition of liquor (the Eighteenth amendment) was ratified at *precisely* the moment in history (1919) when automobiles were ending the farmer's extreme isolation.

Of all his achievements, Henry Ford was proudest of "getting the farmer out of the mud." The Model T brought rural Americans closer to the cultural mainstream than they'd been since the Civil War—though they would comprise an ever-shrinking percentage of the national population. Cars made the farm family's Saturday shopping trip to town a much broader national institution. Schooling, medical care, movies and newspapers suddenly became accessible to people who had been left behind by industrial progress and the novelties of metropolitan living.

History is ironical because it is made up of unforeseen conditions and unanticipated consequences linked together in long chains of perverse cause-and-effect which in turn generate evermore unexpected repercussions. As rural life in America became culturally enriched with the introduction of cars after World War One, American city life deteriorated sharply as cars and trucks overwhelmed the streets, immobilized trolleys, degraded all civic space, and made the public realm uniformly more unpleasant than it had ever been before. In a very short time the need to manage all this new car traffic led to enormous new and unanticipated public expenditures for police, stoplights, railway grade crossings, parking facilities, new bridges, and road improvement on an unprecedented scale. The money for these things was diverted from other public works, especially the great civic improvements of the City Beautiful movement—and that was just the first phase of the equipment needed to support mass automobiling.

The quality of city life suffered so enormously from the onslaught of cars that the majority of Americans soon made up their minds to reject the city, and what they *thought* it represented, for good. America was big, with seemingly endless room to spread out. The tacit promise of the car was that sooner or later everybody could live somewhere outside of town. The mature auto suburb of our time is the reenactment of life on the frontier. The landscape of the auto suburb is the new wilderness, and Americans pretend not to mind it because wilderness is supposedly America's natural social condition. What matters to us is hearth and home. The outside doesn't matter, except as excess space. Everything outside is merely to be traversed and endured. The freeway-scape is exactly this sort of wasteland. The car makes it endurable, even pleasurable with the recent innovations of air conditioning and stereo sound. It's not an accident that many car advertisements on television are filmed in wastelands that look more like the surface of Mars than anyplace Americans really live. The regime of mass car use is an offshoot of our historical aversion to civility itself. The car allows Americans to persist in the delusion that civic life is unnecessary. As a practical matter, this regime is putting us out of business as a civilization.

THE UGLY NUMBERS AND WHY WE DON'T CARE ABOUT THEM

We have all the information we need to persuade us by means of rational argument that using cars the way we do is catastrophic. The trouble is we don't care. I attribute this to a particular set of beliefs held by most educated Americans today. We believe there is a technical solution to every problem life presents. That is why the debate about car use has centered on purely technical issues such as air pollution, which can be easily measured, rather than on the developmental needs of children marooned in suburbia, which are harder to quantify. Notice, by the way, that even our elegant technical solutions to problems such as tailpipe emissions—catalytic converters, new fuel formulas, et cetera—have barely kept up with minimum federal air quality standards, because the total number of cars keeps growing, and we've done absolutely nothing to discourage the aggregate growth of car use (in fact, we encourage it). Meanwhile, there has been next to zero debate on the social or spiritual consequences of suburban sprawl, because such a debate would hinge on issues of quality, not on numbers.

This preoccupation with statistics and technical solutions to problems, especially problems of human behavior, is itself a byproduct of something more insidious in modern culture: the belief that science is an adequate replacement for virtue.* This dangerous habit of mind can also be expressed as *the fallacy of false quantification*. It means that no matter how solid your statistics are, numbers don't necessarily tell the whole story, or even the important part of it. It also means that statistics can be used to lie. We tend to select for debate only those aspects of a question that can be quantified, whether they are relevant or not, because the ability to measure something, *anything*, makes us feel more secure, more in control of our destiny, than grappling with thornier qualitative issues of good and bad or right and wrong. That is why we so often hear the word *methodology* flung about as a verbal weapon in public policy debates, as in "I challenge your methodology!" The jargon of science makes non-scientists feel more authoritative, at least among themselves. Anybody who can even *use* the word *methodology* in an argument sounds more scientifically respectable, whether he has anything worthwhile to say or not. Professionals operating on the fringe of hard science—such as journalists and critics of technology—feel unarmed without the buzzwords of the lab. So, numbers and statistics drive our debates about modern life, to the exclusion of all other frames of reference. What else should we expect from a culture that has ruled "value judgments" to be generally inadmissible?

That few Americans even care about the ominous statistics produced by whatever methodologies (some of them quite sound on their own terms) is something else again. It leads to the inescapable conclusion that this nation doesn't really want to think about the damage cars are causing our society. We lack the will to reflect, and perhaps the requisite virtue to acquire the will. We're too comfortable munching Cheez Doodles on the freeway right now to think about the consequences of continuing this behavior. The relatively feeble public debate about cars currently underway is carried on mainly by a few environmental groups and it is aimed at other environmentalists—in other words, preaching to the choir.

---

*E. Michael Jones elaborates this point nicely in his books *Living Machines* and *Degenerate Moderns* (San Francisco: Ignatius Press, 1995 and 1993, respectively).

Notwithstanding all these possibly fatal equivocations, here are the numbers, down and dirty.*

Americans log two trillion miles a year behind the wheel. Growth in vehicle miles traveled (VMT) far exceeds the growth of population or jobs in the United States. With 5 percent of the world's population, the United States consumes a quarter of the world's oil. Half of this is burned in motor vehicles.

No other country depends as heavily on cars as the United States. The average American drives twice as much as the average driver in Europe and Japan. Americans use cars for 82 percent of their trips compared to 48 percent for Germans, 47 for the French, and 45 percent for the British. In 1990, there were a record 190 million motor vehicles registered in the United States, which amounted to 23 million *more* cars than licensed drivers. More than 60,000 square miles of U.S. land is paved over, amounting to 2 percent of the total surface area, and possibly 10 percent of arable land.

The part of the world with the largest supply of oil is more politically unstable than at any period in our lifetimes. Russia (and its spin-off republics such as Kazahkstan), Iran, Iraq, Turkey, Saudi Arabia, Egypt, Libya, are all at risk of serious social disorder, which would affect world oil markets. Even moderate instability of supply and price could throw the U.S. economy into a state of chaos. Our military presence in the Middle East currently costs $50 billion annually. Waging a two-week-long war in that region in 1991 cost $5 billion.

All told, the costs of driving that motorists and truckers *don't* bear themselves amounted to about $300 billion a year in the early 1990s. User fees

---

*Unless otherwise specified, the following figures come from these sources: *The Going Rate: What It Really Costs to Drive*, by James J. MacKenzie, Roger C. Dower, and Donald D. T. Chen (based on research from the Lawrence Berkeley Laboratory, The Urban Institute, the Federal Highway Administration [of the U.S. Department of Transportation], the Brookings Institution, the National Research Council, the Kennedy School of Government at Harvard University, the Cato Institute, testimony before committees of the U.S. House of Representatives; the Institute of Transportation Engineers, the U.S. General Accounting Office, et. al.), published by the World Resources Institute, Washington, D.C., 1992; and *Road Kill: How Solo Driving Runs Down the Economy*, authors not individually credited (based on studies conducted by Apogee Research, Inc. and supported by the Joyce Foundation), a report published by the Conservation Law Foundation of Boston, 1994.

such as tolls and gas taxes are estimated to cover from 9 to 18 percent of the cost of using cars the way we do. Only part of the rest is covered by government subsidies derived from income, sales, excise, and property taxes. The remainder is fobbed off in the form of government debt onto generations as yet unlicensed to drive. Much of what government "pays" (subsidies plus debt) for driving is not identified as a cost of transportation, but lies buried in the budgets of agencies other than transportation departments. It is also distributed among the legal profession, and the insurance and medical industries, whose operations are themselves intermingled with each other and with stupendously expensive government bureaucracies like Medicaid. The net effect of all these pass-alongs, interminglings, and fobbings-off is to make driving *appear* cheaper than it really is.

Though the interstate highway system is now complete, the United States spends nearly $200 million a *day* constructing, improving, and rehabilitating streets and roads. In a year $20 billion is spent on routine maintenance like snowplowing and pothole filling. (In 1989 about 265,000 miles of pavement was rated in poor condition and 134,000 bridges rated as structurally deficient.) In a year $48 billion is spent nationally for traffic management and parking enforcement by police (at the expense of all other public safety problems, such as crime), on accident response teams, and on the administration of driving by federal, state, and city departments of transportation (DOTs) and state motor vehicle bureaus. A total of $6.3 billion goes to interest and debt retirement on highway bonds and the like.

The costs of air pollution that result in illness, hospitalization, and premature death is calculated to be somewhere between $10 billion to $200 billion a year—given the difficulty of assigning exact causes to some medical conditions and the uncertainty of monetizing the value of human life. The United States accounts for one quarter of worldwide carbon dioxide emissions, which contribute to global warming and possibly catastrophic climate change. The costs of car-generated ozone is estimated at roughly six cents per gallon of gas used. Roughly 50,000 people are killed every year in auto accidents—equal to total deaths in the Vietnam War. The costs in terms of damage to families are hard to quantify, but a study by the Urban Institute for the Federal Highway Administration monetizes the cost of all accidents at $358 billion annually, including 5,000,000 injuries a year, 1,800,000 of them disabling. The same study quantifies the cost of pain, suffering, and reduced quality of life at $228 billion a year. Property damage is estimated at roughly $40 billion a year—mostly in wrecked vehicles. Damage to buildings by noise is calculated at $9 billion; by vibration, $6.6 billion.

The Federal Highway Administration expects freeway congestion to quadruple over the next twenty years and to double on ordinary roads. The National Transportation Board predicts that annual delays in travel time (gridlock) will increase by 5.6 billion hours in the same period, wasting an additional 7.3 billion gallons of fuel, adding 73 million tons of carbon dioxide to the current emission levels, and costing $41 billion more per year. Congestion in Los Angeles has reduced average freeway speed to 31 mph. If the current rate of increase in cars is sustained, average freeway speed will fall to 11 mph by the year 2010. Seventy percent of daily peak-hour travel on urban freeways (that is, roads without traffic lights) now occurs under stop-and-go conditions, a 30 percent increase since 1983. The U.S. General Accounting Office cites estimates of national productivity losses caused by highway congestion at $100 billion a year.

Parking is, of course, "free" to many motorists at malls and shopping centers, with their immense lots. But all that paving raises the rents in malls so that only large national chain stores can afford to risk the long-term leases, which helps to force out local retailers, thus damaging local communities. Eighty-six percent of the workforce (about 85 million people) commute by car and, of these, 90 percent park "free." The average dollar value of a parking space is estimated at $1,000 per year, a subsidy amounting to $85 billion, supposedly paid by American businesses. Except business is able to write off the cost of supplying employee parking on their taxes. In other words, the government eventually bears the cost, partly in the form of debt. This supposedly "free" parking makes car commuting almost irresistible. If commuters had to pay for their parking spaces, it is estimated that the number of solo commuters would drop between 18 and 81 percent, depending on the locality and its standard of public transit.

If you commute 45 minutes twice a day for 49 workweeks a year (figuring three weeks vacation per 52-week year), you are spending 2.18 weeks year sitting in your car going to work and back. The average car costs approximately $6,100 a year to keep on the road in out-of-pocket payments, including installment loans, insurance premiums, maintenance, and gas. If you lived close enough to walk to work, you could take that $6,100 and the

2.18 weeks (plus your three-week paid vacation), and rent a house in the south of France for a month every year. Or, if you don't like to leave home, you could break down the 2.18 weeks into 367.5 extra hours a year to spend with your kids, or to make love with your spouse, or take piano lessons, or work out, or cook fantastic dinners, or do *anything* more spiritually gratifying than sitting in a tin can on the freeway.

The average price of a house where I live is $125,000. Over the thirty years of home ownership, one would spend about $250,000 on principal and mortgage interest payments for such a house, and—assuming *lower* annual real estate inflation rates looking ahead than we've experienced during the past thirty years—one would end up with equity in the form of a house with a market value of $250,000—that is, a sum equal to the amount invested over time. Over the lifetime of that home mortgage, you may *consume* eight cars, assuming you have two cars in the household (which is average), and that each car has a working life of about seven years. The average car now costs $20,000, not including finance charges. Figuring an average annual price inflation of 5 percent per car over the lifetime of your home mortgage, plus finance charges of 10 percent per car (but *not* including regular maintenance, gas, accidents, or insurance), you will spend $440,000 on cars during that thirty-year period (assuming you never graduate to better-than-average cars) and your total equity in cars after all that time (figuring the value of two more-than-seven-year-old cars, which is what you'll be left with at the end), will be little better than zip. It is often said that the most important investment decision in life is your home. These figures belie that bit of conventional thinking. Evidently, the most important decision is *where that home is*—because you will save a fantastic sum of money on cars over time if you live close to both work and shopping.

Those are the ominous figures. I wouldn't blame the reader if he or she felt that they were mind-numbing. It's an understandable human reaction. We see numbers and our eyes glaze over. Perhaps that's because, as awesome as they are, the numbers don't even come close to describing how we *feel* about living under the regime of endless driving.

HERE COME THE TECHNO FOLLIES

We're entranced with statistics, yet we don't really care what they have to say to us. We retain a childlike faith in the ability of science and technology to solve our problems—which is to say problems that have largely been *caused* by our use of science and technology, a curious situation.

It is actually pretty easy to trace the arc of our attitudes toward science and technology, and see how we've gotten into this predicament. From about 1790, when the modern industrial world got underway, through the 1890s, which brought us everything from anesthesia to zippers (also dynamite, electric lights, photography, railroads, recorded music, repeating rifles, steamboats, and telephones), there was every reason to believe that the future would be better than the past. The effects of World War One—the first glimpse of mechanized mass destruction—rocked that faith in a better future through technology, but more so, at first, for Europeans than Americans. Though the United States suffered over 60,000 combat deaths, all the battles took place off American soil, lending a patina of abstraction to the conflict, embodied by the abstract idealism of Woodrow Wilson in the war's aftermath.

For the next decade, the era we call the Roaring Twenties, America actually benefited from a war-dazed Europe, with its hangover of economic and political disruption. By 1929, however, the United States' hyperrobust industrial capacity had saturated its own markets and a steep downturn in our business cycle commenced. It was a downturn in proportion to the gigantic scale that industry had achieved in the early twentieth century, when factories like Ford's River Rouge works sprawled for square miles and employed thousands of workers.

This unprecedented crisis, the Great Depression, shook the nation's faith in technology's companion, industrial capitalism.* Yet even through the Depression, scientific progress and technical innovation proceeded so stunningly that it was possible to look to the future with hope. The years since World War One had brought forth evermore wonders: radio, commercial aviation, mass automobile ownership, rural electrification, talking pictures in color, plastics, air-conditioning. Americans' optimism about technology was neatly summarized in the 1939 World's Fair at Flushing Meadows in New York City, where the most popular exhibition was General Motors' "World of Tomorrow," featuring an enormous model of a "City of the Future," complete with elevated freeways and high–rises a la Le Cor-

*For a more detailed description of forces contributing to the Great Depression, see *The Geography of Nowhere*, Chapter 6.

busier. None of the unpleasant consequences of these innovations were anticipated by yesterday's futurists—for instance, what it might *feel* like to live or work in a tower next to a twelve-lane expressway, or what it might do to the neighborhood.

The World's Fair had barely shut its doors when Germany started another major war that left Europe a smoldering wreck again, only much worse this time, with a radioactive Japan thrown in for good measure. The Europeans were too devastated to remain utopian optimists. The French, shamed by their surrender to Adolf Hitler in 1940, and their subsequent complicity with Nazism under Vichy rule, retreated into the dreary existentialism of Camus and Sartre, until Charles DeGaulle, one of the few Frenchmen with a clear conscience on account of his wartime exile in Britain, rescued them from despair. The formerly avant-garde Russians, numb with victory, and with twenty million war dead, settled for a paranoid, gray, industrial-bureaucratic serfdom—anything for a little physical security! Shellshocked Britain slid into a half-baked version of Fabian socialism. And battered Japan made cheap tin toys for the export market, like a maimed war veteran relearning how to use his hands by stringing beads in occupational therapy. Again, while suffering many combat casualties, America miraculously escaped any physical damage to the homeland.

The atomic bomb can be viewed as an elegant technological solution to a political problem—the problem being Japan's failure to recognize her own defeat. Atomic weapons technology remained top secret until the day that the first bomb exploded over Hiroshima, so Americans did not have time to prepare psychologically for its debut. For all the anxiety it aroused, the bomb left us highly impressed with our ability to *get things done*. That the Soviets soon figured out how to make one was not a testament to their evil genius so much as proof that it is very difficult to keep valuable information secret in this world of human weakness.

The anxious sense of security Americans found in the atomic age doctrine of *assured mutual destruction* was, at best, a problematic adaptation to a deeply disturbing historical development. It was universally assumed that nuclear weapons would sooner or later be used by some new maniac—we had just concluded a war featuring a colorful cast of international maniacs, so we knew there was no shortage of them—and it was universally believed that World War Three would mean the end of the civilization, if not the human race itself. The "Atoms for Peace" program was a kind of consolation prize. Our confidence and pride in technology, and especially in winning World War Two so decisively, was now undermined by a pervasive unease about the apocalyptic danger that winning technology posed. A feeling of having lost control over it saturates the pop culture of the fifties, from movies about radioactive giant ants to the lore of backyard bomb shelters.

Under these anxiety-provoking conditions, America re-embarked on the path to that utopia General Motors had so brightly presented back in 1939, before Hitler and Japan so rudely interrupted us. Perhaps tragically we succeeded in building it. American know-how delivered the complete package right down to the elevated urban freeways and the high–rise housing projects, along with a million-score *little cabins in the woods* outside our soon-to-be-decrepit Cities of Tomorrow.

We've been living in this auto-utopia ever since. We've added to it, and elaborated it, with few public misgivings, despite the fact that it is impoverishing us and literally driving us crazy. Anybody who travels back and forth across the Atlantic has to be impressed with the difference between European cities and ours, which make it appear as though World War Two actually took place in Detroit and Washington rather than Berlin and Rotterdam. We barely endure the endless gridlock of suburbia, and wonder what is so deeply unfulfilling about the American Dream. And having thrown away much of the past to attain it, our disconnection from other elements of human culture is nearly complete. We've gone beyond the idea that the future will not be as good as the past. Judging by our behavior, we don't believe in the future, period. Our faith in everything else is also compromised. Religion is a kind of low-grade showbiz for that half of the nation under the median IQ. Art is a crazed naked woman smeared with chocolate hollering "fuck you" at an audience of masochists. Ironically, all we're really left to believe in *is* technology, which is demonstrably still with us, still providing fresh thrills.

An obvious delusional aspect of our obsession with technical fixes can be seen in the search for evermore-perfect cars, specifically, electric cars, so-called supercars or hyper-vehicles running on combinations of motive power, and on Intelligent Vehicle Highway Systems (IVHS).

The electric car is supposed to fix the problem of air pollution. The idea is that it runs on batteries, periodically recharged, therefore obviating tailpipe emissions. The first problem with this is that it is like the old joke about the guy who decides to make his blanket longer by cutting off twelve inches from the top and sewing it onto the bottom. The electric car presupposes that power will be generated at some central plant that each motorist will tap into for recharges. Unless the central plant generates electricity by solar, water, or wind—which is not technically feasible now at the scale proposed—they will have to operate by burning fossil fuel or by nuclear reactors. Both methods produce pollution. In the case of fossil fuels, power plant emissions (carbon dioxide in particular) would have to be of a magnitude proportionate with the number of vehicles running. In the case of nuclear power, the residue is spent radioactive material with a half-life of thousands of years that we have no idea how to get rid of safely.

The auto industry itself no longer believes in the electric car as a solution to the present set of problems. General Motors, supposedly the furthest ahead of the Big Three, merely goes through the motions as a public relations sop to the government, which mandates that a certain percentage of cars sold must be electric, beginning at 2 percent in 1998 and leading to 10 percent by 2003.* Storing enough energy equal to a gas-tank's worth of fuel (about 300 miles) would require so many pounds of batteries that the car would be too heavy to move. Batteries of realistic weight would have a much more limited range, and relatively long recharge periods. Additional concerns have arisen over lead pollution from the mining, manufacture, and use of lead-acid batteries.†

A more discouraging thing where electric cars are concerned is the economic equation. Batteries would have to be replaced every couple of years at a cost of $10,000 or more, for a car that is expected to be priced at not less than $35,000 (1996 dollars) to begin with. The overall implication is that the electric car is a product that cannot be brought profitably to the mass market. And since driving is a mass phenomenon in our society, it is unlikely to succeed as a replacement for gasoline-powered cars.

Another techno-fix for the fossil fuel quandary is the so-called Supercar or Hypervehicle, highly touted by an environmental group called the

---

*"Expecting a Fizzle, G.M. Puts Electric Car to Test" (*The New York Times*, January 28, 1994, p.1).

†"Lead Battery Used in Electric Car May Pose Hazards" (*The New York Times*, May 9, 1995, p.1).

Rocky Mountain Institute in Snowmass, Colorado, and its directors Amory B. and L. Hunter Lovins.* This vehicle is supposed to operate at rates up to 600 miles per gallon. The fabulous mileage is to be achieved by making cars super-light, aerodynamically super-slippery, and by storing otherwise wasted engine power in a flywheel. The motive power is a combination of internal combustion (fuel variable) and electricity. It is certainly plausible that such a driving machine could be developed. Whether it might be an *affordable* car for the mass of commuters is another question, and if not, the outcome is the same as with the all-electric car: if only a fraction of commuters could afford the damn thing, what about the majority who couldn't? Would it be okay for them to just go on burning gasoline, knowing that their wealthier counterparts were *morally superior*?

Finally, though, and most important, the problem with the Supercar, as with the electric car, is that they do absolutely nothing to address the disastrous social problems caused by suburban sprawl—the environment they are intended to service—or the spiritual damage to people who live in sprawl, which is to say in places that are not worth caring about. Nor will they help the rubble heaps that used to be our city centers. There is every reason to believe that super-hyper-electro-vehicles will only make these problems worse by perpetuating the delusion that we can continue to live vast distances from the places where we sleep, work, shop, and play—or that we should *want* to continue. In this light they are classic follies, short-sighted ideas divorced from any consideration of what constitutes a life worth living, or a decent human habitat, and it is rather appalling that so-called environmentalists would take such ideas seriously.

Another techno-fix of truly comical dimension is the Intelligent Vehicle Highway System (IVHS) or Intelligent Transport System (ITS). The idea here is to use computers imbedded in roadways and in cars to optimize traffic flow so we can move evermore cars on existing roads. Anybody who has driven on a major urban commuter road such as the Long Island Expressway or the Washington, D.C. Beltway really has to wonder whether the folks behind this idea are kidding. These highways are already jammed bumper to bumper. It is proposed that the computer would help drivers find alternate routes off the highway on surface streets. Do you suppose it

*"Reinventing the Wheels," by Amory B. Lovins and L. Hunter Lovins (*The Atlantic Monthly*, January 1995).

will improve the quality of your life to have three times the volume of traffic on the street where you live as you have now? And what happens when we've encouraged more and more car commuting by clever computer routing? Surely in ten years the secondary and tertiary roads will also be jammed. By the way, on-board computers would do nothing to prevent mechanical breakdowns or roadwork. Someone somewhere will still suck a valve on the freeway, and the pavement on every highway in America will have to be repaired from time to time. There will always be roadwork somewhere.

Under IHVS virtually every car on the road would have to be equipped with a computer. The system implies 100 percent compliance. What would prevent any number of miscreants from getting on the freeway without one? Many people already drive without licenses or insurance, with guns, with heads full of drugs and liquor. How could this system work if, say, 10 percent of all drivers were only pretending to have computers on board? They'd have to be pretty good drivers, to say the least, if they were to keep within six inches of the car ahead at 65 mph without screwing up the system.

Finally, if the idea is to make travel as automatic as possible, why not go all the way and establish decent public transit? That's what riding a train or a bus is all about: *somebody else drives the damn thing.* A human brain, after all, is also an on-board computer. It must be obvious that IVHS is a joke.

ISTEA

The good news is that the U.S. government, while often foolish, is not completely insane. The Intermodal Surface Transportation Efficiency Act (ISTEA) of 1991 was an authentic attempt to redirect federal Department of Transportation money from spending strictly on highways to more integral systems that would include trains, light rail, buses, bicycles, and pedestrians. The act was also supposed to give the states and localities more "flexibility" in their spending choices. Predictably, some states, like Missouri and Wisconsin, have chosen to use their federal transportation dollars to continue gold-plating their highways. When I saw him in June of 1995, Milwaukee Mayor John O. Norquist, a New Urbanism activist, deplored the Wisconsin DOT's decision to pour more than half a billion dollars into the *renovation* of a single interchange in his city's downtown. For the same amount of money, Norquist said, the city could have built a light rail system twenty miles out to the suburbs. That same week, WisDOT's commissioner Charles H. Thompson denounced ISTEA before a gathering of highway construction industry bigwigs, saying the act would put them out of business—which was utter nonsense for reasons I shall discuss presently.

Other states, like Maine, Oregon, New Jersey, and New York, have moved aggressively to get people around by means other than single-occupant automobiles. In the fall of 1991, the citizens of Maine voted down a bond issue aimed at widening the Maine Turnpike and then approved a law called the Maine Sensible Transportation Policy Act that reiterated all the goals of ISTEA at the state level. Before that, there had been a perception that the Maine DOT was simply a Department of Highways.*

As I write, Portland, Oregon, is laying the tracks for the second line of its light rail system. The first line, opened in 1990, went east; the new one will run out to the western suburbs. The Portland Metro region has also enacted a .5-cent sales tax to finance a north-south transit axis. New Jersey announced plans for a new electric trolley system along the west side of the Hudson River, from North Bergen to Bayonne. New York City will replace the derelict West Side Highway with a grade-level boulevard along the Hudson River in lower Manhattan. The design includes sidewalks, bike paths, a tree-lined median, and provision for buses. This is a particularly good example of the difference between a monofunctional elevated freeway and a finely detailed, integral, multimodal street. The new boulevard will not only function better as a transportation corridor, but since it is built at street grade, it will also reconnect the life of the city to the Hudson River—which was previously blocked by the menacing wasteland beneath the elevated freeway. By the way, more people already walk to work in New York than any other state. Upstate, NY DOT is turning the towpaths of the Erie and Champlain Canals into a 300-mile recreational bike trail. Both canals are still used by commercial barges and pleasure boats, only they are no longer towed by mules.

The ISTEA law also required every region in the United States with a population above fifty thousand, to create an entity called a Metropolitan

---

*"The Highway Revolution That Wasn't," by Jonathan Walters (*Governing*, May 1995).

Planning Organization (MPO) to finally begin what should have been going on the last seventy-five years: land-use planning that is coordinated with transportation planning, so that suburban sprawl based on bonehead single-use-zoning is no longer the only kind of "growth" that occurs. The MPOs are not off to a rousing start. Hardly any of them employ staff designers—i.e., people who actually draw town plans, street grids, and building types. The MPOs' enforcement powers run from little to zilch. And they are not backed by any sort of public consensus that demands a real alternative to suburban sprawl.

Some parts of the United States are going to make a successful transition out of the golden age of motoring, while some are going to be left behind, and the longterm results are apt to be tragic for the left-behind regions. However, ISTEA also connotes opportunities that are currently unrecognized—as exemplified in the Wisconsin DOT chief's remarks. The construction industry, which now bemoans any reduction in highway building, would benefit greatly from the rebuilding of city and town centers. "We have over eight thousand miles of sidewalks to maintain in New York City alone," said Jeffrey Olson, New York State DOT's ISTEA bicycle and pedestrian coordinator. "In Europe, where pedestrian-oriented city centers have taken off in a big way," he added, "the construction industry is really behind the effort, because there's so much to build. Adding light rail lines, integral streets, sidewalks, textured pavements, new signals, and all the other infrastructure that classic city planning calls for, creates jobs. It's just construction of a different kind than we're used to."

THE END OF THE ROAD?

We ought to know how to assemble a human habitat of high quality that equitably allows citizens of all classes to get around in a dignified, comfortable, even pleasurable manner, that gives children and old people equal access to society's civic institutions, that produces safe neighborhoods for the well-off *and* the less well-off, that promotes a sense of belonging to a community, that honors what is beautiful, and which doesn't destroy its rural and agricultural surroundings. This habitat comes down to us from history in the form of villages, towns, and cities. The suburban sprawl model that has temporarily replaced these forms must be understood to be an aberration, an extreme and abnormal condition, as cancer is an abnormal condition in the tissues of the human body.

The original benefits of automobiles were thought to be convenience, freedom of mobility, and comfort. The first two things vanished entirely under the regime of compulsory commuting. What is left of comfort amounts to little more than air-conditioned imprisonment. I believe that our utter dependence on the automobile must and will come to an end. Society can no longer afford the cultural phenomenon of *mandatory mass car ownership*. Whatever cars might run on in the future, we will have to use fewer of them and less often. We are going to need places that are worth dwelling in, from which we won't feel compelled to escape every moment we are not working. These are precisely the kind of villages, towns, and cities I propose, and I will spell out the particulars of their design in later chapters. I am convinced that they will make us happier.

In the future, car ownership will not be required for first class citizenship. Some people may want to own them. Many others, wishing not to be burdened by the cost of maintaining and storing a personal driving machine that they use perhaps a few dozen times a year, will be happy to rent one when the need arises. You may be sure that the market will provide rental cars that are in good mechanical condition and clean. You will have a choice of models, from a tin can on wheels to luxury and sport vehicles. In fact, that is already the case. I travel a lot, and I have yet to rent a car that is not altogether in better shape than my own 1992 Toyota pickup truck.* Very short-term rental also will be accomplished the same way it is now: taxicabs. Not only do you rent the car by increments of miles or minutes, but it comes with a driver, and the moment you reach your destination, you don't have to worry about the damn thing—where to park, whether it needs gas, or a new muffler, are not your concern.

Otherwise, an intelligently designed town can easily provide access to the needs and wishes of people in everyday life by public transit, walking, and biking. The models for these places already exist. They're called London, Paris, Amsterdam, Prague, Munich, Oxford, Perugia, and Zurich.

I believe that we Americans have managed to go beyond driving ourselves crazy with cars. There is a moral and spiritual dimension to these

---

*I describe my own living situation in Chapter 12.

problems that we are unable to reckon. We have the knowledge to do the right thing; we lack only the will to do the right thing. The inescapable conclusion is that our behavior is wicked, and that we are liable to pay a heavy price for our wickedness by losing things we love, including our beautiful country and our democratic republic.

CHARM

I T is hard to imagine a culture less concerned than ours with the things that make life worth living. Much of what we esteem as life-enhancing and pleasure-giving tends toward the childishly self-destructive: fast cars, goopy microwaved cheese snacks, prolonged television viewing, compulsive shopping, playing with guns, heavy drinking, kinky sex, to name a few. These are the fruits of political liberty in our time, and so, tragically, liberty itself begins to seem a rather trashy thing.

The physical setting that we Americans have lately constructed for our everyday lives reflects this trashiness. It is probably self-reinforcing, meaning the worse it gets, the worse we act, and the worse we act, the worse it gets. One could almost state that the everyday world of the United States seems designed to enable us to dwell in a condition of ever-diminished humanity. Why this should be so has something to do, I suppose, with the self-correcting mechanisms of the teleologic process that we call nature, or *the ever-unfolding universe*, which seeks at many levels to maintain a course toward evermore self-aware intelligence, or grace, and in so doing tends to punish craven stupidity of the kind evinced by American culture in the late twentieth century. In other words, we're getting what we deserve.

This seems pathetic, not least so because historically our national character has been, by and large, generous, diligent, and idealistic—if not always wholly honorable (but what nation ever was?). And so, lately—really since our great victory over the evil Axis in World War Two—we have become, by sheer inertia, a nation of overfed clowns, crybabies, slackers, deadbeats, sadists, cads, whores, and crooks. Most pathetic is that this regression occurred in an era of unprecedented technical innovation, when we have managed to shed light where there had been so much darkness. And so our diminishing humanity in the face of this might seem to call into question the value of technological progress itself.

More to the point, though: why does the experience of standing in the street of a suburban housing subdivision, or in the parking lot of a shopping mall, or beneath the glass-box skyscrapers in downtown Minneapolis or Austin, or under the elevated freeway in Seattle, fill a healthy, normal person with the very primal dread of everlasting darkness? What is in the nature of these things that makes them so unlovable?

Nature appears to consist of things, of stuff we call matter, but more correctly may be said to consist of patterns of energy. The patterns are bound atomically by charm and animated by gravity, which is charm at a higher order of magnitude. At the quantum level nature miraculously springs to being as a set of mere probabilities, and upward from there elaborates itself into evermore complex intersections, or relationships of relationships. It is in the nature of nature to be charming and therefore beautiful. The many patterns of nature are charming at all their levels of intersection. Where patterns live—and here on Earth is so far the only known dwelling place of living patterns, which we call biological organisms—they reach out tropistically, ever-evolving, to become something else, arguably something higher and better.

In terms of human behavior and self-consciousness, charm is the quality of *inviting* us to participate in another pattern, for instance, to glimpse the pattern of another personality through the veil of manners, customs, pretense. When we say that a person is charming, we mean that he makes himself permeable, and, in so doing, invites you to do likewise, so that the two patterns of your personalities may intersect for a while. I think the same principle is true of the things around us. As Christopher Alexander has ably pointed out, what we perceive to be *things* in our everyday surroundings—buildings, walls, streets, fences—are more properly understood as patterns intersecting with patterns, *relationships* between other relationships.* It is when they cease to be relationships and become mere things that patterns lose the quality Alexander calls "aliveness." A window in a house is a relationship between the inside of the house and the outside world. It transmits light and air, and it affords glimpses between the private and public realms. When it fails to operate in these ways, it becomes a mere hole in a wall. From this point of view, it is easy to understand how various relationships and patterns in our everyday world either possess the qualities of "aliveness" or "deadness." It is this quality of aliveness that I propose to call charm for the purpose of this discussion. Charm promotes the intersection of relationships and invites one set of patterns to interact with other patterns, including the complex patterns of individual human minds.

WHY LATELY WE PREFER UNREALITY

So, we stand out in the street of the suburban housing subdivision. There are the ranks of the split-level houses, each with a different cosmetic cladding—harlequin brick, vinyl, asbestos, or aluminum siding, redwood board-and-batten, et cetera—marching up the gently curved suburban street. The houses are large by world standards and filled with wondrous amenities for cooking, bathing, and regulating the room temperature. They stand set back on spacious lawns, the foundations concealed behind the familiar clumps of juniper or rhododendron. Trees frame the house on its lot. The scene is peaceful as can be. At worst, the peace is disturbed by occasional automobiles motoring by. Now, why would a casual observer viewing this tranquil scene want to jump out of his skin and shriek?

A key element commonly perceived by critics of this scene—even by its

---

*A *Pattern Language*, Christopher Alexander, et al. (New York: Oxford University Press, 1977). For an extremely condensed discussion of Alexander's ideas, see *The Geography of Nowhere*, Chapter 13.

kitsch devotees—is its plodding artificiality, its unreality, its inauthenticity. The suburban housing subdivision is not what it pretends to be. It is emphatically not a community, certainly not a village or a town. What you feel most strikingly is the perverse absence of those qualities. The subdivision is an abstraction: a metaphor. It is an assemblage of *little cabins in the woods* or *little manors in a park* or some hybrid of the two. It is essential to this metaphor that each of these houses be understood as existing in isolation. The fact that there are, say, 350 of them distributed around a tract of 175 acres only elevates the unreality of the metaphor. We want them to behave as an ensemble, as a living pattern, but the houses refuse. To do so would contradict their splendid isolation.

Behind this particular metaphor, as we've previously touched on, stands the compulsion to reenact the national experience of life on the frontier, each family lodged in its own sacred grove, surrounded by wild beasts and skulking redskins. We cherish this image. We're like a dysfunctional family playing a beloved home video of a family camping trip over and over. Americans could have set out to use the fantastic economic windfall that followed World War Two in embellishing the real patterns of real life, as found in the systems of our existing towns and cities. We chose not to. We opted for fantasy instead.

Despite this raiment of metaphor and fantasy, the housing subdivision fails to satisfy. Its constituent parts do not add up to the organic whole of a human settlement. It fails by deliberate design because the individual houses are not *supposed* to be part of a whole. It also connects very poorly with other patterns outside its boundary, including other subdivisions. Even when streets are geographically proximate, they will not connect, because to do so would mean admitting that there is a larger social context beyond the individual houses.

Further proof of this refusal to acknowledge the larger social context is the political outrage that always greets the announcement of a new subdivision to be built next to an older one. The inhabitants of the older one feel betrayed, as though some special social contract should have protected them from the consequences of the very thing that they demand of their elected officials: economic growth in the only form that it is currently understood, at any cost. Often the "victims" will resort to expensive legal measures to defeat the new proposal. The town hall—a cinderblock box between the strip malls—will resound with their lawyers' cries of indignation. What right has the developer to destroy their illusion of living *in the country*!

Of course, it turns out he has every right by law—the zoning law, that is. The new subdivision gets built because it meets all the technical requirements of the codes. New fry pits and chain stores are added to the nearby highway strip in anticipation of more customers, more fields and woods are bulldozed to accommodate the new junior high school and its parking lots, and whatever remnant of rural charm the area had is destroyed, without being mitigated by the creation of authentic human civic constructs, i.e., real towns.

Why do we enjoy the countryside, by the way? What is rural charm? It is the opportunity to live in connection with the rich patterns of other organisms, namely plants and animals, and their interactions with natural patterns like the seasons or the cycles of day and night. These patterns include the processes of birth and decay, and they excite our senses in ways that their artifact replacements do not. A hike through meadows and woods in real farm country in May is exhilarating because of the extravaganza of patterns of emerging life operating in concert: the buds unfurling on the trees, the trilliums blooming, the insects buzzing in the air, the birds singing as they build their nests, the little wild mammals scurrying about, the perfumes and tantalizing stinks of the cow pastures and the sloughs. We feel more alive in places like this. We are literally drawn into sensual participation with these patterns, charmed by the living activities of creatures and organisms with whom we share a kinship. We are hard-wired to appreciate these patterns. It is part of the neurological pattern of our own nature to be excited by them.

The artifact replacements for these rural things in the form of a suburban housing subdivision turn out to be rather paltry. They end up acting more as sinister barriers to other living patterns, leaving us in a kind of neurobiological slum. There is the numbing undertone of the lawnmowers in their ceaseless battle to discipline the monoculture of grass. There is the sound of radios and the smell of soapy water evaporating on warm asphalt as the cars are washed in the driveways. The odor of pesticide wafts off the rose bushes, making us shudder with intimations of cancer or mutant offspring. One is neither in nature, nor in an authentic human community (which is also in and *of* nature). This unreality turns out to be very costly. Maintaining the artifice of millions of *little cabins in the woods* like these causes a tremendous amount of what we call environmental damage, meaning it disrupts or destroys existing patterns in nature, and lately it does so at a scale that begins to threaten the larger intersecting patterns of the organism that constitute our planet.

While natural patterns and ecosystems appear to be fragile and highly susceptible to the assault by human artifacts, they may in the end prove more resilient than we are. The damage that we do to the natural patterns in our surroundings and to our own nourishing patterns of culture represents the substitution of deadness for aliveness, a push toward stasis and changeless equilibrium. It may put us out of business as a species long before the earth loses its ability to restore the dynamic disequilibrium that has been its chief characteristic since life began. In fact, getting rid of us may be necessary, even desirable, for a teleologic cosmos bent on evolving to ever-higher states of self-aware intelligence.

Then again, we may yet prove to be the angelic instrument of its evolution. We're not doomed to go on living in the late twentieth century automobile dystopia, with all its death-dealing trappings, nor are the other industrial nations doomed to copy our follies. There is reason to believe that we can reform our living arrangements and find a way to dwell much more sympathetically with the rich organic processes of the planet, without plundering, insulting, and destroying them in order to carry on our own activities. A more optimistic view of technology, for instance, might pose the great advances of our time as the prelude to an evolutionary leap that would permit us to live much more equitably among other living patterns. Almost all the damage we've caused has occurred in the past 200 years, a nanosecond in geological time. Our great-great-grandchildren may look back at these crude industrial centuries as some ghastly stage of human development like puberty, complete with all the physical disfigurement and idiocy that we associate with puberty.

Yet, for the moment, we are still stuck in it. It has been in the nature of this phase for us to revel heedlessly in our new technological prowess, like fifteen-year-olds preoccupied with their newly activated sexual endowments, and the result for human culture has been correspondingly unattractive.

DEMOCRACY UNBOUND

Our triumph in World War Two was a victory of industrial production. The American army was structured not much differently than our enemies' armies. Many of our generals were professional soldiers and so were theirs. Their conscripts were drawn from all the ranks of society as ours were. The salient difference in the conduct of the war was that we could bomb the shit out of their factories, while our factories were never touched.

After the war, we continued in this successful mode of activity, producing Levittowns, freeways, Chevrolets, TVs, and refrigerators instead of tanks and artillery shells. Meanwhile, our notion of democracy mutated from a set of political institutions to a merchandise distribution scheme: everybody deserved lots of new *stuff* as a reward for whipping the Nazis and the Japanese, and this *stuff* would be standardized, affordable, and sufficiently vulgar to ensure the broadest appeal among the democratic masses.

The catch was that vulgarity militates against excellence: for instance, the idea that some things might be better than other things, or that some people might be better than other people—an obscene notion in the aftermath of Auschwitz. To protect society against future political obscenities, American intellectuals of what was then called the political left led a revolt against elitism that was strangely consistent with the psychology of mass consumer culture. The revolt soon featured a campaign against standards in the arts and humanities, including a ban against "value judgments," which led to an inability to make distinctions in the quality of anything, and a paradoxical devaluation of intellectual excellence itself. Next came the battle against hierarchies and authorities in the 1960s, leading to the demoralization of higher education in the 1970s, and climaxing in the Political Correctness wars of the 1980s and 1990s, which were induced by the wish among academic zealots to compel the toleration of "diversity" (differences minus standards)—especially those forms of diversity officially sanctioned by the campus Thought Police. Cultural relativism beat a quick path to cultural despotism, the dictatorship of the mediocre.

The refusal to allow value judgments, or recognize hierarchies in civic affairs and the arts, or to assert that some things might be better than others, was certainly reflected in the charmlessness of public architecture through this period, out of which every building in some way or other took on the democratic characteristics of a parking garage. I am picturing, for instance, the many new buildings erected on my state university campus, circa 1966–1970, the brutal, raw poured concrete exteriors and cinderblock classrooms. Whether they were psych labs for running rats or art history lecture halls, the look and feel was the same: democratically dismal.

Perhaps all the wars and disruptions of the twentieth century were *so* cumulatively terrible that western culture decided in some collectively subconscious way that it was no longer worthy of beauty or delight. The idea that *form follows function* expressed by Louis Sullivan in 1896 was adopted with maniacal rigor as the basis for nearly all western architectural theory and practice in the twentieth century, particularly in the universities. That Sullivan himself did not mean it to be applied so literally is indicated by the remarkably rich and structurally functionless ornamentation of his own buildings. As a dictate, *form follows function* is a curious perversion of the much more durable precept in Vitruvius (reiterated by Jacques-François Blondel in 1752) that architecture is composed of the triad *commoditas, firmitas, and venustas,* or function, structure, *and* beauty. Somehow, in the twentieth century, beauty ended up in the garbage can.

CHARM, SANITY, AND GRACE

Many failures in human pattern-making ensue from the dismissal of beauty as a legitimate constituent of cultural artifacts. The consequences have been unanticipated and fraught with paradox and irony. Perhaps the most glaring is that during America's financially richest period, 1950 to 1990, we put up almost nothing but the cheapest possible buildings, particularly civic buildings. Look at any richly embellished 1904 firehouse or post office and look at its dreary concrete box counterpart today. Compare the home of a small-town bank president dating from the 1890s, with its masonry walls and complex roof articulation, to the flimsy house of a 1990s business leader, made of two-by-fours, sheetrock, and fake fanlight windows. When we were a far less wealthy nation, we built things with the expectation that they would endure. To throw away money (painfully acquired) and effort (painfully expended) on something guaranteed to fall apart in thirty years would have seemed immoral, if not insane, in our great-grandfathers' day.

The buildings they constructed paid homage to history in their design— including elegant solutions to age-old problems posed by the cycles of weather and light—and they paid respect to the future through the sheer expectation that they would endure through the lifetimes of the people who built them. They therefore evinced a sense of chronological connectivity—one of the fundamental patterns of the universe—an understanding that time is a defining dimension of existence, particularly the existence of living things, such as human beings, who miraculously pass into life and then tragically pass out of it, perhaps forever—we do not know—our self-awareness of this fate making it tragic.

Chronological connectivity lends meaning and dignity to our little lives. It charges the present with a more vividly conscious validation of our own aliveness. It puts us in touch with the ages and with the eternities, suggesting that we are part of a larger and more significant organism. It even suggests that the larger organism we are part of *cares* about us, and that, in turn, we should respect ourselves, our fellow creatures, and all those who will follow us in time, as those preceding us respected us who followed them. In short, chronological connectivity puts us in touch with the holy. It is at once humbling and exhilarating. I say this as someone who has never followed any formal religious practice. Connection with the past and the future is a pathway that literally charms us in the direction of sanity and grace.

The antithesis to this can be seen in the way we have built things since 1945. We reject the past and the future and it shows in our graceless constructions. Our houses, commercial, and civic buildings are constructed with the fully conscious certainty that they will disintegrate in a few decades. There is even a name for this condition: the *design life*. Strip malls and elementary schools have short design lives. They are not expected to endure through the span of a human life. In fact, they fall apart in under fifty years. Since there is no expectation that these things will last, nor that they will speak to any era but our own, we seem to believe there is no point in putting any money or effort into their embellishment—except for the sort of cartoon decoration that serves to advertise whatever product is sold on the premises. Nor do we care about the age-old solutions to the problems of weather and light, because we have technological artifacts to mitigate these problems, namely electricity and central heating. So the windows don't open in many new office buildings. In especially bad buildings, like the average WalMart, there may be no windows. Yet this process of disconnection from the past and the future, and from the organic patterns of weather and light, all done for the sake of expedience, ends up diminishing us spiritually, impoverishing us socially, and degrading the aggregate set of cultural patterns that we call civilization. We register these discontinuities as *ugliness*, or the absence of beauty.

The everyday environments of our time, the places where we live and work, are composed of dead patterns. They infect the patterns around them with disease and ultimately with contagious deadness, and deaden us as they do. They are patterns which fail to draw us in, to invite us to participate in the connectivity of the world. They frustrate our innate biological and psychological needs—for instance, our phototropic inclination to seek natural daylight, our need to feel protected, our need to keep a destination in sight as we move about town. They violate human scale. They are devoid of charm.

Our streets used to be charming and beautiful. The public realm of the street was understood to function as an outdoor room. Like any room, it required walls to define the essential *void* of the room itself. Where I live, Saratoga Springs, New York, there once existed a magnificent building called the Grand Union Hotel. It was enormous—the largest hotel in the world in the late nineteenth century—occupying a six-acre site in the heart of town. The hotel consisted of a set of rather narrow buildings which lined the outside of the unusually large superblock. Inside the block was a semipublic parklike courtyard. The sides of the hotel that faced the streets incorporated a gigantic veranda twenty feet deep, with a roof three stories high supported by columns. This facade functioned as a marvelous street-wall. Its size—a central cupola reached seven stories—was appropriate to the scale of the town's main street, called Broadway. The facade, or street-wall, was active and permeable. The veranda that lined it was filled with people sitting perhaps eight feet above the sidewalk grade, talking to each other while they watched the pageant of life of the street. These veranda sitters were protected from the weather by the roof, and protected from the sun by elm trees along the sidewalk. The orderly rows of elm trees performed an additional architectural function. The trunks were straight and round, like columns, reiterating and reinforcing the pattern of the hotel facade, while the crowns formed a vaulted canopy over the sidewalk, pleasantly filtering the sunlight for pedestrians as well as the hotel patrons. Notice that the integral soundness of all these patterns worked to enhance the lives of everybody in town, a common laborer on his way home as well as a railroad millionaire rocking on the hotel veranda. In doing so, they supported civic life as a general proposition. They nourished our civilization.

When I say the facade of the Grand Union Hotel was permeable, I mean that the building contained activities that attracted people inside, and a number of suitably embellished entrances that allowed people to pass in and out of the building gracefully and enjoyably. Below the veranda, and one-half a story below the sidewalk grade, a number of shops operated, selling cigars, newspapers, clothing, and other goods. So the street wall was permeable at more than one level and with a multiplicity of uses.

The courtyard park that occupied the inside of the six-acre block had winding gravel paths lined with benches among more towering elm trees. It was a tranquil place of repose—though sometimes band concerts and balls were held there. Any reasonably attired person could walk in off the street, pass through the hotel lobby, and enjoy the interior park. This courtyard had even more overt characteristics of a big outdoor room than the street did. It was much more enclosed. Like the street facade, the courtyard facade also featured a broad permeable veranda with a high roof.

THE GRAND UNION HOTEL, SARATOGA SPRINGS, NEW YORK, A CENTURY AGO. (SARATOGA SPRINGS HISTORICAL SOCIETY)

The veranda functioned as a mediating zone between the outdoor world and the world of the hotel's interior, with its many public, semipublic, and private rooms. One passed through this hierarchy from public to private in a logical sequence, and the transition was eased at each stage by conscious embellishment. It was, by nature, a more formal order of things than we are accustomed to in our sloppy, clownish, informal age. The layers of intersecting patterns at work in this place were extraordinarily rich. The patterns had a quality of great aliveness, meaning they worked wonderfully as an ensemble of patterns, each pattern doing its job while it supported and reinforced the other patterns in functioning optimally. The hotel was therefore a place of spectacular charm. It was demolished in 1953.

While nothing lasts forever, it was tragic that this magnificent building was destroyed less than a hundred years after it was built. In 1953 America stood at the brink of the greatest building spree in world history, and the very qualities that had made the Grand Union Hotel so wonderful were antithetical to all the new stuff that America was about to build. The town

THE GRAND UNION SUPERMARKET STRIP MALL, SARATOGA SPRINGS, NEW YORK, 1960, OCCUPYING THE FORMER SITE OF THE GRAND UNION HOTEL. (SARATOGA SPRINGS HISTORICAL SOCIETY)

demolished it with a kind of mad glee. What replaced the hotel was a strip mall anchored by, of all things, a *Grand Union* supermarket. This Grand Union shopping plaza was prototypical of its time. Tens of thousands of strip malls like it have been built all over America since then. It is in absolutely all its details a perfect piece of junk. It is the anti-place.

What had been the heart and soul of the town was now converted into a kind of mini-Outer Mongolia. The strip mall buildings were set back from Broadway one hundred and fifty feet, the setback now comprising a parking lot. The street and the buildings commenced a non-relationship. Since the new buildings were one story high, their scale bore no relation to the scale of the town's most important street. They failed to create a street-wall. The perception of the street functioning as an outdoor room was lost. The space between the buildings and the street now had one function: automobile storage. The street, and consequently the public realm in general, was degraded by the design of the new strip mall. As the street's importance as a public place declined, townspeople ceased to care what happened in it. If it became jammed with cars, so much the better, because individual cars were understood not merely as "personal transportation" but as *personal home delivery vehicles*, enabling people to physically haul home enormous volumes of merchandise very efficiently, at no cost to the merchandiser—which was a great boon for business. That is why the citizens of Saratoga in 1953 were willing to sacrifice the town's most magnificent building. It was okay to simply throw away the past. The owners of the supermarket chain that anchored the strip mall didn't live in town. They didn't care what effect their style of doing business would have on the town. They certainly didn't care about the town's past, and their interest in the town's future was limited only to technicalities of selling dog food and soap flakes.

What has happened to the interrelation of healthy, living patterns of human ecology in the town where I live has happened all over the country. Almost everywhere, the larger patterns are in such a sorry state that the details seem irrelevant. When my town invested tens of thousands of dollars in Victorian-style street lamps in an effort to create instant charm, the gesture seemed pathetic, because there was no awareness of the larger design failures. It is hard to overstate how ridiculous these lampposts look in the context of our desolate streets and the cheap, inappropriate new buildings amid their parking lots in what remains of our downtown. The lamppost scheme was like putting Band-Aids on someone who had tripped and fallen on his chainsaw.

The one-story-high Grand Union strip mall building must be understood as a pattern in itself, a dead one which infects surrounding town tissue with its deadness. Putting up one-story commercial buildings eliminated a large number of live bodies downtown, and undermined the vitality of the town. The pattern of one-story commercial buildings in the form of strip malls became ubiquitous across the United States after the war. In most places, it became a *requirement* under the zoning laws. You couldn't build anything *but* a one story strip mall if you obeyed the rules. This eliminated a form of affordable market housing that exists virtually everywhere else in the world.

By the way, it is a common misconception that apartments over shops are inhabited by the shopowners. More often than not, the owner of a business like a drug store or a dry cleaner has enough income to live in a regular house elsewhere in town. Apartments over stores are necessary, however, for many other categories of decent people who don't happen to need a whole house, especially single working young adults without children. This is a group of people with a very high need for social interaction in public places. They seek out the public life of the streets and the cafes, and their presence enriches the life of the town tremendously. A critical mass of inhabitants must be present in a neighborhood to generate an informal social scene, so there must be plenty of places for them to live. The dwellings must be physically close to the places of work, shopping, and relaxation. A young person must be able to leave his or her dwelling on a whim and meet his or her friends at the cafe within a short walk. This does not now happen anymore, with very few exceptions. We have not built things in this pattern for half a century, so isolation and loneliness broods across this land.

This is the tragedy of single-use zoning, which has infected every quarter, every country mile, every cul-de-sac. The towns and cities across America were decanted of their middle-class residential populations, who were then scattered across the "cheap" land of the countryside, connected only by cars. The civic life lost in this process could not be reconstituted in the suburbs, because proximity was made illegal. Single-use zoning made everybody a commuter. What's more, the pure experiential *quality* of commuting by private car was low, despite such luxuries as air-conditioning and on-board digital stereo systems. Each commuter had to act as pilot as well as passenger. This took concentration, and was especially vexing after eight hours of work. The landscape around the freeway was so hideous that simply gazing out the windshield made your head hurt. You couldn't exactly sit back and read the *Atlantic Monthly* going 45 mph on the freeway. Forget about ordering a cocktail. Where traffic was really bad, as in Los Angeles, people got so angry and hateful they fired pistols at each other.* Even under normal conditions, commuting left people psychologically exhausted.

Having suffered to get home, leaving home after work to socialize in suburban sprawl becomes problematical, even for highly motivated young people. Not only are the live bodies thinly distributed over vast areas, but there are often few social destinations, and they are generally not concentrated in one area, meaning you have to get back into the goddam car, which you just struggled to get out of. And finally you're stuck with the low-grade experience of driving up and down the highway strip in the pall of night, a tedious, futile, and rather sordid enterprise. Meanwhile, the tawdry blandishments of the boob tube and the microwave oven combine with this feeling of futility to defeat normal, healthy individuals in their quest for social connection. They sink into the sofa for another night of microwaved cheese dips and canned laughter. . . . When we refer to the suburbs as "dead," we couldn't be more precise.

THE HOUSE AS TOTEM OBJECT

Having made the public realm of towns and cities desolate, and our civic buildings laughable, Americans are left with the private realm of the house. Since the 1980s, the *Little Cabin in the Woods* or the *Manor in a Park* has again mutated to a higher level of abstraction in our collective national fantasy life, especially as it is expressed in pop culture. The fanatical obsession with individual houses and the comforts they must provide today is striking. Upon returning from Dallas, Texas, where he was taken on a tour of suburban villas to get an idea of what the upscale market expected

---

*In July 1994, I was in Los Angeles, idly listening to the local TV news while dressing for a speech. The news featured reports of monumental traffic tie-ups due to an accident on the Santa Monica Freeway. An advertisement then came on for a car toilet, a sort of bedpan designed for people stuck in traffic jams on limited access highways.

in the way of a house, the architect and town planner Andres Duany declared, "We no longer refer to the main bedroom as the master *suite*. From now on we call it the master *resort!*" The level of luxury was mind-boggling, he said. Walk-in closets and Jacuzzies were just the beginning. Nowadays the buyer expected a virtual home Health & Racquet Club, with square footage for Nautilus weight training machines, treadmills, Stairmasters, NordicTracks, rowing devices, sauna, and a juice bar.

I am fascinated by the so-called "shelter" magazines like *House Beautiful* and *Country Living*, with their tableaux of domestic felicity—a world where the cookies are always warm from the oven; and $5,000 worth of polished copper cookpots hang in size order from an iron rack over the Vulcan restaurant-grade stove; and the country quilts speak of loving handwork passed from one generation to the next; and the moldering antique duck decoys remind us of those bracing afternoons out in the marshes getting wild meat for the supper table.... Wait! There's glamorous Martha Stewart, the goddess of hearth and home herself, radiating health, wholesomeness, and not a few pheromones, gilding pumpkins out in the potting shed! Ah, home, home, home sweet home! Home at last. Home.

Here, unlike the miserable outside world, the patterns of things can be lovingly and carefully arranged to work in harmony to create places that will satisfy our neural and spiritual needs. Here, the moronic zoning laws are not in force and all the conventions of homemaking, acquired painfully over the epochs of human history, still operate—unlike, say, the acquired conventions of architecture and town planning, which are on the garbage barge steaming off to Nowhere. Here, within these comforting walls, bathed in amber candlelight, surrounded by rich fabrics and burnished wooden artifacts, the conventions of decoration, of *honoring* the private realm with our own heartfelt embellishments, intersect with our longings for a place where we can truly feel we belong, not just like transients temporarily installed in a commodity called *housing*. Within these painstakingly rag-rolled and faux-marbled walls, we can bring our mere existence *to life*, we can *charm* our surroundings into a condition of animation, sanity, and grace, using correct proportions, appropriate scale, and choice materials, and nobody can stop us because this is home, the sanctuary. And, wonderfully enough, since there is no end to the diversity of patterns, and patterns working within other patterns for us to employ, there are endless versions of this domestic fantasy to spin out, so one never tires of the shelter magazines, month after month after month. The rooms are always fresh, new, different, and deeply satisfying.

Notice that we almost never see the setting of these fabulous palaces, that is, what lies beyond the property line. Probably nine-tenths of such showplaces picked at random stand within shouting distance of some horrific boulevard of chain stores and frypits, or a housing subdivision designed by subnormal developers for subnormal home buyers, or a Spend-Rite Shopper's Klub in a 12-acre parking lot, or a stock car racetrack. We never see the context because it's universally assumed that the context is horrible, and we don't even want to know about it. Forget about showing the nearest street—we don't even want to see the driveway. The shelter magazines *never* feature automobiles, except for the ads. Their mere presence in them would spoil the picture. Give the slightest hint that a real world of freeway on-ramps and supermarket parking lots exists beyond the rose arbor, and a stench invades the fantasy, like a heap of dog shit on the stenciled solarium floor. Notice that there are no magazines in America called *Neighborhood Living*, or *Towns Beautiful*. What would we show? The supermarket parking lots of Beverly Hills are just as depressing as those in any *lumpenprole* subdivision town outside Scranton, Pennsylvania.

It is also worth noting that connubial bliss has not exactly kept pace with this cult of domesticity. If anything, there appears to be an inverse relationship between our growing obsession with the home as a totem object and the disintegration of families that has become the chief social phenomenon of our time. We worship this idealized container for family life, and yet it turns out that the family cannot be sustained without the larger container of community life. Husbands and wives, parents and children, brothers and sisters cannot be all things to each other.

Oddly, too, real live people, like cars, are rarely pictured in the idealized photos of the shelter mags, I suppose for a couple of reasons. One is that we are expected to project ourselves into the picture, to imagine what it would be like if these were *our* homes, and so, of course, they cannot be already occupied by strangers. Another reason is that when people are photographed at leisure in such settings, standing around the butcher-block kitchen *island* with balloon glasses of cabernet in their hands, and little tidbits of goat cheese focaccia in their fingers, they take on the appearance of idle, overprivileged twits, of people whom we are disposed to dislike, because whatever they do in the world, they're being paid too much, compared to us, who aren't paid enough to afford a Vulcan restaurant-grade stove, and who the hell has time to marbleize baseboards, make focaccia, and gild pumpkins, anyway? So by association we then decide not to like their unbelievably expensive, overly precious house with the phony-baloney quilts sold through a catalog outfit located in some dreary suburb of Minneapolis, and the pretentious $5,000 copper cookery set that the chatelaine never really uses. So that's why the live bodies are kept to a minimum.

There is also evidently an inverse relation between our obsession with the fabulous houses presented in the shelter media and the kind of *dreck* market houses that actually spring up in the cornfields after the bulldozers and the guys with plastic hats have paid their little visit. Whether these are $78,000 starter homes for junior actuaries, or three quarter of a million dollar palaces for thoracic surgeons, they are apt to be designed equally poorly, and built of equally inferior materials, incompetently assembled.

A WINDOW INTO METAPHYSICS

It is amazing how terrible new houses look these days. That they are isolated objects without civic connection or context is bad enough. But in other societies, and in history, people have managed to put up isolated houses that look pleasing. A popular argument is that Americans simply have very low standards. I wonder whether Americans have any standards. Whatever was known about design patterns that worked, that came alive, in terms of human psychology and neurology has been forgotten or dismissed.

A hundred years ago, for instance, there was general agreement in our culture about the regulating proportions of windows. One almost never sees a horizontal window in a house built before 1900, and there is a reason for it. Human beings project anthropomorphic qualities on the things they build. Picture the front end of a 1949 Buick and how uncannily it resembles a snarling face, its massive chrome radiator grill set like the teeth of a flesh-eating fiend—not unlike the frightful masks used by primitive tribespeople to scare their enemies. I suppose a car like that expresses the abnormally high testosterone levels of men who had just returned in triumph from war.

Houses, too, express human qualities. Historically windows are vertical.

VERTICAL VERSUS HORIZONTAL WINDOWS

WE PROJECT HUMAN QUALITIES ON HOUSES AND THEY REFLECT THEM BACK AT US. VERTICAL WINDOWS FRAME THE HUMAN FIGURE IN AN UPRIGHT, NEUTRAL, AND DIGNIFIED WAY. (J.H. KUNSTLER)

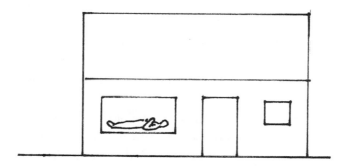

HORIZONTAL WINDOWS FRAME THE HUMAN FIGURE IN A WAY THAT IMPLIES THAT THE INHABITANTS ARE EITHER SLEEPING, HAVING SEX, OR DEAD. WE DON'T WANT TO THINK ABOUT THEM THAT WAY. (J.H. KUNSTLER)

The pattern holds across all cultures until very recent times. This configuration allows for load-bearing walls, and distributes more light into the interior rooms. But there is something else going on: anthropomorphically, vertical windows frame the standing human figure. They represent *the idea* of people standing erect inside the house. This appeals to our minds. Horizontal windows are rather disturbing at a subconscious level. If they frame the human figure at all, they do so in ways that make us vaguely uncomfortable: they suggest that the inhabitants are either sleeping, having sex, or dead.

Now, sleeping, sex, and being dead are all obviously part of the human condition, but as casual observers we don't want to project them onto the house and its denizens. Most of the time, the people inside are strangers to us. Our minds want to conceive them in the most dignified condition possible. That's what standing up signifies. It is generalized, formal, composed, and dignified, like a portrait. The convention of vertical windows, therefore, is a device for regulating a house's sense of dignity.

I use the word convention because it means an idea that has been agreed upon by the members of a given society and instated in their culture. Often it represents the solution to some practical problem arrived at by trial and error over a long period of time. The convention makes further experimentation, and further argument, unnecessary. It also performs a unifying design function, within which diversities of details can freely operate. There are many ways that one can design and embellish a vertical window, but verticality itself can unify all windows in a building. Conventions have the drawback of becoming ossified rules. Sometimes, they result in customs perpetuated for reasons that few people remember—like the Jewish dietary injunction against eating lobsters. But in some cases, conventions persist for good reasons, and we should at least take some care when we set out to disregard them.

The agreement about vertical windows fell apart in the twentieth century. Modern construction materials and methods of assembly obviated the need for load-bearing exterior walls. For Modernist architects, horizontal windows became a way of declaring that the "skin" of a building could look like anything. It could even violate the needs of human psychology. The vertical lines of a building imply the existence of gravity, and the natural fact that things on earth tend to be *grounded*. Geological features, trees, animals, human beings all express the condition of groundedness. Horizontal windows violate this sense of groundedness in a building by visually interrupting the vertical elements. Modernists liked this because they were in favor of defying history and convention. A building that appeared to levitate in defiance of gravity delighted them, and if it made *bourgeois* individuals uncomfortable, so much the better. Defying gravity seemed especially ultramodern, like the idea of space travel.

Frank Lloyd Wright, who was emphatically not a member of the Modernist club, but was a creature of his time nonetheless, detested ordinary, double-hung, vertical sash windows of the kind universally used in houses at the turn of the century. He called them "guillotines." He, too, employed horizontal windows and exploited horizontality as a general principle, but his designs were so rigorously regulated by other conventions that they brought his buildings miraculously back into a state of groundedness that the brain could accept.

Modernism provided an intellectual rationale for discarding age-old conventions, like vertical windows; technology made it feasible. With cheap electric lighting, natural light seemed dispensable. This led to another peculiar development. People began designing their houses from the inside out. It used to work the other way around. The great Palladio hardly concerned himself with the interiors of his famous country villas. It really wasn't until the mid-nineteenth century, with its advancements in plumbing and heating, that the design of the interior of a house became at least equally important as the outside—royal palaces and the like being obvious exceptions. Today the outside is nearly meaningless. We have shifted 180 degrees. I often come across new subdivisions full of houses that have whole exterior walls with *no* windows at all. They are not needed for light. Nobody wants to look at their neighbor's side yard, nor do they want anybody in the side yard looking into the house. In fact, they don't want to acknowledge the neighbor's existence. What's more, windows are expensive—not to mention curtains and shades. Why add another $10,000 to the cost of construction? So the solution today is to eliminate "excess" windows wherever possible.

This results in a house that is built like a television set. Only the front matters, and it only matters insofar as it can broadcast some cartoonish image of what we want others to think about it—for instance, that it vaguely conjures up Scarlett O'Hara's plantation house, or William Shakespeare's birthplace. The windowless sides of the building are of no consequence. Often the sides are clad in a cheaper material than the front, and completely incompatible with it. Around here, you get harlequin bricks on the front and yellow vinyl "clapboards" on the side. And, of course, the rear is where the plug comes out, so to speak. The rear of such a subdivision house is usually a hodgepodge of ventilation caps and weirdly shaped windows that have no relation to anything but the interior position of master beds, hot tubs, and kitchen sinks. That's where the odd-shaped windows go, the little octagons from Home Depot.

Many houses built after 1950 have a garage door—or doors, since multiple car ownership is now nearly mandatory in suburbia—occupying up to 50 percent of their facades. This dominating feature invariably compromises whatever remains of the building's dignity. Jonathan Hale's discussion of "regulating lines" in *The Old Way of Seeing* is pertinent here.* One of the historical conventions in architecture—including vernacular houses—is that the visible features of buildings conform to hidden geometric patterns. We don't notice them, but they are there. For instance, you can draw a diagonal line across the photo of a 1790 house and the corners of the windows and doors will magically fall on this line. The hidden diagonal exists, therefore, as a means of regulating the proportions of the facade elements.

A given building may be rich with many hidden regulating lines, and this charms our minds, inviting us to take delight in the building's many intersecting patterns, its *aliveness*. Frank Lloyd Wright's houses are meticulously loaded with these hidden regulating diagonals, which are not always present in buildings by his less talented contemporaries, That is the reason that Wright's houses emit such a sense of organic aliveness, despite their gross horizontality.

Other powerful geometric devices seem to have magical properties and have been known and used for thousands of years. The golden section is one of these. The golden section is a mathematical formula that is imbued with such power that Renaissance artists and philosophers referred to it as the divine proportion. A golden section is created by the point C on line AB if AC/AB = CB/AC. The algebra derived from this arrangement yields the ratio 1:1.618.

The same proportion is produced by the Fibonacci series in mathematics, in which the succeeding number in a series is the sum of the two previous numbers, as in 1, 1, 2, 3, 5, 8, 13, 21, 34, 55, 89, and so on. Dividing

The Old Way of Seeing, by Jonathan Hale. (Boston: Houghton Mifflin Co., 1994).

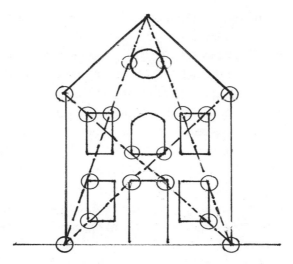

IN OLDER HOUSES, INVISIBLE DIAGONALS (BROKEN LINE) REGULATE THE PROPORTIONS OF DOORS AND WINDOWS. NOTICE HOW MANY POINTS LINE UP ALONG THE REGULATING LINES. THIS KIND OF VISUAL AGREEMENT PLEASES THE HUMAN MIND. (J. H. KUNSTLER)

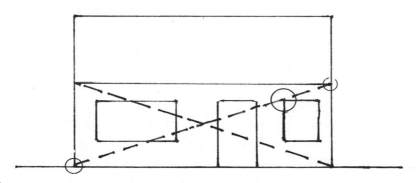

IN THE POSTWAR HOUSEBURGER, THE INVISIBLE DIAGONALS DO A POOR JOB OF REGULATING PROPORTIONS. THE MIND IS SUBCONSCIOUSLY DISTURBED BY THE LACK OF VISUAL AGREEMENT. (J. H. KUNSTLER)

one figure in the series by its successor produces a golden section ratio—with greater accuracy as the numbers increase. Both Hale and Turner make the point that this ratio, or proportion, shows up repeatedly in nature.*

*Beauty: Value of Values, by Frederick Turner. (Charlottesville: University of Virginia Press, 1991).

Translated visually, it produces the Fibonacci spiral, which expresses the dynamic form of evolving organic growth. The spiral pattern can be discerned in a chambered nautilus seashell and sunflower seed heads. The golden section manifests mathematically in the proportion of lines that compose a five-pointed star and a pentagram, which are represented by such natural forms as starfish, sand dollars, and maple leaves. The proportions of tree branch sections to one another also conform linearly, and the crowns of many trees, when framed geometrically, result in rectangles with golden section proportions. Turner writes: "Psychophysical experiments show that irrespective of culture and education, people prefer rectangles, the lengths of whose sides are related by golden section ratio, to any other shape of rectangle. Thus, the rudiments of visual beauty are founded upon the ratio of organic growth."*

The golden section happens to have many analogs in the proportions of the human body. Hale points out that it corresponds to the ratio of the distance from the feet to the navel to a person's overall height. The human face contains golden section proportions, and we may conclude that this accounts to some degree for a consensus of human beauty in any given culture. These many synchronisms indicate that when we make things that are part of our world, we are inclined to follow existing orders in nature, and that these orders are not arbitrary or absurd, as many epistemologies of the twentieth century have proposed. There is the further implication that we defy these organic patterns in our constructed surroundings at some hazard to our humanness.

"One purpose of pattern is to ground the building in nature and connect it to our bodies by imitating the ordering discipline of life forms, especially our own," Hale states.† Turner says, "The physical world already possesses a powerful consensus of its own, to which we must adapt, and out of which we grow."‡

I'm not proposing per se any strict mathematical method for proportioning man–made forms. The dogmas of Modernism were hyperrational, if anything, and they did not produce a humane architecture. Le Corbusier was well aware of golden section relationships in human anatomy, and he

*Ibid. p. 95.
†*The Old Way of Seeing*, p. 67.
‡*Beauty: Value of Values*, p. 71

worked out a rational proportioning system based on them that he called the "Modulor." It didn't make his buildings any more livable. His atrocious Unite d'Habitation apartment block in Marseilles was based on thirteen Modulor dimensions. Its failures had at least as much to do with Corb's apparent ignorance about ordinary domestic concerns such as the desire for privacy, or the spatial needs of cooks.

Other rigorous proportioning systems for building things have existed in history, with equally legitimate claims on our neurology—for instance, Renaissance systems based on musical intervals and harmony. There are many ways of making connections with what is elemental in our nature. One "magical" property of such mathematical phenomena such as the golden section (1.618 . . .), or of Pi (3.14159 . . .), is that they are irrational numbers that go back and forth irresolvably between infinite microdimension and macrodimension. This, along with the tantalizing implications of chaos theory and of the fractal geometries described by Mandlebrot and others suggests a reality that takes the form of a questing intelligence in a state of disequilibrium, in perpetual pursuit of equilibrium, or resolution, pursuing this goal in beautiful patterns based on irresolvable numbers. Aliveness itself might be defined by such irresolvable tensions. Tension is at the core of sexuality. One could describe the music of Johann Sebastian Bach as an orchestration of tensions. I suspect that whatever arithmetical patterns we *can* discern point to ever-deeper tensions, paradoxes, and yearning harmonics at work in a universe we only superficially understand. These mysteries are what we call beauty.

I suppose I am making a general argument in favor of readmitting metaphysics to the humanities. Empirical science is not the only way of knowing things. Not everything is demonstrable by double-blind experiments. Our attempts to turn the arts and humanities into pseudosciences in this century have proceeded from the fallacious idea that nothing but the empirically demonstrable is real, and this has led to the abolition of virtue, beauty, and grace from many sectors of human enterprise, particularly the sectors where they are most needed: the realms of human conduct and art. The fundamental nature of the holy, after all, is that we *sense* it exists, though we have no way of proving it.

Now we have come rather a long way from my original point in all this, but it is still pertinent: the result of breaking the conventions about window proportions is that you get houses with no dignity and a world without charm. This is the price that we pay for ignoring our own psychology and millenniums of tradition that proceeded from it in the form of practical wisdom. I daresay many Americans don't care what their own houses or their neighbors' houses look like. We chalk this off to good old American pragmatism, or patriotic individualism, but the consequences are rather serious: a world outside the confining walls of the home that nobody cares about, a country made up of places that are not worth caring about, and a nation that is not worth defending.

REINSTATING BEAUTY AND VALUES IN GENERAL

First we have to care about our everyday world. The private world of the house as a repository for consumer goodies has taken precedence in recent decades. The public realm of the everyday world was relinquished to the cars which serviced the private world of the house. This behavior was supported by a set of conditions that enabled us to forsake our local communities, in other words, to forsake our sense of place. Cheap gasoline made it possible for the majority of Americans to live great distances from their workplace, which diminished their ability to care about either the place in which they lived or the place in which they worked—and especially the places in between. It allowed giant national retail chains to ship enormous volumes of merchandise vast distances at tiny profit margins, and still make tons of money, and in the process to exterminate a whole class of local business people who formerly played crucial roles in the economic and civic life of our home-places. Cheap gas made it possible to maintain single-use zoning, which has put civic life out of the reach of children, old people, and those without the means to own a car.

The regime of cheap gas and mandatory driving demolished human scale in the everyday world. It turned every journey between point A and point B into the same experience of sitting in a steel capsule listening to canned entertainment. It impoverished the rich patterns of connectivity that had existed in human settlements throughout history. These patterns developed out of natural orders and served our natural needs. Their complexity and aliveness manifested as palpable charm in man–made forms from the smallest detail on a single building to whole towns.

The regime of cheap gas is near its end, and I believe we will respond to it—though with some neurotic resistance—by recondensing the everyday life of our nation into human-scaled neighborhoods in towns and cities that will be worth living in. The reinstatement of human scale alone has broad and deep implications. It implies that the outside will once again matter. We will care about the world beyond our thresholds because every little detail will be in our face, so to speak; there will be no avoiding them, no more whizzing past them at sixty miles per hour.

If we live and work in the same place, as is increasingly the case for many people, mixed use will come to supersede single-use zoning, and it will enliven our towns by naturally reintegrating dwellings, shopping, and business of many kinds. We have already reached the point where significant numbers of people work out of a home office, and increasingly they demand more from their surroundings than the monotony suburbia has to offer. I've been self-employed for twenty years, and this has led me to choose a classic Main Street town as my headquarters because living, shopping, and business were already integrated in the town's physical fabric. I have been very happy in this situation, and consider myself fortunate. I don't waste my time commuting.

However, my town is a cultural vestige. Tourists by the thousands come here to gawk at a way of life that has been nearly exterminated elsewhere in America, a way of life that was once common. My town is regarded as *charming* because it is so *unlike* the places that visitors come from, the northeastern big-city suburbs. Here they recognize relationships between things that are deeply pleasing, relationships that can't be duplicated or re-created under their own zoning laws back home. They may speak of my town as *charming* in a superficial sense, but that doesn't mean that they do not apprehend its deeper implications. Americans are just beginning to awake from the long coma of complacency that they fell into half a century ago.

We are also exiting a regime of mind which devalued every way of measuring the quality of human happiness except that which could be demonstrated by empirical experiment or by statistical analysis. As I've mentioned, one consequence of that worldview was to make all value judgments inadmissible, especially among the educated classes. This was a tragic thing. It denied validity to other dimensions of human experience. It made us incapable as a society of defining the spiritual properties of a life worth living.

It is most unfortunate that under this regime the moral dimension of life was relegated to the domain of the supernatural, and therefore in our time moral issues have become the special province of evangelical religious bullies, political extremists, and maniacs like the abortion clinic assassins. These are our arbiters of right and wrong, of goodness and badness. The discussion has not taken place on a higher level. Those truly equipped to lead the discussion of values—as Hamilton, Madison, and Jefferson did in their day—have dropped out under the assumption that all cultural values are relativistic and equally valid. This assumption has been solidly lodged in most college curricula, where its influence on impressionable minds is hard to overstate. It is embedded in much of what passes these days for higher culture.

I sense that this is changing, that it is once again becoming possible, if not yet exactly respectable, for educated people to make value judgments, and that is a very good thing. Our times demand it. Our national civitas is failing, and it will not do any longer to pretend that all forms of conduct are equally okay, or that all economic choices are equally favorable, or that all products of human ingenuity are equally beneficial.

The times demand that educated people debate issues of good and bad, right and wrong, beauty and ugliness. Educated people must readmit notions such as virtue and wickedness into the realm of ideas, and arrive at a humane consensus about what they mean. It will no longer do to say that virtue is too complex to be understood—and that, therefore, we prefer *no* definition of virtue to a possibly imperfect one. In restoring these notions of value to respectability, we may even resurrect the fundamental source of beauty in our world, which is the shame, the original sin, of our innate human imperfection.

CREATING SOMEPLACE

I T is literally against the law almost everywhere in the United States to build the kind of places that Americans themselves consider authentic and traditional. It's against the law to build places that human beings can feel good in, or afford to live in. It's against the law to build places that are worth caring about.

Is Main Street your idea of a nice business district? Sorry, your zoning laws won't let you build it, or even extend it where it already exists. Is Elm Street your idea of a nice place to live—you know, the houses with the front porches on a tree-lined street? Sorry, that's against the law, too. All you can build where I live, in upstate New York, is another version of Los Angeles. The zoning laws say so.

This is not a gag. Our zoning laws comprise the basic manual of instructions for how we create the stuff of our communities. Most of these laws have only been in place since World War Two. For the previous 300-odd years of American history we didn't have zoning laws. We had a popular *consensus* about the right way to assemble a town, or a city. Our best Main Streets and Elm Streets were not created by municipal ordinances, but by cultural agreement. Everybody agreed that buildings on Main Street ought to be more than one story tall, that corner groceries were good to have in residential neighborhoods, that streets ought to intersect with other streets to facilitate movement, that sidewalks were necessary, and that orderly rows of trees planted along them made the sidewalks much more pleasant, that rooftops should be pitched to shed rain and snow, that doors should be conspicuous so you could easily find the entrance to a building, that windows should be vertical to dignify a house. Everybody agreed that communities needed different kinds of housing to meet the needs of different kinds of families and individuals, and the market was allowed to supply it. Our great-grandfathers didn't have to argue endlessly over these matters of civic design. Nor did they have to reinvent civic design every fifty years because everybody forgot what they agreed about.

Everybody agreed that both private and public buildings should be ornamented and embellished to honor the public realm of the street, so they built the kind of town halls, firehouses, banks, and homes that today are on the National Register of Historic Places. We can't replicate any of that stuff. Our laws actually forbid it. Want to build a bank in Anytown, USA? Fine. Make sure that it's surrounded by *at least* an acre of parking, and that it's set back from the street by *at least* 75 feet, and that it be no more than one story high. There's your bank. The instructions for a church or a muffler shop are identical. That's exactly what your laws tell you to build. If you deviate from the template, you will actually be punished by not receiving a building permit.

Therefore, if you want to make your communities better, begin at once by throwing out your zoning laws. Get rid of them. Throw them away. Don't revise them. Set them on fire if possible and make a public ceremony of it—public ceremony is a great way to announce the birth of a new consensus. While you're at it, throw out your "master plans" too. They're invariably just as bad. Replace these things with a new traditional town-planning ordinance, which prescribes a more desirable everyday environment.

The place that results from zoning is suburban sprawl. It must be understood as the product of a particular set of instructions. Its chief characteristics are the strict separation of human activities (or *uses*), mandatory driving to get from one use to the other, and huge supplies of free parking.

CURRENT ZONING CODES

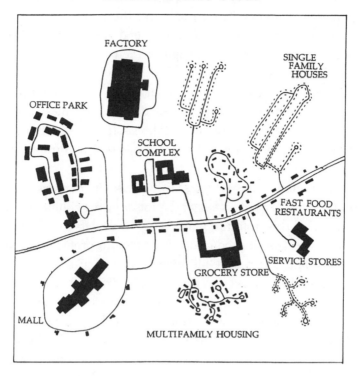

UNDER CURRENT ZONING, ALL ACTIVITIES ARE SEPARATED FROM ONE ANOTHER IN SINGLE-USE PODS, ISOLATED ON CUL-DE-SAC STREETS, ACCESSIBLE ONLY BY CAR. (CATHERINE JOHNSON)

After all, it's called *zoning* because the basic idea is that every activity demands a separate zone of its very own. You can't allow people to live around shopping. That would be harmful and indecent. Better not even allow them within walking distance of it. They'll need their cars to haul all that stuff home, anyway—in case you haven't noticed, most supermarkets don't deliver these days. While you're at it, let's separate the homes, too, by income gradients. Don't let the $75,000-a-year families live near the $200,000-a-year families—they'll bring down your *property values*—and, for Godsake, don't let some $25,000-a-year recent college graduate live near any of them, or a $19,000-a-year widowed grandmother on social security. There goes the neighborhood! Now, put all the workplaces in a separate office "park" or industrial "park," and make sure nobody can walk to them either. As for nice public spaces, squares, parks, and the like—forget it, we can't afford them because we spent all our public funds paving the four-lane highways and collector roads and the parking lots, and laying sewer and water lines out to the housing subdivisions, and hiring traffic cops to regulate the movement of people in their cars going back and forth to these segregated uses.

It soon becomes obvious that the model of the human habitat dictated by zoning is a formless, soulless, centerless, demoralizing mess. It bankrupts families and townships. It causes mental illness. It disables whole classes of decent, normal citizens. It ruins the air we breathe. It corrupts and deadens our spirits.

The construction industry likes it because it requires stupendous amounts of cement, asphalt, steel, and a lot of heavy equipment and personnel to push all this stuff into place. The car dealers love it. Politicians *used to* love it, because it produced big short-term profits and short-term revenue gains, but now they're all mixed up about it because the voters who live in suburban sprawl don't want any more of the same stuff built around them—which implies that at some dark level suburban sprawl dwellers are quite conscious of its shortcomings. They have a word for it: *growth*. They're now against growth. Their lips curl when they utter the word. It has the same appeal as the word *fungus*. They sense that any new construction is only going to make the place where they live worse. They're convinced that the future is going to be worse than the past. And they're dead-on right because, in terms of their everyday surroundings, the future *has been getting worse* throughout their lifetime. They're not hallucinating. Growth means only more traffic, bigger parking lots, and ever-bigger-and-uglier buildings than the monstrosities of the sixties, seventies, and eighties.

So the suburbanites become NIMBYs (Not In My Back Yard) and BANANAs (Build Absolutely Nothing Anywhere Near Anything). If they're successful in their NIMBYism, they'll use their town government to torture developers (i.e., people who create growth) with layer upon layer of bureaucratic rigmarole, so that only a certified masochist would apply to build something there. Eventually, all this unwanted growth leapfrogs over them to cheap, vacant, rural land farther out (controlled by politicians hungry for "rateables"), and then all the new commuters in the farther-out suburb are choking the NIMBY's roads anyway to get to the existing mall in NIMBYville.

Unfortunately, the NIMBYs don't have a better model in mind. They go to better places on holiday weekends—Nantucket, St. Augustine, little New England towns—but they think of these places as *special exceptions*. It never occurs to NIMBY tourists that their own home places could be that good, too. *Make Massapequa like Nantucket? Christ, where would I park?* Exactly.

These special places are modeled on a pre-automobile template. They were designed to the human scale and in some respects *maintained* that way, too. Such a thing is now unimaginable to us today. We *must* design for the automobile because . . . because all the weight of our laws and habits tell us we must. Notice, by the way, that you *can* get to all these special places in your car. It's just a pain in the ass to use the car while you're there—so you stash it someplace for the duration of your visit and get around perfectly happily on foot, bike, cab, or public transit. The same is true, by the way, of London, Paris, or Venice.

NANTUCKET STREET

AMERICANS PAY PREMIUM PRICES TO VACATION IN TOWNS WITH TRADI-TIONAL STREETS LIKE THIS. MOST OF THE RELATIONSHIPS YOU SEE HERE VIOLATE COMMON ZONING LAWS, ESPECIALLY THE DENSITY OF HOUSES PER ACRE. (CATHERINE JOHNSON)

Now, I have already made the point that the future will not allow us to continue using cars the way we've been accustomed to in the unprecedented conditions of the late twentieth century. So, whether we adore suburbia or not, we're going to have to live differently. Rather than being a tragedy, this is actually an extremely fortuitous situation, a wonderful opportunity, because we are now free to redesign our everyday world in a way that is going to make all classes of Americans much happier. We are fortunate also that the knowledge needed to accomplish it already exists. We do not have to come up with tools and techniques never seen before. The principles of town planning can be found in excellent books written before World War Two. Three-dimensional models of the kind of places that these principles can create also exist in the form of historic towns and cities. In fact, after two generations of educational amnesia, this knowledge has been reinstalled in the brains of professional designers in active practice all over the country, and these designers have already begun to create an alternate model of the human habitat for the twenty-first century.

What's missing is a more widespread public consensus—i.e., cultural agreement—in favor of the new model and the will to go forward with it. Large numbers of ordinary citizens haven't heard the news. They're stuck in old habits and stuck in the psychology of previous investment, and political leadership reflects this all over America. NIMBYism is one of the results, a form of hysterical cultural paralysis. *Don't build anything, don't change anything!* The consensus that exists, therefore, is a consensus of fear, and that is obviously not good enough. We need a consensus of hope.

In the absence of a new widespread consensus about how to build a better everyday environment, we'll have to replace the old set of rules with an explicit set of new rules. Or, to put it a slightly different way, replace zoning laws with principles of civic art. It will take time for these principles to become second nature again, to become *common sense*. It may not happen, in which case we ought to be very concerned. In the event that this body of ideas gains widespread acceptance, think of all the time and money we'll save! No more endless nights down at the zoning board watching the NIMBYs scream at the mall developers. No more lawsuits. We will have time, instead, to become better people and to enjoy our lives on a planet full of beauty and mystery. Here, then, are some of the things citizens will need to know in order to create a new model of the everyday environment in America.

A SHORT COURSE IN THE GENERAL PRINCIPLES OF CIVIC ART

The principles apply equally to villages, towns, and cities. Most of the principles apply even to places of extraordinary high density, like Manhattan, with added provisions that I will not go into here, in part because there are so few special cases like Manhattan, and because I believe that the scale of even our greatest cities will necessarily have to become smaller in the future, at no loss to their dynamism. (London and Paris are plenty dynamic with few buildings over ten stories.)

The pattern under discussion here has been called various *neo-traditional planning, traditional neighborhood development* (or the *TND*), *low-density urbanism, Transit Oriented Development* (or the *TOD*), *the New Urbanism,* or just plain *civic art*. Its principles produce a setting that resembles the American town prior to World War Two.*

1. The basic unit of planning is the neighborhood. A neighborhood standing alone can be a village or a town. A cluster of neighborhoods becomes a bigger town. Clusters of a great many neighborhoods become a city. The population of a neighborhood can vary, depending on local conditions.

2. The neighborhood is limited in physical size, with a well-defined edge and a focused center. The size of a neighborhood is defined as a five-minute walking distance (or a quarter-mile) from the edge to the center, thus a ten-minute walk edge to edge, or one-half a square mile. Human scale is the standard for proportion in buildings and their accessories. Automobiles and other wheeled vehicles are permitted, but do not take precedence

---

*The principles outlined here are derived from a consensus among members of the Congress for the New Urbanism. Other lists of principles exist and have been articulated in various formats by Elizabeth Plater-Zyberk and Andres Duany, Peter Calthorpe, Daniel Solomon, Peter Katz, and Anthony Nelesson. A complementary list, called the Ahwahnee Principles, was drawn up in a 1991 conference at the Ahwahnee Lodge in Yosemite Park. Among the participants were Duany and Plater-Zyberk, Katz, Stefanos Polyzoides, and Elizabeth Moule, architects and planners, and Michael Corbett, a former mayor of Davis, California. The book *Town Planning in Practice*, by Raymond Unwin (1863–1940) republished in 1994 by the Princeton Architectural Press, is also a classic source.

A NEIGHBORHOOD

A FIVE-MINUTE WALK FROM EDGE TO CENTER DEFINES THE AREA OF THIS CITY NEIGHBORHOOD, BEACON HILL IN BOSTON. THIS AMOUNTS ROUGHLY TO AN AREA OF HALF A SQUARE MILE. (CATHERINE JOHNSON)

over human needs, including aesthetic needs. The neighborhood contains a public transit stop.

3. The secondary units of assembly are corridors and districts. Corridors form the boundaries between neighborhoods, both connecting and defining them. Corridors can incorporate natural features like streams or canyons. They can take the form of parks, natural preserves, travel corridors, railroad lines, or some integral combination of all these things. In towns and cities, a neighborhood or parts of neighborhoods can comprise a district. Districts are composed of streets or ensembles of streets where special activities get preferential treatment. The French Quarter of New Orleans is

an example of a district. It is a whole neighborhood dedicated to enter-tainment in which housing, shops, and offices are also integral. A corridor can also be a district—for instance, a major shopping avenue between ad-joining neighborhoods.

4. The neighborhood is emphatically mixed-use and provides housing for people with different incomes. Buildings may be various in function, but compatible in size and disposition to the street. The daily needs of life are accessible within the five-minute walk. Commerce is integrated with residential, business, and even industrial use, though not necessarily on the same street in a given neighborhood. Apartments are permitted over stores. There is a mixture of housing types, including apartments, single-family, duplex, accessory apartments, and out-buildings, disciplined in mass and location. (Over time, streets will inevitably evolve to become less desirable and more desirable. But attempts to preserve "property val-ues" by mandating minimum square-footage requirements, outlawing rental apartments, or other strategies to artificially exclude lower income residents must be avoided. Even the best streets in the world's best towns can accommodate people of various incomes.)

5. Buildings are disciplined on their lots in order to successfully define public space. The street is understood to be the preeminent form of public space and buildings that define it are expected to honor and embellish it.

In the absence of a consensus about the appropriate decoration of build-ings, an architectural code may be devised to establish some fundamental unities of massing, fenestration, materials, and roof pitch, within which many variations may function harmoniously. Buildings also define parks and squares, which are distributed throughout the neighborhood and ap-propriately designed for recreation, repose, periodic commercial uses (e.g., farmers' markets), or special events such as political meetings, concerts, theatricals, exhibitions, and fairs.

6. The street pattern is conceived as a network in order to create the greatest number of alternative routes from one part of the neighborhood to another. This has the beneficial effect of relieving vehicular congestion. This network can be a grid. Networks based on a grid must be modified by parks, squares, diagonals, T-intersections, roundabouts, and other devices that relieve the grid's tendency to monotonous regularity. The streets exist in a hierarchy from broad boulevards to narrow lanes and alleys. In a town or city, limited access highways may exist only within a corridor, preferably

DEFINING PUBLIC SPACE—STRIP MALL

THE DEEPLY SET-BACK ONE-STORY BUILDINGS OF A STRIP MALL WITH THEIR VAST PARKING LOTS FRONTING THE STREET DO A POOR JOB OF DEFINING PUBLIC SPACE. THE RESULT IS A WASTELAND RATHER THAN AN OUTDOOR ROOM. (CATHERINE JOHNSON)

in the form of parkways. Cul-de-sacs (dead ends) are strongly discouraged except under extraordinary circumstances—e.g., where rugged topography requires them.

7. Civic buildings (town halls, churches, schools, libraries, museums) are placed on preferential building sites such as the frontage of squares, neighborhood centers, and where street vistas terminate, in order to serve as landmarks and reinforce their symbolic importance.

PARTICULARS

Some features of these principles may be self-evident, while others bear detailed explanation. I will attempt to clarify these points in a question and answer format.

What's the difference between zoning and civic art, anyway?

Civic art has existed as long as people have lived in permanent settlements. As primitive settlements evolved into true towns and cities, people learned to solve many of the practical and spiritual problems of life by controlling the physical arrangement of things in their everyday world. They learned that it was good to leave a central open space in the center of town for markets and public ceremonies. This evolved into a convention—an accepted feature of culture—called the plaza or town square. They learned that buildings more than one story high had economic advantages. They learned to control the flow of water and distribute it among buildings. They learned to erect special large buildings for reflecting on life's meaning, calling them temples and churches. Over time, new conventions were adopted, while others become obsolete—for instance, fortifications around towns. But many conventions have a timeless quality because the physical size of people and their psychological nature has not changed that much over 5,000 years of recorded history. Doors and stairways have not changed

DEFINING PUBLIC SPACE—MAIN STREET

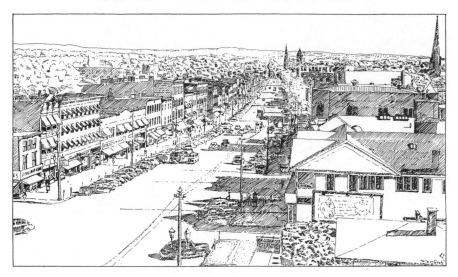

IN AMERICA, THE STREET IS OUR PREEMINENT FORM OF PUBLIC SPACE AND MAIN STREET IS OUR PREEMINENT TYPE OF STREET. BUILDINGS MEET THE SIDEWALK EDGE, FORMING A WALL THAT GIVES MAIN STREET THE FEELING OF AN OUTDOOR ROOM. AMPLE SIDEWALKS GIVE PEDESTRIANS EQUITY WITH AUTOMOBILES. PEOPLE CAN LIVE AND WORK IN THE UPPER STORIES ABOVE THE SHOPPING. (CATHERINE JOHNSON)

STREET SYSTEMS

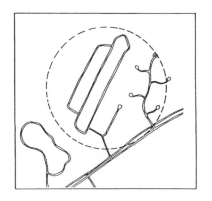

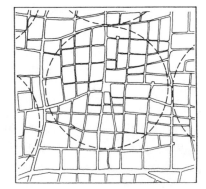

ARTERIAL AND CUL-DE-SACS
(CATHERINE JOHNSON)

GRID OF STREETS

TRADITIONAL NEIGHBORHOOD DESIGN

IN A TRADITIONAL TOWN, ACTIVITIES ARE INTEGRATED IN AN INTERCONNECTED NETWORK OF STREETS. BUILDINGS (INDICATED IN BLACK) DEFINE THE PUBLIC REALM. HOUSING EXISTS IN A VARIETY OF FORMS, INCLUDING APARTMENT BUILD-INGS, ROWHOUSES, AND SINGLE-FAMILY HOMES. (CATHERINE JOHNSON)

PUBLIC BUILDINGS

PUBLIC BUILDINGS DESERVE ARCHITECTURAL EMBELLISHMENT IN ORDER TO EXPRESS THE DIGNITY OF THE INSTITUTIONS THEY HOUSE AND TO HONOR THE PUBLIC REALM OF THE STREET. THEY ALSO DESERVE IMPORTANT SITES. (CATHERINE JOHNSON)

that much. Shopping streets have existed for thousands of years. The human need to be surrounded by beauty has not changed, and civic art until very recently was as concerned with beauty as it was with practicality. Ideas about beauty certainly evolve and change over time, and these changes are expressed as *style* or *fashion*. But the essential human hunger for beauty remains constant (whether we recognize it or not), and we have reason to believe that it is keyed to some of the fundamental ordering systems of nature, and of the human need to see our place within these systems expressed in physical form. (See Chapter 4, *Charm*.) Civic art, then, is the practice of assembling human settlements so that they maximize the happiness of their inhabitants.

Zoning has existed only since the early twentieth century. It resembles civic art in its attempt to regulate the everyday environment, but it lacks all of civic art's historical refinements. Zoning is not an art, but a limited set of crude classification techniques. It is distinguished from civic art especially in its lack of concern for the human scale and for human psychological needs.

Zoning began as a political response to the obnoxious effects of industry on human settlements. Originally, its intent was to keep factories away from houses, to create separate zones for industry to carry on its noisy and dirty activities. Over the twentieth century, the imposition of motor vehicles brought the obnoxious noise and danger of industry to every street, virtually to every doorstep, and so zoning eventually became preoccupied with problems posed by the movement and storage of cars. The problem became so pervasive that zoning completely replaced civic art as the ordering principle of human settlement, especially in the years since 1945. Over time, zoning became evermore elaborate in its tendency to segregate all human activities into separate zones. In the present era, it has even enabled developers to sort households into rigorously separate mini-zones based on small increments of income.

Zoning now identifies shopping as an obnoxious industrial activity that must be kept separate from houses. It makes no distinction between a steel mill and a cabinet shop. Zoning is quantitative rather than qualitative. Zoning is abstract, not particular. Zoning is the practice of assembling human settlements in order to minimize human unhappiness. Zoning has never been concerned with the question of beauty. It produces a cartoon of a human settlement.

What are the social ramifications of zoning versus civic art?

There are many serious differences between the two systems' effects on the quality of daily life. Zoning is a reaction to industrialism, and industrialism is a two hundred-year-old social experiment whose outcome we do not yet know. It is already clear, however, that zoning has produced as many unanticipated problems as it has putatively solved. Zoning inevitably results in sprawl by mandating that all the components of the human settlement be separated. Under current zoning, the only acceptable connecting device is the car and its expensive infrastructure. Therefore, it

CURRENT ZONING VERSUS TRADITIONAL NEIGHBORHOOD DESIGN

CURRENT ZONING CODES — TRADITIONAL NEIGHBORHOOD DESIGN

Sprawl Commercial

City Blocks

Apartment Complex

Small Town

Housing Subdivision

Village

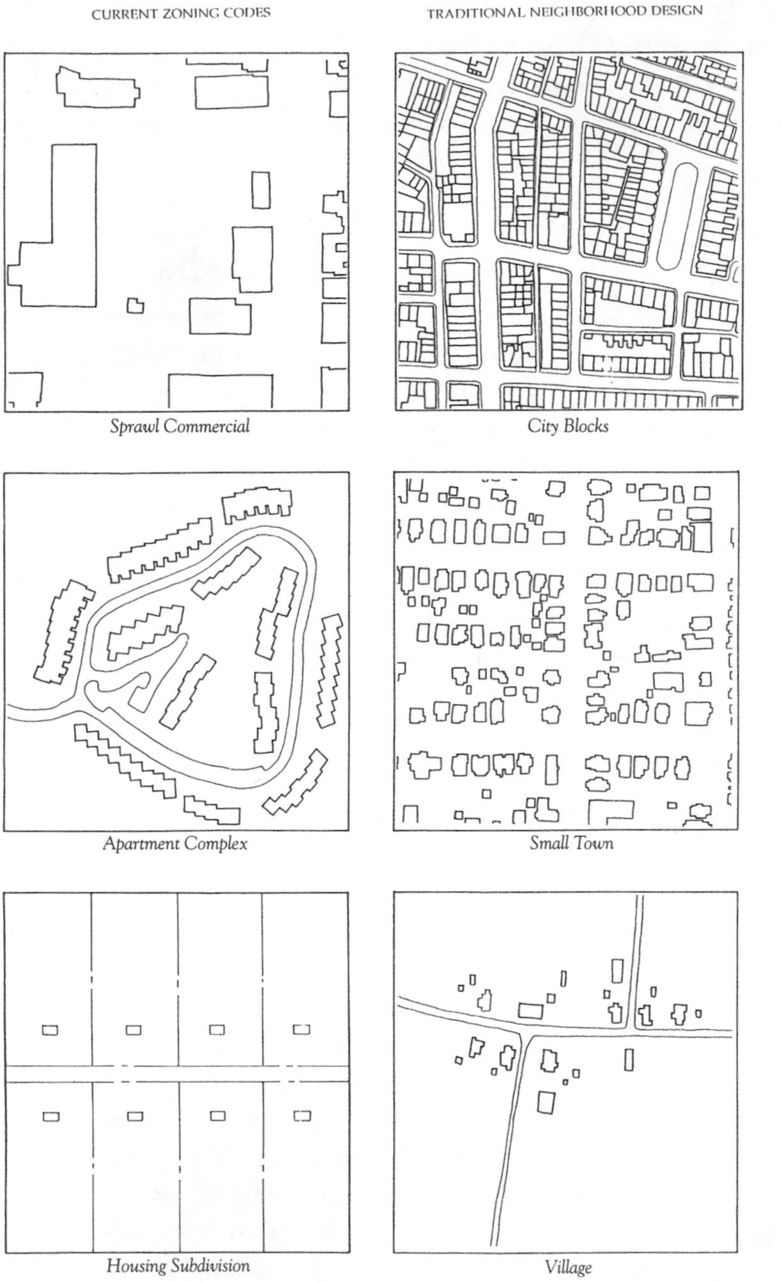

(CATHERINE JOHNSON)

makes car ownership mandatory, and those who cannot participate—e.g., children, senior citizens, the poor—are made dysfunctional and cannot use the everyday world. Mandatory car use causes catastrophic amounts of air pollution. Zoning destroys immense amounts of rural and agricultural land, even in regions, like greater New York and its environs, where there has been no absolute increase in population for decades. Zoning degrades the public realm of our streets by favoring cars over the human scale, making the streets unpleasant. It diverts public spending from civic amenities to the asphaltic infrastructure of highways and their accessories. Instead of parks, it provides landscaped parking lot medians and other useless, meaningless "green space." It *dis*-integrates the formerly *integrated* human settlement. In doing so, it destroys the fibers of civic connection and the patterns of civic life. It sows distrust and paranoia between different categories of citizens. It disconnects the young from cultural institutions. It is neither economically nor ecologically sustainable. Zoning destroys the bonds of communities and, ultimately, whole cultures.

Civic art concerns itself with making all the functions of a community integral, affordable, and spiritually pleasing. It allows all classes of citizens equal access to the civic and cultural equipment of the community. In doing so, it brings many different kinds of people into proximity where they learn mutual respect and tolerance. It recognizes the importance of the public realm as embodied in real places, and therefore reinforces a shared idea of the common good.

The New Urbanism is the reinstatement of the primacy of civic art over zoning.

What's so significant about a five minute walk? And why is walking such a big deal, anyway?

One of the transcultural constants of town-making in history is the idea that a quarter mile is the maximum distance that the average person will walk to get somewhere on a routine basis. Beyond the quarter mile, some people will either seek transport or not bother going. This theory is born out in many different cultures around the world and is clearly due to the universality of the human scale. The quarter-mile standard therefore seems to present an *optimum* arrangement. It permits people to go about routine business without a car. Chores that require many separate, tedious car trips in sprawl can be accomplished in a single outing on foot. (In a culture of walkable neighborhoods, shop owners adapt by offering home delivery of bulky merchandise.) Walking allows a person to visit many different types of shops—thereby promoting small scale, locally owned businesses, which, in turn, promote manifold civic benefits from the support of local institutions to the physical caretaking of the street. Walking down the street permits casual socializing. Pedestrians make streets safer by their mere presence in numbers. Finally, walking down the street is spiritually elevating. When neighborhoods are used by pedestrians, a much finer scale of detailing inevitably occurs. Building facades become more richly ornamented and interesting. Little gardens and windowboxes appear. Shop windows create a continuity of visual spectacle, as do outdoor cafes, both

STREET HIERARCHY

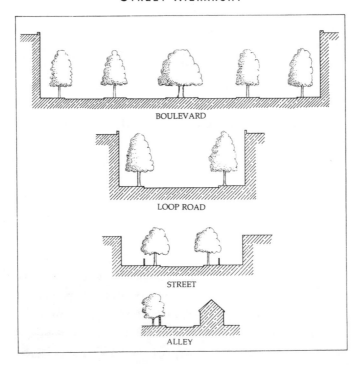

BOULEVARD

LOOP ROAD

STREET

ALLEY

NOWADAYS WE BUILD ALL STREETS TO THE SPECIFICATIONS OF COUNTY HIGH- WAYS. TRADITIONAL TOWN PLANNING RECOGNIZES THAT DIFFERENT PARTS OF TOWN CALL FOR DIFFERENT TYPES OF STREETS. (CATHERINE JOHNSON)

for walkers and the sitters. There is much to engage the eye and the heart. In such a setting, we feel more completely human. This is not trivial.

What is meant by a "hierarchy of streets"?

Streets are of greater and lesser importance, scale, and quality. What's appropriate for a part of town with small houses may not be appropriate as the town's main shopping street. These distinctions are properly expressed by physical design.

Under the regime of zoning, and the professional overspecialization that it fostered, all streets were made as wide as possible because the specialist in charge—the traffic engineer—was concerned solely with the movement of cars and trucks. In the process, much of the traditional decor that made streets pleasant for people was gotten rid of. For instance, street trees were eliminated. It is hard to overstate how much orderly rows of mature trees can improve even the most dismal street by softening its hard edges and sun-blasted bleakness. Under zoning, street trees were deemed a hazard to motorists and chopped down in many American towns after World War Two.

The practice of maximizing car movement, at the expense of all other concerns, was applied with particular zeal to suburban housing subdivisions. Suburban streets were given the speed characteristics of county highways, though children played in them. Suburbs notoriously lack parks. The spacious private lots were supposed to make up for the lack of parks, but children have an uncanny tendency to play in the street anyway—bicycles don't work too well on the lawn. In the suburbs, where street trees were expressly forbidden, we see those asinine exercises in romantic landscaping that attempt to recapitulate the North Woods in clumps of ornamental juniper. Sidewalks, in a setting so inimical to walking, were deemed a waste of money.

In the New Urbanism, the meaning of the street as the essential fabric of public realm is restored. The space created is understood to function as an outdoor room and the building facades are understood to be street walls.

Thoroughfares are distinguished by their character as well as capacity. The hierarchy of streets includes, at the greatest dimension, the grand boulevard, featuring express lanes in the center, local lanes on the side, and tree-planted medians between the express and local lanes, with parallel parking along all curbs. Next in the hierarchy is the multilane avenue with a median down the center. Next is a main shopping street, with no median.

MAKING SAFE SIDEWALKS

THE SIDEWALK IS AN ENSEMBLE OF PARTS THAT INCLUDE NOT JUST THE PEDES-
TRIAN PATH ITSELF, BUT ALSO A PLANTING STRIP WITH ORDERLY ROWS OF TREES
AND A CURB THAT CAN ACCOMMODATE PARKED CARS, ALL OF WHICH CONTRIBUTE
TO THE SAFETY OF PEDESTRIANS. (CATHERINE JOHNSON)

This is followed by two or more orders of ordinary streets (apt to be residential in character), and finally the lane or alley, which intersects blocks and becomes the preferred location for garages and accessory apartments.

Parallel parking is emphatically permitted along the curbs of all streets, except under the most extraordinary conditions. Parallel parking is desirable for two reasons. (1) Parked cars create a physical barrier, and a psychological buffer, that protects pedestrians on the sidewalk from moving vehicles; (2) a rich supply of parallel parking can eliminate the need for parking lots, which are extremely destructive of civic fabric. Anyone who thinks that parallel parking "ruins" a residential street should take a look at some of the most desirable real estate in America (as reflected by house prices): Georgetown, Beacon Hill, Nob Hill, Alexandria, Charleston, Savannah, Annapolis, Princeton, Greenwich Village, Marblehead, et cetera. All permit parallel parking.

The dimensions of residential streets can and should be narrower than current specifications permit. In general, cars need not move at speeds greater than 20 mph within the neighborhood. Higher speeds are reserved for boulevards, or parkways, which occupy corridors. Otherwise, the explicit intent is to calm and tame vehicular traffic within the neighborhood. This is also achieved by the use of corners with sharper turning radii, partially textured pavements, and "T" intersections. The result of these practices is a more civilized street.

Even under ideal circumstances, towns and cities will always have some streets that are better than other streets. Over time, streets tend to sort themselves out in a hierarchy of quality as well as size. The New Urbanism recognizes this tendency, especially in city commercial districts, and designates streets "A" or "B" streets. The "B" streets can contain less desirable activities—for instance, parking garage entrances, pawnshops, homeless shelters, Burger King—without disrupting the "A" streets in proximity. This does not mean that "B" streets are allowed to be deliberately squalid. Even here, the public realm deserves respect. Cars are still not given dominion. A decent standard of detailing applies to "B" streets in respect to sidewalks, lighting, and even trees.

Don't alleys promote crime and squalor?

Under zoning, alleys have not been permitted, so many localities have no experience with them, and hence, fear the idea. Our popular image of an alley derives from movies and cartoons of the industrial city, circa 1930–1950, an era of semi-dereliction. This is a very limited view. To the contrary, the alley is a simple device of civic art that produces many beneficial results. It allows the garage to be removed from the front of the house. Without the ugly garage door dominating the facade, houses can be dignified and beautiful again. The alley is the place where your garbage cans go, too. Also the utility lines. Even where alleys with outbuildings already exist, such as the town where I live, rental apartments are currently discouraged under zoning. Under the New Urbanism, they are once again permitted. Alleys are made much safer when people live along them, namely renters in outbuildings. For the ultra-paranoid, there are simple new devices, such as light switches triggered by motion, that would provide an extra measure of security at little cost.

The argument has been made lately that cul-de-sac streets or gated streets are safer than connecting streets because evildoers have a hard time getting in and out.* This is a drastic remedy for an uncivil society and must not be thought of as normal. It is one thing to tame traffic, it is another to create paranoidal fortifications. The best way to bring security to streets is to make them delightful places that honorable and decent citizens will want to walk in. They become, in effect, self-policing. The disadvantages of an interrupted street network in all other respects far outweigh any supposed gain in security.

If streets are narrower than the traffic engineers want them to be, how do fire trucks get down them? And especially alleys?

Any modern fire truck can get down a minor residential street scaled at 30 feet across. They can likewise easily get down a 24-foot-wide right–of–way, which is the width proposed for alleys in the New Urbanism. By the way, the most common location of house fires is the kitchen. Kitchens are generally in the rear of the house, closer to the alley than the street. Hence, if a fire starts in a kitchen, it can be reached *more easily* by a fire truck in the alley. Under the New Urbanism, a house fire can be addressed from both the street *and* the alley.

Defensible Space: A New Physical Planning Tool for Urban Revitalization, by Oscar Newman (Journal of the American Planning Association, Vol. 61, No. 2, Spring 1995).

How do you preserve property values in a neighborhood that allows "affordable housing"?

Under zoning, it became necessary to create "affordable housing" artificially because the rules of zoning zoned out the very conditions that formerly made housing available to all income groups and integrated it into the civic fabric. Accessory apartments became illegal in most neighborhoods, particularly in new suburbs. Without provision for apartments, an unmarried sixth-grade schoolteacher could not afford to live near the children she taught, never mind the cleaning lady or the gardener—they had to commute a half hour from some distant low-income ghetto. In many localities, apartments over stores also were outlawed under zoning. You may have noticed that few modern shopping centers are more than one story in height, and I know of no suburban malls which include integral housing. In eliminating these arrangements, we've eliminated the most common form of affordable market housing found virtually all over the rest of the world. By zoning these things out, we've zoned out Main Street USA.

During the 1970s and 1980s, the home-building industry and the banks supporting it skewed their operations toward ever larger and more expensive houses, because these produced greater profits per unit. Legal covenants in subdivisions soon reflected this bias in minimum square footage requirements which said, in effect, *"To live in this new part of town, your house must be at least a 3,000-square-foot mini-mansion"*—the idea being that only "nice people like us" could afford such a big house. This would theoretically "protect property values" against slumification.

THREE WAYS TO PROVIDE AFFORDABLE HOUSING

Apartments over Shops

Small and Large Lots Together

(CATHERINE JOHNSON)

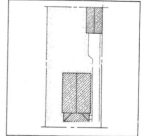

Apartment over Garage

After a few decades of this behavior, the median price of a house in America was much higher than the ability of the average family to pay for a house. Also, according to the 1990 census, only 27 percent of American households were made up of traditional two-parent families with children. Even where smaller, cheaper new houses were built—say, out on the fringe of the Mojave Desert—homeowners were invariably saddled with the burden of owning two cars in order to commute to the two jobs necessary to support the house and the two cars. This naturally produced social discontent. Thus "affordable housing" as a political remedy.

It has not worked. As always, distortions imposed on an organic market system produce unanticipated perversities in market behavior. Affordable housing carries a stigma, and for good reasons. One popular gimmick for providing it has been the deed restriction, a legal provision which forbids owners from reselling their "affordable" house at market price—for the purpose of keeping the price forever artificially low (i.e., "affordable"). Unlike the regular homeowner, therefore, owners of officially designated "affordable" houses are denied one of the chief benefits of home ownership: equity appreciation. This makes them second-class homeowners. The other most common form of owner-occupied affordable housing available these days is the trailer. Not only is it an inferior dwelling, but in many places it is restricted to "mobile home parks," trailer ghettos, usually in distant hinterlands reachable only by cars. Nothing in government policy on affordable housing addresses the actual problems caused by government planners: the outlawing of integral rental housing, or the officially sanctioned extreme segregation by income group.

The best way to make housing affordable is to eliminate mandatory car ownership, which means building and restoring compact mixed-use traditional American neighborhoods. The way to preserve property values is to recognize that a house is part of a community, not an isolated object, and to make sure that the community itself maintains high standards of civic amenity in the form of walkable streets, easy access to shops, recreation, culture, and public beauty.

In towns built before World War Two there are more desirable and less desirable residential streets, but even the best can have income-integrated housing. A $350,000 house can exist next to a $180,000 house, part of which includes a $600-a-month garage apartment (which has the added benefit of helping the $180,000 homeowner pay a substantial portion of his mortgage). Such a street might house two millionaires, eleven professionals, a dozen wage-workers, sixteen children, three full-time mothers, a college student, two grandmothers on social security, and a bachelor fireman. That is a street that will maintain its value and bring people of very different ages and occupations into informal contact.

The New Urbanism calls for houses to be built on smaller lots than conventional suburban subdivisions. Doesn't this lead to congestion?

Congestion was the scare word of the past, as growth is the scare word of our time. The fear of congestion springs first from the atrocious conditions of the urban slums at the turn of the century. The Lower East Side of Manhattan is estimated to have contained more inhabitants per square mile in 1900 than modern-day Calcutta. If the issue had been confined to the slums, it might not have made such an impact on the public imagination. But urban congestion was aggravated by the revolutionary effects of the elevator, the office skyscraper, the sudden, mass replication of large apartment buildings, and finally the introduction of the automobile on a massive scale. These innovations drastically altered the scale and tone of city life. Within a generation, cities went from being dynamic to being— or at least seeming—frighteningly overcrowded in a way that *all* classes had never experienced before. Those with the money to commute were easily persuaded to get out, and in the 1920s, therefore, we see the first mass evacuation to new automobile suburbs. The movement was halted by the Great Depression and World War Two.

The memory of all that lingers. Consequently, there is still tremendous confusion in America today about density and congestion, even though most urban areas and even many small towns (like my own) now suffer from density deficits. There are not enough people living, or business activities, at the core to maintain the synergies necessary for civic life. The New Urbanism proposes a restoration of synergistic densities within reasonable limits. These limits are regulated by building size. The New Urbanism calls for higher density than zoning does, more houses per acre, closer together. However, the pattern that the New Urbanism models is not the urban slum, but the traditional American town. This is not a pattern of life that should frighten reasonable people. Millions pay forty dollars a day to walk through a grossly oversimplified version of it at Disney World. It complies exactly with their most cherished fantasies about the ideal living arrangement.

In the New Urbanism, houses may be freestanding, but the lots are smaller than in sprawl subdivisions. Streets of connected rowhouses are also deemed desirable. What is being eliminated are the useless front lawns. The New Urbanism compensates for this loss by providing squares, parks, greens, and other useful, high-quality civic amenities. The New Urbanism also provides streets of beauty and character.

This model does not suffer from congestion. Occupancy laws remain in force—you don't have sixteen families jammed into one building as in the tenements of yore. There is plenty of privacy in back yards and houses can be large and spacious on their lots. People and cars are able to circulate freely in the network of streets. The car is not needed for trips to the store, the school, or other local activities. This pattern encourages good connectivity between people and their commercial and cultural institutions.

Zoning, in contrast, mandates the spreading out of houses on large lots separated by enormous lawns. Car use is unavoidable. The street has little meaning as a shared public space. There are no parks, squares, or greens because it is assumed that the private lawn fulfills that need—though it is not a good place to meet people. Zoning mandates a foolish redundancy of privatized amenities, for instance, swimming pools in every backyard—children really *prefer* to swim in pools with other children. The crude street pattern of zoning, with its cul-de-sacs and collector streets actually promotes congestion because absolutely every trip out of the single-use residential pod must be made by car onto the collector street. The worst congestion in America today takes place not in the narrow streets of traditional neighborhoods such as Georgetown or Alexandria, but on the six-lane collector streets of places created by zoning, such as Tyson's Corner, Virginia. Because of the extremely poor connectivity inherent in them, such products of zoning have all the equipment of a city and the culture of a backwater.

Isn't it un-American to concoct codes that "discipline" buildings in terms of siting, windows, doors, materials, roof pitches?

The public consensus about how to build a human settlement that is practical, affordable, socially equitable, and spiritually gratifying has collapsed. Standards of excellence in architecture and town planning have collapsed. Civic art has collapsed into the pseudo-science (or pseudo-art) of zoning. To say that a consensus never existed in highly individualistic America would be erroneous. Dozens of historic towns and urban neighborhoods testify to its previous existence. Not long after its founding in 1633, Cambridge, Massachusetts, enacted laws specifying build-to lines (six feet from the street), and roofing materials (slate or board, not thatch). Colonial Williamsburg had similar laws governing the placement of houses next to the street. Until the advent of cars, there was widespread general agreement about the ways that buildings should behave in the civic setting. We threw these agreements away in order to become a drive-in civilization.

What was thrown away must now be reconstructed, spelled out, and reinstated. The New Urbanism proposes to accomplish this through formal codes. These codes will restore the basic unities of design within which a wide variety of individual expressions can function happily. The codes will invoke in words and graphic images standards of excellence that previously existed in the minds of ordinary citizens but which have been forgotten and forsaken. The codes, therefore, aim to restore the collective cultural consciousness.

This sounds authoritarian!

Authorities can exist without being despotic. Indeed authorities must exist if a culture is to remain healthy. We are in the unfortunate and dangerous condition of a culture that has de-legitimized all authorities, that doesn't believe in anything. The New Urbanism is an unapologetic effort to reestablish one particular authority: that of civic art. Its principles may be subject to discussion—a healthy skepticism about ideas is normal and desirable—but they are stated with the confidence of an underlying legitimacy rooted in history and practice. The codes and principles are stated explicitly so that years, perhaps decades, need not be wasted reinventing practices of civic design that are already understood and proven.

The codes are lists of what is desirable and what is undesirable in our surroundings. They are given the force of law. This may sound scary, but, in fact, we already have such codes. Zoning is a set of codes given the force of law. The trouble is that zoning codes are crudely numerical and schematic in their application and they produce a poor model of an everyday environment. They say nothing about the quality or character of the things we build in the places we live. The New Urbanism seeks to replace them with rules that redefine standards of quality and character.

In the New Urbanism, a distinction is made between the urban code and the architectural code. The urban code is the skeleton and large muscles of a town, the architectural code is its small muscles and skin. The urban code defines the hierarchy of streets, type and size of blocks, corridors, location of the neighborhood centers, transit stops, parks and squares, and above all how the buildings must behave in respect to the public space of the streets.

The architectural code is subordinate to the urban code. It attempts to spell out desirable standards of design in elements such as roof pitches, window proportion, facade treatments, porch dimensions, and cladding materials. The architectural code introduces an extra layer of rigor that may be thought of as optional. It is recommended as a remedy for the unprecedented incompetence of architects in practice today.* In theory, many of the refinements spelled out in the architectural code might evolve naturally back into general use in response to a good urban code. For instance, if we had great streets, we might once again want to build balconies on the second floors of our houses.

How can you say that buildings "behave"? People behave. Buildings just sit there.

It might be more accurate to say that buildings foster certain kinds of behavior in humans. Even so, buildings possess anthropomorphic qualities that reflect human qualities and aspirations (see Chapter 4, *Charm*) which we, in turn, project onto them—a self-reinforcing feedback loop. When buildings fail to reflect human qualities, they fail as elements of civic design. So for the sake of clarity we will apply the human characteristics of "behavior" and "attitude" when discussing how buildings affect civic life.

The human desire for enclosure in an everyday setting is probably in-

---

*This extraordinary incompetence can be attributed to the education of architects—rooted in Modernist dogma—which encourages them to be heroic geniuses before they become adept practitioners. The buildings of heroic geniuses must be like nothing ever seen before in history. They are also designed to exist in splendid isolation. They therefore occupy space rather than define space. They are anti-social by nature. They necessarily cannot fit into an established fabric of buildings by non-heroic non-geniuses.

nate; it is expressed in things we build. Whether in the garden at home, or on Main Street, people like to feel sheltered and protected. We're attracted to arbors, pergolas, street arcades, even awnings. We enjoy the shade and enclosure afforded by mature trees. We especially enjoy room-like spaces outdoors. People are repelled by the abyss, or by conditions that suggest the abyss. Traditional design all over the world reflects this. Buildings, therefore, are used to define and control space, and, by making it comprehensible to the human mind, make that space appear safe and welcoming.

In the New Urbanism buildings are not categorized by use but rather by their mass, their height, and their attitude toward the street. Buildings that share unities of size and mass and behave harmoniously can accommodate a wide variety of uses. Certainly shops and offices can be re-integrated with apartments. Most light industrial activities need no longer be rigorously segregated. Institutional buildings like schools, town halls, and museums can be made integral by giving proper attention to the creation of parks and squares on which such buildings deserve to be sited.

In order for the street to achieve the intimate and welcoming quality of an outdoor room, the buildings along it must first compose a suitable street wall. While they can vary in style and expression, there must be some fundamental agreement, some unity, which pulls buildings into alignment. Think of one of those fine side streets of rowhouses on the Upper East Side of New York. They may express in masonry every historical fantasy from neo-Egyptian to Ruskinian Gothic. But they are all close to the same height, and, even if their windows don't line up precisely, they all run to four or five stories. They all stand directly along the sidewalk. They share a basic unity of materials: stone or brick. They are not interrupted by vacant spaces or parking lots. About half of them are homes, the rest may be diplomatic offices or art galleries. They co-exist in harmony. This is the essential unity of 82nd Street between Madison and Fifth Avenues in New York City. The same may be said of streets in Chicago's North Side, Savannah, Beacon Hill, Georgetown, Pacific Heights, and many other ultra-desirable neighborhoods across the country.

Similarly, buildings must be sized in proportion to the width of the street. Low buildings do a poor job of defining streets, especially overly wide streets, as anyone who has been on a postwar commercial highway strip can tell. The road is too wide and the cars go too fast. The parking lots are fearsome wastelands. The buildings themselves are barely visible—that is why gigantic internally lit signs are necessary. The relationship between buildings and space fails utterly in this case. In many residential suburbs, too, the buildings do a poor job of defining space. The houses are low, the front lawns and streets are too wide. Sidewalks and orderly rows of trees are absent. The space between the houses is an incomprehensible abyss.

The New Urbanism advances specific solutions for these ills. Commerce is removed from the highway strip and reassembled in the form of a town or neighborhood center. The buildings that house commerce are required to be at least two stories high and perhaps higher, with the additional benefit of apartments and offices above the stores to bring vitality to the center, plus extra rents. The code states that provision for retail business must be made on the ground floor of buildings on designated shopping streets near the center.

The build-to line determines how close buildings will stand to the street and promotes regularity of alignment. Zoning has a seemingly similar rule called the setback line, but it is intended to keep buildings far away from the street in order to create parking lots all around the building, particularly in front, where parking lots are considered to be a "welcome" sign to motorists. When buildings stand in isolation like this, the unfortunate effect is their complete failure to define space: the abyss. In the New Urbanism, the build-to line intends an opposite outcome: the positive definition of space by pulling buildings forward to the street. If parking lots are necessary, the place to put them is behind the buildings, in the middle of the block, where they will not disrupt civic life.

Additional codes govern building heights, recess lines where upper stories may be set back, and "transition lines" which denote a distinction between first floor retail use and upper floor offices and apartments. (Paris, under Baron Haussmann, was coded for an 11-foot-high transition line, which is one reason for the phenomenal unity and character of Parisian boulevards.)

In traditional American town planning, the standard increment for lots has been 25 feet, which allowed for 25-foot rowhouses and shopfronts, and also allowed for 50, 75, and 100-foot lots suitable for free-standing houses. Automobiles are now with us. Unfortunately, the old standard is slightly out of whack with what is needed to park cars efficiently. Therefore, the

STREET PROPORTION: MAKING A STREET FEEL MORE LIKE A ROOM

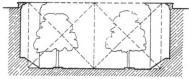

RENAISSANCE PROPORTIONS DESCRIBE STREETS THAT HAVE PROPORTION OF BUILDING HEIGHT TO STREET WIDTH NO GREATER THAN 1:6. A TYPICAL RESIDENTIAL CROSS STREET OF ROWHOUSES, FOR EXAMPLE, THREE OR FOUR STORIES HIGH, 75' TO 100' WIDE, WOULD HAVE A 1:2 PROPORTION.

STREETS LINED WITH ONLY SINGLE STORY OR ONLY OCCASIONAL TWO STORY BUILDINGS DO A POOR JOB OF DEFINING THE STREET. AS A RESULT, THE STREET MAY BE PERCEIVED TO BE WIDER THAN IT ACTUALLY IS. HUMANS PREFER TO BE IN SPACES THAT ENCLOSE THEM, AND SEEK OUT URBAN SPACES WITH PLEASING PROPORTIONS. A 125' WIDE STREET WITH BUILDINGS 18' TO 28' HIGH HAS A PROPORTION OF 1:7.

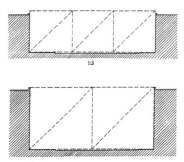

INCREASING BUILDING HEIGHT SO THAT A 1:3, 1:2 OR 1:1 PROPORTION IS ACHIEVED WILL CREATE A NICER STREET. FOR A 125' WIDE STREET, THE MINIMUM BUILDING HEIGHT SHOULD BE 42' (FOR BEST RESULTS 65').

(CATHERINE JOHNSON)

increment for platting lots becomes 16.5 feet, the rod, a classic unit of measurement. This allows a minimum rowhouse lot of 16.5 feet with room for parking one car in the rear (off an alley) plus a few feet for a pedestrian passageway around the car. The 1.5-rod (24+ feet) townhouse lot is more generous and allows two cars to park in the rear. The 2-rod lot (33 feet) allows a townhouse with parking for two cars plus a small side yard. Three

PLATTING

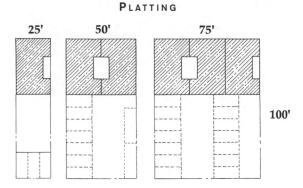

PLATTING IN 25' INCREMENTS IS VERY COMMON IN THE U.S. HOWEVER, IT DOES NOT YIELD THE MOST EFFICIENT PARKING LAYOUTS POSSIBLE. (DOUBLE SIDED HEAD-IN PARKING REQUIRES A WIDTH OF 60'.) EFFICIENCY IS NOT POSSIBLE IN MOST LOTS.

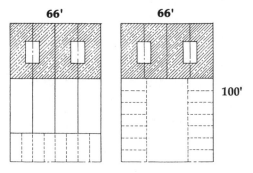

PLATTING WITH A ROD OF 16.5' AVAILS GREATER FLEXIBILITY: 4 LOTS @ 16.5' WIDE X 100' LONG YIELDS 14 SPACES.

(CATHERINE JOHNSON)

rods (49.5 feet) permits a standard detached house with on-site parking in different configurations. The four-rod lot (66 feet) provides room for a very large detached building (house, shops, offices, or apartments) with a ten-space parking lot in a rear lot.*

*The new standard of the rod is derived from *Architectural Graphic Standards*, 9th Edition, Chapter 2, Land Planning and Site Development, by Gary Greenan, Andres Duany, Elizabeth Plater-Zyberk, Kamal Zaharin, and Iskandor Shafie. American Institute of Architects, 1994.

New Urbanist codes recognize zones of transition between the public realm of the street and the semiprivate realm of the shop or the private realm of the house. In the world of zoning, these refinements are nonexistent. Successful transitions are achieved by regulating *devices of transition* such as the arcade, the shopfront, the dooryard, the ensemble of porch and fence, even the front lawn. These devices play a crucial role in softening the visual and psychological hard edges of the everyday world, allowing us to move in between these zones with appropriate degrees of ease or friction. Notice they are also absent in the harsh geometries and polished surfaces of Modernism.

The arcade, for instance, affords shelter along the sidewalk on a street of shops. It is especially desirable in southern climates where both harsh sunlight and frequent downpours occur. The code specifies that the arcade must shelter the entire sidewalk, not just a portion of it. Otherwise it tends to become an obstruction rather than an amenity. A code may specify that porches on certain streets be located at a "conversational distance" from the sidewalk, literally to aid communication between the public and private realm. The low picket fence plays its part in the ensemble as a gentle physical barrier, reminding pedestrians that the zone between the sidewalk and the porch is private, while still permitting verbal and visual communication. There are conditions where a front lawn is appropriate. Large, ornate civic buildings often merit a lawn because they cannot be visually comprehended close up. Very large private houses merit lawns for similar reasons.

The architectural codes operate at a finer level of detail and refinement than the urban codes. In theory, a good urban code alone can create the conditions that make civic life possible by raising the standard of excellence in a town's basic armature. Architectural codes raise the standard of excellence for individual buildings, particularly the surface details. It is important to emphasize that in the New Urbanism, variances to codes may be granted to buildings on the basis of architectural merit. The New Urbanism does not favor any particular style.

Nowadays houses are often designed from the inside out. A married couple decides that it would be nice to have a fanlight window over the bed, or a little octagonal window over the Jacuzzi, and a builder or architect designs the house around those wishes. This approach does not take into account how the house ends up looking on the outside. To make mat-

A GRAPHIC URBAN CODE

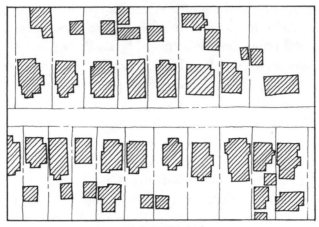

BLOCK PLAN

URBAN CODE
    Lot Size 48' x 112' (3 x 7 Rods)
    Setbacks Required: 15' front, 12'side, 5' side, 5' rear
    Building Height: min. 2 stories
                     max. 2 1/2 stories

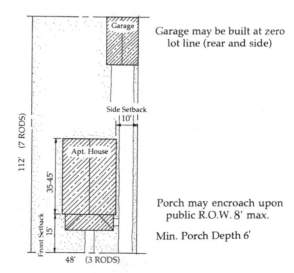

Garage may be built at zero
lot line (rear and side)

Porch may encroach upon
public R.O.W. 8' max.

Min. Porch Depth 6'

LOT PLAN

A TRADITIONAL TOWN-PLANNING ORDINANCE PRESENTS ITS CODES IN PICTURES
THAT ORDINARY CITIZENS CAN UNDERSTAND. ZONING PRESENTS ITS CODES IN
LEGALISTIC VERBIAGE THAT ELECTED OFFICIALS OFTEN CANNOT UNDERSTAND.
(CATHERINE JOHNSON)

A GRAPHIC ARCHITECTURAL CODE

TYPICAL STREET

ARCHITECTURAL CODE
Story Heights: 9' first floor, 9' second floor, 8' top floor
Height of First Floor Above Grade: min. 30", max. 60"
Roof Pitch: 6:12 or steeper
Stoop May Encroach Upon Public R.O.W. : max. 8'
Building Materials: wood clapboards or shingles, stucco

ELEVATION

AN ARCHITECTURAL CODE ESTABLISHES SOME FUNDAMENTAL UNITIES OF DESIGN WITHIN WHICH MANY PERSONAL TASTES MAY BE EXPRESSED. IT CAN BE CONSIDERED AN OPTIONAL OVERLAY TO THE URBAN CODE.

(CATHERINE JOHNSON)

ters worse, electric lighting has made windows optional in the opinion of some people and so we get entirely blank walls, usually the side. The outside ceases to matter. This is socially undesirable. It degrades the community. It lessens surveillance on the street, reduces the opportunities for making connections, and in the long term causes considerable damage to the everyday environment.

The New Urbanism declares that the outside *does* matter, so a few simple rules reestablish the necessary design discipline for individual buildings. For example, a house will include a minimum percentage of window area in proportion to the total area of each exterior wall, and all sides of the house must have windows. Suddenly, houses no longer look like television sets, where only the front matters. Another rule may state that windows must be vertical or square, but not horizontal. This rule reinstates a basic principle in architecture that, unfortunately, has been forgotten and abandoned in America—and has resulted in millions of terrible-looking houses.

The front porch is regarded as an important and desirable element in some neighborhoods. It can be stated categorically that a porch less than six feet deep is useless except for storage. There is not enough room for furniture and the circulation of human bodies. Builders tack on inadequate porches as a sales gimmick for "curb appeal" so the realtor can drive up with the customer and say, "Look, a front porch!" The porch becomes an applique cartoon stuck onto the house, like the little fake cupola on the garage. This saves the builder money in time and materials. Anyway, it is assumed that the street will be too repulsive to sit next to.

Why do builders even bother with pathetic-looking, half-hearted cartoon porches? Apparently Americans desire, at least, *the idea of a porch* in order to pretend that they live in real communities. It reassures them symbolically that they're decent people living in a decent place. Of course, the cartoon applique only compounds the degradation of the public realm, making it evermore phony and unappealing.

In America today, flat roofs are the norm in commercial construction. This is a legacy of Modernism, and we're suffering because of it. The roofscapes of our communities are boring and dreary. An interesting roofscape can be a joy—and a life worth living is composed of many joys. The flat roof came into fashion with early twentieth century European political dogma, which stated that pitched roofs, and especially fancy roofs with towers and domes, were evil symbols of the "ruling classes." Modernism therefore got rid of these symbols, with the expectation that Socialism would get rid of the ruling classes themselves—which didn't happen—and we are stuck with the flat roofs and buildings that inspire only dread and depression.

The reason we're stuck, long after the symbolism of the flat roof lost its meaning, is that once Modernism fled Europe for America, it developed a hidden agenda: to give developers a moral and intellectual justification for putting up cheap buildings. One of the best ways to save money on a building is to put a flat roof on it. Altogether, this strategy generated more work for architects while it nullified the complaints of ordinary citizens by painting them as Philistines if they objected to the design.

To aggravate matters, the United States was so affluent after World War Two that we began to regard buildings as throwaway commodities, like cars. They weren't built to last for the ages. So it didn't matter much that flat roofs tend to leak after a few years, because by then the building would be a candidate for demolition. That attitude has now infected all architecture and development. Low standards that wouldn't have been acceptable in our grandparents' day—when this was a less affluent country—are today perfectly normal. The New Urbanism seeks to redress this substandard normality. It recognizes that a distinctive roofline is architecturally appropriate and spiritually desirable in the everyday environment. Pitched roofs and their accessories, including towers, are favored explicitly by codes. Roofing materials can also be specified if a community wants a high standard of design.

I must reemphasize that an architectural code should be viewed as a supplement to an urban code. An architectural code is not intended to impose a particular style on a neighborhood—Victorian, neo-classical, et cetera—though it certainly could if it was sufficiently detailed and rigorous. Style is emphatically *not* the point. The point is to raise the standard of excellence in design for the benefit of the community as a whole. Is there anything wrong with standards of excellence? Or should we continue the experiment of trying to live without them?

GETTING THE RULES CHANGED

Replacing the crude idiocies of zoning with true civic art has proved to be a monumentally difficult task. It has been attempted many places around the United States the past ten years, mainly by developers, professional town planners, and architects who are members of the New Urbanist movement. It has succeeded in a few places. The status quo is a tremendous drag, no matter how miserable it makes people, including the local officials who support it and who have to live in the same junk environment as everybody else. An enormous entrenched bureaucracy at state and federal levels also supports zoning and its accessories. The Departments of Transportation, the Federal Housing Administration (FHA), the various tax agencies, and so on, all have a long–standing stake in policies that promote suburban sprawl, and heavily subsidize it. They're not going to renounce them without a struggle. Whenever you change a rule about land development, you make or break people who seek to become millionaires. Ban sprawl and some guy who bought twenty acres to build a strip mall is out of business, while somebody else with three weed-filled lots downtown suddenly has more valuable property.

While I believe we have entered a kind of slow-motion cultural meltdown due largely to our living habits, many ordinary Americans wouldn't

BUILDING WITH CURRENT ZONING CODES

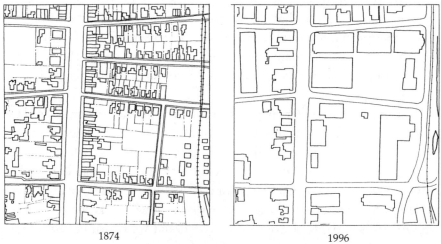

1874   1996

THIS DOWNTOWN, LIKE MANY AMERICAN CITIES, WAS SAVAGED BY REDEVELOPMENT PATTERNED ON MODERN ZONING. THE ONCE-THRIVING MIXED-USE NEIGHBORHOOD WAS ERASED AND REPLACED BY SUBURBAN-STYLE STRIPS. NO NEW HOUSING WAS BUILT WHERE ONCE HUNDREDS OF PEOPLE LIVED. (CATHERINE JOHNSON)

agree. They don't perceive a crisis. They may or may not be doing okay in the changing economy, but they have personal and psychological investments in business as usual, and they don't want to hear about changing things. Many Americans have opted for suburbia out of sheer hatred for the historic crumminess of American cities, and particularly in fear of the underclass that dwells there. They would sooner move to the dark side of the moon than consider city life.

Americans still have considerable affection for small towns. But over the past fifty years, many towns have received a suburban sprawl zoning overlay which in many cases has made them indistinguishable from the sprawl matrix that surrounds them. In my town, strip malls and fast food joints have invaded what used to be a much denser core and nearly ruined it.

Notwithstanding all these obstacles, zoning must go, and zoning will go. In its place we will reestablish a consensus for doing things better, along with formal town planning codes to spell out the terms. I maintain that the change will occur whether we love suburbia or not. Economic forces are underway that will require us to live differently. The only question in my mind is whether the fabric of society will be torn apart in the process. This depends to a great extent on how clearly we recognize the social costs incurred by our present chosen way of living.

Fortunately, a democratic process for making these changes exists. It has the advantage of being a highly localized process, geared to individual communities. It is called the *charrette*.* In its expanded modern meaning, a charrette is a week-long professional design workshop held for the purpose of planning land development or redevelopment. It includes public meetings that bring together all the players in one room—the developers, the architects, the citizens, the government officials, the traffic engineers from the DOT, the environmentalists, and so on—so as to get all issues on the table and settle as many of them as possible, avoiding the otherwise usual, inevitably gruesome, process of conflict resolution as performed by

---

*Charrette is French, meaning *little cart*. It derives from a tradition, in the old Ecole des Beaux Arts, of architecture students working on their final project drawings up until the very last moment, when the drawings were collected by a teaching assistant on a little cart trundled about the studio. Legend has it that some students would climb upon the little cart with their pens and erasers, making last-minute corrections. Thus, the term *charrette* describes a design workshop carried on in the spirit of a collegiate "all-nighter."

lawyers—which is to say, a hugely expensive waste of society's resources, benefiting only the lawyers (who then end up with so much money that they build million dollar homes on ten-acre lots, causing additional problems for society).

The object of the charrette is to produce results on paper in the form of drawings and plans. The object is not to produce verbiage. This highlights an essential difference between zoning codes and traditional town planning based on civic art. Zoning codes are invariably 27-inch-high stacks of numbers and legalistic bullshit that few people but technical specialists understand. Because this is so, local zoning and planning board members frequently don't understand their own zoning laws. Zoning has great advantages for the specialists, namely lawyers and traffic engineers, because they profit financially by being the sole arbiters of the regulations, or benefit professionally by being able to impose their special technical needs (say, for cars) over the needs of citizens—without the public being involved in their decisions.

Traditional town planning produces pictorial, or graphic, codes that any normal citizen can comprehend. This is democratic and ethical as well as practical. It elevates the quality of the public discussion about development. People can *see* what they're talking about. Such graphic codes show a desired outcome at the same time they depict formal specifications. They're simply much more useful than the reams of balderdash found in zoning codes.

An exemplary town planning code devised by Duany, Plater-Zyberk and others, can be found in the 9th Edition of *Architectural Graphic Standards*. The code runs a brief fourteen pages. About 75 percent of the material is devoted to pictures of street sections, blocks, building lots, building types, and street networks. While it is generic, there's no reason why a code of similar brevity could not be devised for localized conditions all over America. The charrette process is premised on the idea that all localities present special problems that call for an individualized approach.

The most common by-product of the status quo under zoning is that it ends up imposing fantastic unnecessary costs on top of bad development. It also wastes enormous amounts of time. And, as they say in the construction industry, "time is money." Projects are frequently sunk by delays in the process of obtaining permits. The worst by-product of the status quo is that it actually makes good development much harder to do than bad development.

Because citizens have not been happy with the model of development that zoning gives them, they have turned it into an adversarial process. They have added many layers of procedural rigmarole so that only the most determined and wealthiest developers can withstand the ordeal. In the end, after all the zoning board meetings, flashy presentations, and environmental objections and mitigation, and after both sides' lawyers have chewed each other up and spit each other out, what ends up getting built is a terrible piece of shit anyway, because it's a piece of sprawl equipment—a strip mall, a housing subdivision. Everybody is left miserable and demoralized, and the next project that comes down the road gets even more beat up, whether it's good or bad.

Now, as far as I'm concerned, many projects deserve to get beat up and delayed, even killed. But wouldn't it be better for society if we could agree on a model of good development and make it relatively easy for people to go forward with it? This is the intent of the Traditional Neighborhood Development (TND) ordinance as proposed under the New Urbanism.

Human settlements are like living organisms. They must grow and they will change. But we can decide on the nature of that growth, particularly on the quality and the character of it, and where it ought to go. We don't have to scatter the building blocks of our civic life all over the countryside, impoverishing our towns and ruining farmland. We can put the shopping and the offices and the movie theaters and the library all within walking distance of each other. And we can live within walking distance of all these things. We can build our schools close to where the children live, and the school buildings don't have to look like fertilizer plants. We can insist that commercial buildings be more than one-story high, and allow people to live in decent apartments over the stores. We can build Main Street and Elm Street and still park our cars. It is within our power to create places that are worthy of our affection.

BEYOND SEASIDE

A s America emerges squawking and bleating from the aphasia of Modernism and its regime of zoning, efforts are being made around the country to restore city, town, or neighborhood life in places that already exist, or to create new places of authentic civic character from the ground up, using traditional design principles of the New Urbanism. Some of these efforts are more successful than others, some more sound, some idealistic, others rather cynical. On the whole, this work represents a tremendous struggle against the currents of cultural inertia and business as usual. As a challenge to the status quo, this movement has already spawned lots of controversy, political rancor, professional backbiting, and animadversion.

A favorite target of abuse has been Seaside, the 80-acre "new town" development on the Florida panhandle designed by the team of Duany and Plater-Zyberk. Critics charge that it is nothing more than a resort for rich yuppies, a "Victorian" theme park, and a private despotic dukedom of its developer, Robert Davis. This obloquy is undeserved and unfair.

Seaside was the first bold attempt *by anybody* to create a life-sized working model of a radically better form of land development than the sort of crap Americans have been blandly accepting for fifty years. As such, Seaside quickly became an icon for architectural reformers, and an object of scorn for the retro avant-gardists. It is true that Seaside functions as a resort town. So what? Has anyone proposed that resorts ought to be abolished in America? Are all the hard-core leftists and diehard Modernists marching with flaming torches on Bar Harbor and Aspen? I don't think so. Seaside was built as a resort for two simple reasons: (1) the land that Robert Davis inherited from his grandfather happened to be beachfront property in Florida; and (2) it was an excellent way to support an architectural and social experiment that otherwise might not have been financeable at all.

After ten years, Seaside exhibits the salient attribute of a large-scale experiment: some of its features work better than others. On the whole, many of its parts work excellently and it must be regarded as a huge success. It has spawned scores of imitations of varying quality around the country. The prices of lots and houses at Seaside—which started pretty modestly at around $15,000 for a lot and $125,000 for a house—have soared astronomically compared to comparable houses along the Gulf Coast. Part of this is due to its status as an icon, but mostly it reflects the current scarcity of equally good places. Quality is a commodity in short supply.

It has taken longer than expected to develop the commercial core of Seaside, and to determine what will really work there. The town may never support much more than basic service retail—groceries, a few restaurants, ice cream, resort gear, and a bookshop. There is not much demand for office space yet, and may never be. The small outbuilding apartments originally intended for waiters and grocery clerks have been bid up by tourists to premium prices. The ornamental plantings have grown out of control because the houses act as windbreaks.

Altogether, though, Seaside works as it was intended. It proves most of its major points: that buildings must be used to define public space, and that a public realm of quality makes the difference between a real town and a mere housing development; that building to the human scale nourishes the human spirit; that people desperately want to be able to walk to shopping, and that shopping does not ruin neighborhoods; that streets can be designed for human beings and cars to share equitably. Otherwise, Seaside ought to be regarded as an experiment still in progress. Time and nature will operate on it, and if a hurricane doesn't blow it away, our grandchildren will be better critics of it than we can possibly be.*

A more general complaint about the New Urbanism is that many projects undertaken in its name have been so-called "greenfield developments" on previously undeveloped land rather than efforts to fix up existing places. While this criticism is philosophically sound, it fails to apprehend the grotesque forces in society that overwhelmingly militate against fixing up derelict towns and cities. Current zoning and tax policy, along with corrupt and incompetent city governments, aggravated by self-defeating political attitudes, make it exceedingly difficult, if not impossible, for even the most dogged entrepreneurs to redevelop existing fabric. They can't assemble the property parcels, they can't gain approvals for their plans, they can't get building permits. The NIMBYs and BANANAs crowd the public meetings with their snarling lawyers. Commercial banks won't lend money for urban rehabilitation projects—red-lining is still silently in force. Every step along the way is attended by such idiocy, delay, procedural hugger–mugger, and needless cost that hardly any sane individual or corporation will venture to do it. Since the private sector is thwarted, it's currently left to these selfsame incompetent city agencies, in league with equally incompetent state and federal agencies, to attempt redevelopment under the impossible burdens of racial politics and governmental insolvency.

Despite these awesome obstacles, the rehabilitation of existing urban fabric advances miraculously on a few fronts. There are heroic efforts to rehab small towns that have been mutilated by zoning, to make something better out of seemingly hopeless suburban smarm. And there is the phenomenon of new towns, both good and bad, that have come along since Seaside.

*In the fall of 1995, Hurricane Opal slammed into the Florida Gulf Coast. The eye of the storm passed a few miles west of Seaside. Beachfront property on both sides of Seaside was devastated. Seaside survived the storm nearly unaffected, losing only the stairways that led from the dunes down to the beach. The town's survival is attributed to its position well behind the dunes and the storm surge, and the quality of its construction.

GROUND ZERO

There's a good reason why cities and towns are where they are. They occupy the best sites. Usually there is some advantageous geographic condition where people have formed settlements—a river or a harbor, or something else having to do with water. New York's harbor is unsurpassed for shelter from the ocean, combined with proximity to it, ease of entry, and the sheer miles and miles of usable waterfront. Yet today New York finds itself in the amazing and pathetic circumstance of having practically no maritime economy whatsoever.

Detroit occupies a site of strategic and commercial importance on a river between two Great Lakes—desolate as that city may be today, with its boarded-up downtown skyscrapers and square miles of formerly grand residential blocks turned into rubble fields. Chicago sits like a well-fed hog on its cushion of prairie beside Lake Michigan, but these days it uses the lake for little more than a summer wallow. San Francisco's rugged peninsula looms above another fantastic natural harbor. Seattle is perched on a world of water. Ditto Boston. All things, many of them good, flow down the Mississippi to New Orleans. Pittsburgh, St. Louis, Cincinnati, Charleston, Kansas City, Bangor, Savannah, Des Moines, Minneapolis, Portland, all are river towns. Even dusty Los Angeles was founded on a little river—today it is a concrete-lined drainage ditch. My small town, Saratoga, grew up around a set of naturally carbonated mineral-water springs. There are a few exceptions to the rule of water. Denver is one, developed as an accessory to cattle trails and railroads. Orlando, Florida, is almost wholly a hallucination of the Highway Builder's Association (and of an evil corporation in the entertainment racket that will go unnamed, but whose mascot is, appropriately, a rodent).

The best sites are already taken. New settlements now form on leftover land, on farmland outside the old cities, or in places that would be inhospitable without air-conditioning and subsidized commuting, such as the far-out desert suburbs of Los Angeles. Lately, being close to the freeway interchange has seemed to confer the greatest locational advantage. But the freeway must be understood as a human artifact, not as a natural landscape feature. Affluent as we have been, we are now just barely able to maintain our freeway systems and to individually pay for all the necessary cars running on them. The time may come soon when the money isn't there, and then proximity to a poorly maintained freeway with an undependable car will have no benefits.

Since midcentury we've been behaving as though all our cities and towns were disposable. The trashing of these places carries dire portents, but also hints at golden opportunities. On the dire side of the equation, what we have thrown away are the prime generators of economic prosperity. That's what cities are, not just because products are made and shipped from them, but because a critical mass of people in them generates the fresh ideas and innovations that are necessary to the sustained organic process of self-renewal that occurs in a healthy civilization. The formless sprawl that we've built *outside* all of our cities will prove not to be an adequate replacement. It doesn't bring people together, it keeps them isolated, and at a fantastic cost. In every way that matters, the automobile suburbs are demonstrably a social disaster and an economic liability. What we've done, in effect, is spend our national wealth on an empire of junk that will soon lose even the marginal utility it may have possessed in the short term.

On the more positive side of the equation, we're now presented with dozens of the best development sites in North America which have, for all intents and purposes, been utterly abandoned. Places like Detroit, Cleveland, St. Louis, Memphis, Providence, Buffalo, and many other towns great and small represent fortunes waiting to be made. They contain large tracts of essentially empty land, or severely underutilized land, begging to be redeveloped. What's more, the site work has already been done. The streets are already there. The services—water, sewer, electricity, phone lines—are all in place and waiting to be reconditioned and reused. As I shall argue ahead, our property tax system does nothing to encourage urban rehabilitation. For the sake of this discussion, though, let's assume the most optimistic outcome: that the idiocies of our current property tax laws can be overcome. That in itself will go a long way to rectifying many of the market perversities currently in operation: the artificial scarcity of land, the underuse of urban property, the incentives for maintaining derelict buildings, even the lack of beauty in our common surroundings.

The replacement of real towns and cities by automobile suburbs has represented, more than anything, lots of wasted time and motion—billions of miles driven for trivial reasons and billions of hours frittered away in traffic. Every economic trend and social augury suggests that from now on we are going to have to live in a more settled, centered, localized, focused way. It makes sense that in order to do this we will return to the best sites for settlement. Just because a place like Detroit looks terrible today does not mean it can't be as beautiful as Prague forty years from now. But do we have the will to reimagine city and town life as a general proposition? And will our standards be high enough to produce results worth caring about?

AN EXEMPLARY PROJECT: DOWNCITY PROVIDENCE

Providence, Rhode Island (pop. 183,000), is the state capital and a harbor city. The site was chosen by Roger Williams, the Puritan apostate who was thrown out of Massachusetts in 1635 for saying that civil magistrates had no legitimate authority to regulate people's thoughts. In its heyday, Providence was a silverware, jewelry, and textile manufacturing center. The devastating hurricane of 1938 hit it square in the face and downtown business never quite recovered from the floods that ensued. That was after nearly a decade of the Great Depression. By the time World War Two was over, Providence was decanting itself down the gold-plated freeway like every other American city.

Providence is perhaps more fortunate than most, though. It withstood two generations of failed grandiose urban renewal schemes with its commercial core of buildings physically intact, if more or less abandoned. The old downtown, or "Downcity," as the locals call it, is about thirty gridded blocks of urban fabric. The perfectly good streets were made uncivil by traffic engineers who designated them one-way and abolished parallel parking in their myopic zeal to afford maximum traffic flow. This gave the streets the characteristics of expressways, and all it really accomplished was to make them horrible places for walking and shopping. By the early 1990s, Downcity was a ghost town.

The building stock there happens to be exceptional, including many gems, like the Arcade Building, the oldest indoor shopping mall in America, erected in 1828. Most of the buildings, though, date from the period 1890 to 1920, when America was pioneering the elevator building. The majority are office buildings, but some were vertical factories and department stores. Few are more than ten stories high. They were built to endure, and they have. They are artful and ornate, and they have features that seem luxurious by today's cheesy construction standards: glorious lobbies, 10-foot ceilings, and large windows that actually open. They were so undervalued that in 1994, one could buy a typical seven-story 60,000-square-foot Downcity office building for $400,000—which is about the same as you'd pay for a new 2,500-square-foot "colonial" in an upscale Boston suburb these days. They were undervalued because nobody could conceive of a use for them. It happened that a very small group of elderly speculators owned most of the important buildings. They had acquired them in the 1970s, when the oil shocks and federal tax credits for gentrification made urban rehab look like a smart investment. Then, in the eighties, Americans forgot about oil, Congress junked the tax credits, and Edge City became the next big thing, so the same group of speculators were stuck with a lot of unwanted buildings in a part of town that now seemed irrelevant. They just sat on them, waiting for their value to go up, which never happened. Some of the speculators retired to Florida, and quit paying attention. Some died, leaving the property to less-interested heirs. Slow rot set in. After a while the only business left Downcity was social services, with its troublesome clientele.

Providence was fortunate in some other respects, though. The scale of everything is pretty small and manageable, even the rot. The city's demographic profile is much more representative of the nation's racial mix than that of other northern cities, with roughly 112,000 whites, 23,000 African-Americans, and 23,000 Hispanics, so the prospect of urban redevelopment did not take on the flavor of *a war against poor people of color*. Anyway, nobody was actually living Downcity, so there was no question of dispossessing any particular group. The city has also long been the headquarters of the New England Mafia, which, ironically, has kept the level of obnoxious street crime down, because gangsters have a particular sensitivity to the issue of safe neighborhoods (and they have ways of enforcing public order that are unavailable to the police). The historic and architecturally rich east side of the city is the home of an Ivy League school, Brown University, and the venerable Rhode Island School of Design. There was a very active historic preservation group operating in town. Its members were drawn from a core of old wealthy New England families who had strong emotional attachments to the city. Finally, the New Urbanism came along and catalyzed a propitious situation.

Back in 1987, Duany and Plater-Zyberk, the architects and planners, had been hired to work on an interesting redevelopment project that involved an aging shopping center in Mashpee on nearby Cape Cod (discussed later in this chapter). The redevelopers, Buff Chace and Douglas Storrs both lived in Providence and their company had its offices there. Duany and Plater-Zyberk began spending time in Providence on the Mashpee project. They noticed that Downcity was a classic American business district preserved as though in amber. Fresh from all the hoopla surrounding Seaside, they were eager to demonstrate that their principles and strategies, based on traditional civic art, could be used to revive American cities in ways that all those zillion-dollar abstract Modernist urban renewal schemes and government social engineering programs had failed to do. Duany himself became buddies with Chace and Storrs—they were all in their late thirties—and as the Mashpee project went forward, they informally brainstormed Providence. Years passed. In the winter of 1994, the firm of Duany/Plater-Zyberk (DPZ) was hired to lead a week-long Downcity charrette.

What they'd realized was that earlier renewal schemes had failed because they insisted on viewing Downcity as strictly a commercial district: single-use zoning. Since the 1960s, though, suburban malls had totally replaced Downcity. DPZ's insight was that the fine old infrastructure of buildings was perfectly suited to other uses, namely to people living there. It had just never occurred to anyone that this was possible or desirable. All those former office buildings and department stores could be converted into apartments, and of a particular kind, loft space with minimal kitchens and baths, for a very particular market: young people without a lot of money to spend, especially artists, of which Providence had a healthy supply because of the Rhode Island School of Design, which pumped out hundreds of graduates every year, many of whom stuck around town to be artists.

From the practical point of view, the idea was that the cost of construction for this kind of high-rise renovation was quite low compared to, say, doing luxury condominiums with fancy baths and Martha Stewart kitchens in every unit. There were other less obvious advantages in this scheme. Youngsters with little money to spend were precisely the kind of people who would be happy to forgo burdensome car ownership if they could live in a walkable neighborhood with basic retail—so parking wouldn't be a live-or-die issue for them. Likewise, it was believed that bringing live bodies downtown twenty-four hours a day would encourage just the sort of small business that would enliven the moribund streets.

The streets themselves would be refurbished in ways that involved little public expense—for instance, reinstating two-way traffic and parallel parking, replacing the mercury-vapor "cobra" streetlamps with smaller fixtures, paving the intersections with brick, and planting some trees.

There were some additional parts to the plan beyond the residential program. One was to create a square surrounded by cafes and shops that would serve as a public gathering place and neighborhood focal point. Another was to enlist a local culinary college called Johnson and Wales, which had been planning a move out of town, to expand Downcity instead and bring more live bodies in day and night. Finally, there was the belief that if enough people could be induced to live Downcity, it would inevitably evolve into a new entertainment district with bistros, bars, galleries, cinemas, and the rest of the equipment one finds in similar places full of youthful energy, like Soho, or Seattle's Capital Hill neighborhood.

It wasn't as though you had to be a card-carrying artist or a certified youth to move into the district. Junior accountants, garage mechanics, and grandmothers would be welcome, too. Mixed use also meant mixed population. The animating idea behind the entire plan was common sense: just keep the up-front costs down and encourage conditions that would naturally synergize. Even with reinvestment and repopulation, Downcity would remain, well, *funky* for quite a ways into the future. There would be A and B streets. Some buildings would be more desirable than others. Social services would continue to be a presence. A livable city is what they had in mind, not Utopia.

The charrette brought all the players together in one room for a week: the mayor, the traffic engineers, the public safety department, the state economic development crew, property owners, preservationists, the bankers, representatives from the colleges, and ordinary citizens. The charrette process was designed to generate a clear consensus among all parties as to methods and goals. For instance, in order to avoid bickering and delay later on, it was important to establish what the building inspectors would require for a department store converted into dwelling units (sprinkler systems and fire stairs). The banks had to be persuaded that urban, mixed-use buildings represented investment-worthy development. The colleges had to be urged to stick around.

To bypass the inevitable incompetence of government agencies, all parties (including the city and state government) agreed to create a private non-profit partnership called the Coalition for Community Development (CCD). This enabled them to act swiftly to acquire buildings crucial to the plan as they came on the market. In mid-1995, CCD bought three buildings totaling 450,000 square feet with the intention of creating 150 to 180 dwelling units. CCD selected a Chelsea (Massachusetts) firm called the Architecture Team to design the renovations. They'd had previous experience turning derelict factories into apartments in the old industrial district of Cambridge. The city of Providence selected a private developer to create the new square, called Grace Park, and the buildings around it. Johnson and Wales reversed an earlier decision to move out to the suburbs and instead bought the old Arcade Building, which they are currently renovating as a mixed-use classroom and student housing center, with retail at street level. The state of Rhode Island bought an old department store building that occupied an entire block and has renovated it to contain the University of Rhode Island's continuing education program. (Continuing ed students are typically people who work regular day jobs and take classes at night, so here was another source of live bodies to enliven the streets after dark.) A convention center, planned before the charrette, opened for business in 1993. Lacking an adjacent district of memorable streets and civic vitality, it could easily have been a multimillion dollar exercise in futility. Now it has a good chance of joining the synergy of Downcity. Finally, in 1993 the state of Rhode Island liberated the little Woonasquatucket River, which had been decked over by a six-lane highway in the 1950s. Its fine granite embankments with pedestrian paths, dating from the nineteenth century, remained intact, and today kayakers and casual strollers can be seen along it from CCD's office window. So far, only the government traffic engineers have been unwilling to do their part—to reinstate two-way traffic and parallel parking throughout Downcity—which is a great matter of consternation among the other parties.

Providence is poised to become an exemplary case for the reuse of American downtowns. We really don't know what form cities will assume in the twenty-first century, but the strategy being used in Providence is flexible, sensibly scaled, and geared toward private investment. It is not racially driven. It makes use of resources that already exist. It will provide housing for young people who have been shortchanged by a construction industry that seeks profits only in expensive suburban houses, and the banks and government policies that support this activity. And the people who come to dwell in Downcity will share a memorable and attractive public realm. Altogether, it may begin to give city life a good name in America.

SUBURBIA INVADES THE CENTRAL CITY

I couldn't get the lyrics from the Randy Newman song out of my head the whole time I was in Cleveland. For those of you too young to remember, back in 1969, the super-polluted Cuyahoga River, which runs through Cleveland into Lake Erie, caught on fire and the city had a hell of time putting it out.

"Burn on, big river, burn on . . ."

Actually, the state of Ohio did an admirable job cleaning up the riverfront, and Lake Erie itself is in much better shape these days, thanks to the federal Clean Waters Act. Where the Cuyahoga empties into the lake, a neighborhood called "the Flats" has morphed from an industrial dead zone to an entertainment district. The river corridor is now lined with restaurants and jazz clubs, with decks overlooking the water, and on summer nights the mouth of the river is so jammed with pleasure boats that it's said a person can cross the river by jumping from deck to deck. Just up a bluff from the Flats, the turn-of-the-century civic center, with its Beaux Arts courthouse and dignified municipal buildings, is one of the finest examples of an urban architectural ensemble in America. A half mile away stands Jacobs' Field, the town's brand-new, perpetually sold-out ballpark, which is generating some gentrification of old rowhouses around it. And, of course, there is the new Rock and Roll Hall of Fame on the lakeshore.

"Cleveland city of light, city of romance. . . ."

Cleveland is a city of many virtues, the main one being that it's not Detroit. Its initial growth was explosive—from 20,000 inhabitants on the eve of the Civil War to half a million in 1910. Seeing the few remnant mansions of the industrial millionaires (including John D. Rockefeller's first trophy house) among the weed-filled wastelands on Euclid Avenue today, one can easily imagine how exciting and wonderful and vibrant such a booming town full of new things must have been in its day. In the twentieth century, Cleveland has been a city of industrial might and cultural distinction, with fine museums, a renowned regional theater, and a first-rate medical establishment. It reached its zenith right after World War Two, when it was America's seventh largest city in population at 914,000. Since 1950, it has lost nearly half its population. They have evacuated to plentiful land in the surrounding suburban townships. No geographical barriers hinder this exodus, and the state of Ohio has been exceedingly accommodating with evermore freeways.

What remains of Cleveland today east of the Cuyahoga River and the ballpark strikes the casual observer as the proverbial hole in the donut. The old inner residential neighborhoods are so wiped out that it seems as if a major war had been fought for the Great Lakes around the time of my college career—and perhaps I was too stoned to hear about it. Rubble fields punctuated by rows of slums occupy block after block of the old grid. Here and there a once-grand Victorian house totters darkly like the ghost of something from an Edward Hopper painting. You round a corner in your rent-a-car and there, suddenly, is the most incongruous sight, a brand-new suburban "colonial" on a quarter-acre lot with its complete kit-of-parts: the lawn, the driveway, the garage door, the juniper shrubs along the foundation, the scraggly saplings—right in downtown Cleveland, surrounded by hectares of desolation. The only nod to urban reality is the iron grill-work over the "picture" window to keep burglars out. I realized, naturally, that this was nothing more than the *little cabin in the woods*, inserted into a new kind of wilderness.

I saw dozens of these on my tour of the city in the summer of 1994. It alarmed me to think that this was the city's idea of residential redevelopment—as though the city itself had forgotten what being urban meant, what being Cleveland meant, and had capitulated completely to some numbskull Leave-It-to-Beaver fantasy imposed on it by the vengeful Rotarians of suburban Chagrin Falls—for clearly the city must have given its permission for these things to be built.

Then, in roughly the same neighborhood, I came upon another startling site: a brand-new suburban-style supermarket strip mall inserted into an old city block. It came complete with *its* kit of parts, including the huge parking lot. Nearly all of the structure was one story high—except for two gesture-like second-story corner "towers" that couldn't have exceeded 2,500 square feet in total. The rear of the strip mall turned its back completely to Chester Avenue, which had once been an important residential thoroughfare. All that Chester Avenue got were the ventilation ducts from the Fry-o-later hoods in the Chinese take-out joint and the deli department of the supermarket. It turned out that this strip mall was a highly touted piece of "urban redevelopment." The remaining denizens of the neighborhood had lacked the most basic shopping amenities for years. In desperation the city had come up with this "contemporary retail offering" and named the thing Church Square, with the mindless flair of suburban developers, though there was no church and no square. President Bill Clinton had flown in for the dedication ceremonies. At a conference I attended, the city held it up as an example of "getting things done." It was pathetic.

What was striking about these things is that it's so obvious we should be building *neighborhoods* in places like Cleveland, not *little cabins in the woods* and strip malls, and that the basic components used should be traditional urban forms—at the very least buildings more than one story high. The very idea that the structure was oriented to motorists was the most ridiculous part, since the residents of the neighborhood were supposedly too poor to afford decent housing, let alone cars. For one-tenth of the money that it costs to keep a car, they could have spent $10 a week in cab fares going back and forth to the supermarket. In an even more intelligent universe, the supermarket could have delivered to their homes.

In short, Church Square could have been assembled in a manner much more appropriate for the city, at not much greater cost. The land squandered on the parking lot could have been a real square with trees and benches. Parallel parking on the surrounding streets would have sufficed. Just based on the land wasted on a ten-foot setback along Chester Avenue—which did nothing to mitigate the obnoxious ventilators—there would have been plenty of room on the site to build a church "on spec," too. Scores of affordable apartments could have been built above the stores for the cost of construction alone. The stores themselves could have faced the street, and a service alley in the center of the block could have easily accommodated all the Fry-o-later ducts and delivery trucks. The whole package couldn't have been more poorly designed for this particular site. In fact, it might not have been designed at all—merely expropriated full-blown from some existing suburban site elsewhere and air-dropped into place as a module.

This represents a standard of thinking and a standard of behavior that is unworthy of civilized people. The appropriate model for neighborhood development still exists in Cleveland for anyone who opens his eyes or wanders around town with a tape measure. There are enough fragments of the model still standing for a city planning official to see. The streets alone instruct you what to build. There are photographs and drawings in the Cleveland library of mixed use development that once stood on these rubble fields. The current city planning crew is obviously referencing the wrong model. The model they have in mind is suburban sprawl and they are inviting its components into the heart of town. My guess is that they may be doing this because the impoverished and uneducated citizens of the inner city see these things on television and demand stuff like it. Or maybe the suburban developers are calling the shots. But holding a job as a city planner presumes some education, and the position as city official presumes some responsibility for leadership, and both of these things presume higher standards than the lowest common denominator. What they are allowing to happen on Cleveland's east side is not a solution for the twenty-first century, but a recipe for a new Dark Age.

MIRACLE IN THE SHORT NORTH

Two hours south of Cleveland via I-71 (there is no train) in Ohio's state capital, Columbus, a private developer was able to infill an exemplary urban neighborhood in exactly the right way with no help from any layer of government and to do it entirely on market terms.

Jack Lucks, fifty-five, is a hyperenergetic, self-described "Type-A personality" who runs marathons and made his fortune developing what he now recognizes as award-winning suburban schlock outside of town, which is to say that he is a creature of his times. Yet he has lived in the city of Columbus virtually all his life. Columbus suffers from the same civic diseases as any other American city. For instance, 70 percent of the old central business district is surface parking. ("We're Nagasaki. It's all flattened. As a developer, I go around here licking my chops," Lucks said as we plied the streets in his Mercedes convertible.) He owns and has renovated a number of the few remaining downtown office buildings built before 1930, including the one that contains his office.

Ringing Columbus's old downtown, however, are several impressive urban residential neighborhoods in excellent condition. Just south of the in-

ner expressway loop stands German Village, a splendid enclave of solid little 1850s-vintage brick gable-end houses and rowhouses on narrow, leafy
streets paved with brick. There is a lot of it, too, perhaps as much as
Georgetown, and it is occupied by gainfully employed people who take
care of their property. The neighborhood is dotted with restaurants and
corner stores. Adjoining German Village is the Brewery District, where
half a dozen elaborate old industrial buildings have been rehabbed into
condominiums.

On the north side of the inner freeway loop stands Victorian Village, a
neighborhood of enormous nineteenth century houses of the type that in
most cities inevitably end up as funeral homes, but which, in Columbus,
are occupied by upper-middle-class families. The street grid in this neighborhood contains service alleys, and the intersections feature roundabouts
scaled just perfectly to slow down cars to 10 mph, which is exactly the kind
of behavior you want in a place like that where children play.

Jack Lucks himself lives in a neighborhood called Bexley, which is
the local version of Cleveland's Shaker Heights, a turn-of-the-century
streetcar suburb of very large houses three miles from his office. Lucks
often bikes to work. His seven-year-old Mercedes has less than 25,000
miles on the odometer. Noontimes, he runs, training for his marathons.
His running route takes him from the office downtown to the Ohio State
University campus and back. Halfway between downtown and OSU,
and adjoining Victorian Village, is the neighborhood called the Short
North.

Ten years ago, the Short North had become the drug and prostitution
center of Columbus. The area was a slum and rents were accordingly low.
There was good fabric there, however—some excellent buildings, especially along High Street, the city's main drag, which becomes OSU's student commercial drag twenty blocks north. Many people travel up and
down High Street day and night. In the late 1980s, some urban pioneers
took advantage of the great buildings, low rents, and high traffic volume,
and opened a bunch of art galleries and restaurants along High Street in
the Short North. Within a few blocks, a pretty lively scene developed. In
a way, it was the natural occurrence of what was now being done deliberately in Providence—letting artists and bohemians serve as the shock
troops of urban rehabilitation. Meanwhile, many of the drug dealers and
whores naturally gravitated away because trashy people function best in

trashy surroundings and, in fact, flee civic improvements like cockroaches scattering at the throw of a light switch.

Anyway, right in the center of this gallery district was a two-block wasteland that had been the site of the old White Cross Hospital. "It was a moonscape, a pile of rubble," Lucks told me. "It looked like a huge missing tooth out of the fabric of High Street." It was owned by an insurance company. They had been sitting on it for years. As High Street in the Short North showed some twitchings of life with the galleries and restaurants, the insurance company put out a request for development proposals and finally chose Lucks' out of six others, becoming partners in his venture as a consequence.

The development Lucks went forward with was nothing more exotic than traditional Short North fabric: two blocks of three-story brick row buildings, with, ultimately, 160 units of mixed-income apartments and townhouses, plus shopfronts along the High Street side of the blocks— none of it subsidized. It was designed to fit the original plan. He called the project "Victorian Gate," which perhaps sounds both hokey and antisocial, except that it actually functioned as a gateway to the adjoining Victorian Village neighborhood, so it made sense in the local parlance.

The project has taken five years. As of the fall of 1995, Lucks had finished 118 of the apartments. They are all rental units and when I was there the project had 100 percent occupancy. The dwelling units are sized from studio apartments to three-bedroom duplexes. Rents run from about $500 to above $1,000, which is still strikingly inexpensive compared to rents in other habitable cities, especially for new construction. The quality of the design is excellent. Because he is such an athletic nut himself, Lucks made sure that every apartment, from smallest to largest, came with a big utility room for the storage of bikes, skis, and other stuff. The kitchens are large. The design quality and attention to detail on the exteriors was way above the present national standard.

Why was Jack Lucks able to build an excellent mixed-use, mixed-income, urban infill project entirely on market terms at a time when such a feat is either unthinkable or impossible in other American cities? There are a few technical answers. He was able to acquire a big enough site—in effect, two whole blocks—to economically rationalize the project. (The total dollar investment will be $10 million at completion. However, Lucks estimates the total value of the property will be $60 million.) He had access to fi-nancing through his partner, the insurance company. (In most American cities, including Columbus, Ohio, banks still virtually "redline" city projects. They just don't view urban redevelopment as a plausible investment.) It is surely significant that Lucks was willing and able to bypass the incompetence of the government.

Finally, though, it becomes obvious that what made this project possible was nothing other than Jack Lucks's faith in city life, and an awareness that the suburban fantasy had run its course. He did things so simple and obvious that others elsewhere would not dare dream of doing. For instance, he respected the traditional pattern of the site. He followed the instructions of history and built pretty much what had been there before—unlike Cleveland, with its ridiculous suburban ranch houses and strip malls plopped into similar neighborhoods.

The whole 160-unit Victorian Gate project occupies a mere 3.2 acres of land. Yet out of that tiny parcel he has created tremendous social and economic value. He's created a place where people can live happily and affordably with a high degree of social amenity. His tenants can walk around the corner to a cafe and be with other people at 8:30 in the morning or ten at night. The cafes and bars, bakeries and shops are an extension of their homes. This is the essence of city life. Lucks believed that ordinary working people would enjoy this sort of arrangement, and he was right. That's why every single unit is rented. He himself waxes eloquently on the subject of boredom in suburbia, including the stuff he had built out there himself. Recognizing the difference between city and suburbs, he didn't get hung up on the issue of parking, and he refused to let the city of Columbus jerk him around about it. His instinct again proved to be correct. Twenty percent of his tenants do not even own cars. (Those who do have access to parking in the middle of the block.) They are ten blocks from the Statehouse, twenty blocks from OSU, and regular city buses run to each. Best of all, he has brought a large number of live bodies to a part of town that will now be active most hours of the day.

When I was there in the fall of 1995, Jack Lucks was negotiating for a thirty-acre site less than a mile away from the Short North. The site is an obsolete industrial research facility just off the southern tip of the vast OSU campus. Much of it is currently weed-filled wasteland. His ambitions for the site are substantial and he appears to know exactly what he is doing.

A WORLD-BEATIN' DEVELOPMENT

In 1987, a Memphis developer named Henry Turley, about fifty years old, who had been in the real estate business "forever," and was a creature of his time and place, and therefore had built a fair amount of suburban sprawl in his career, and tended to hide a considerable intellect behind his folksy manner, bought one-third of a 400-acre island in the Mississippi River a stone's throw from downtown (well, maybe a Ken Griffey, Jr. throw), and had a vision.

Mud Island, as it was called, had never been developed in the long history of the city because it was sometimes under water. Back in the 1970s, it was acquired by east Tennessee bank baron C. H. "Jake" Butcher. Butcher's banking empire collapsed in 1983, but not before he had used his political influence to get a bridge built from the island to downtown Memphis, and had gotten the Army Corps of Engineers to dredge up enough material to create an artificial bluff that was perfect for home sites above the 100-year flood line. Butcher subsequently took a long, involuntary vacation at the Atlanta Federal Penitentiary for bank fraud. The FDIC repossessed his 130 acres on Mud Island and Henry Turley bought it.

"It's an odd piece of property and it demanded a pretty good solution," he began at our interview, using his slow drawl as artfully as a bottlenecking blues singer bending guitar strings. "I struggled over whether we should develop it in an urban or suburban way, and one day I woke up and said, *We must put these labels aside.* They sounded tired and trite, like liberal and conservative. So, I just started with the environmental needs. It's hot as hell here: create some shade, which turned into porches and street trees. And shade calls for walkways, and walkways require destinations, and destinations bein' public in nature, and thereby mixed use—it started coming together in my mind like a picture."

On short notice, Turley asked for a Sunday meeting with RTKL, a big architectural firm in Baltimore that had done a lot of work rehabing that city.

"Sumbitch if the four principals didn't turn out for me," he continued. "So, I show 'em these pictures and get up and ramble on about an hour. They were just nice fellas, not full of shit. Capable. Then they drove me around Baltimore and pointed out these utterly nondescript buildings, and I just loved it. I have come to understand these as contextual, but at the time I thought they were just not *Big Ego* pieces. So I liked 'em right off.

Thirteen days later they called, and I went back up there. They laid out this perfect thing and explained what they were doing. And we have sub-sequently proceeded with buildin' it almost unaltered. From my vague ramblings to their rather precise drawings, nothing has changed. Well, maybe ten percent."

What happened was that Turley had conceived virtually, point for point, in isolation, his own version of Traditional Neighborhood Develop-ment. He hadn't even heard of Seaside, which was then in the early stages of construction. In fact, some of the elements that he envisioned, like ser-vice alleys between blocks, hadn't been done at Seaside, though they would turn up in later projects by DPZ, Peter Calthorpe, Dover/Kohl, and other New Urbanists. Perhaps it was an instance of what the psychologist Carl Jung would call *synchronicity*, an idea whose time had come, popping up mysteriously in different places because the collective unconscious of humanity demanded it. Anyway, Turley was not nearly so pretentious him-self as to speculate along those lines, but he explained to me just how out-of-the-loop he was:

"Early on in the development process, I realized that a bank loan would depend on a good appraisal. So, I get the appraiser I think is most likely to be given the assignment in Memphis, and I bring him up to the office, and kind of clue him in on what I'm doing: 'I'm gonna do something different, George, and this is what it's gonna be, and this is why.' I tell him the whole story. Two hours. And he sits at my desk and kind of stares blankly at me. And then he goes about appraising houses and leadin' the simple life. Two weeks later he calls me and says, 'Henry, you seen the *Atlantic Monthly?*' He says, 'Remember all that bullshit you were tellin' me? It's all in there.' So I jump out of my seat and run down and get it, and sure enough there's [Philip] Langdon's article.* I start readin' it, walkin' back, stumblin' over curbs and whatnot. I don't know if you'd call it an epiphany. I was thrilled that I wasn't out in left field. I'd thought about these things and they seemed so clear and self-evident to me, but I knew that everyone else was buildin' something different. And here was a guy talkin' word-for-word about what I was thinkin'. On the other hand, I was pissed off that I wasn't that smart, that I hadn't figured out somethin' new like Copernicus or Ke-

---

*Philip Langdon later elaborated his article into a lucid and excellent book, *A Better Place to Live: Reshaping the American Suburb* (Boston: MIT Press, 1994).

pler. On balance, I decided to be overjoyed. Then I went out and looked around. I went to see Portland, to Battery Park City in New York (which was disappointin'), and to Seaside, and I had a good time."

Harbortown, as he called his development on Mud Island, was built in short order. There was no charrette, because Turley had never heard of such a thing. The plan called for a great many traditional design elements that drive planning officials crazy—it was mixed use, and therefore against the first law of conventional zoning; it called for densities of eight house lots to the acre; the streets were narrow, with sharp corner radii, there were orderly rows of street trees to menace motorists, and so on. The Memphis planning department had to review it because Mud Island was part of the city. They didn't like parallel parking on 28-foot streets. They fretted about fire trucks and street trees. Finally, they wouldn't issue variances, but agreed to permit these things if the streets remained the responsibility of the homeowners' association.

"It was a *tabula rasa* out there," Turley told me. "Had we not proposed such a world-beatin' development, I imagine some people would've smarted off, but what could you say? We're in a place where there's nothin', nobody to object, nobody to say that the density is too great, that the lots are too small—except some tired old catfish."

As it was built, the 130 acres of Harbortown has three neighborhoods organized on a traditional network of connecting streets intersected by diagonal boulevards, all of which terminate at formal parks or squares. The Harbor district is the town's commercial center. The shopping street is on an axis with a hotel, a marina, and a yacht club. If you live in Harbortown, either as a homeowner or apartment renter, you automatically become a member of the yacht club. Originally there was some idea of making the shopping street a tourist attraction in the "festival marketplace" vein, but so many rubberneckers were already coming over to the island making a nuisance of themselves that this was scaled back to basic retail: a grocery store, some restaurants, a laundromat, and a few other shops. Over time, the market will adjust to what the residents of Harbortown really want. The buildings along the shopping street include eighty-seven apartment units over the stores. Altogether, Harbortown will comprise 450 houses of different types—townhouses, semi-attached, and regular stand-alone houses—and 430 apartments. At this writing, 260 houses and 345 apartments had been built.

In the planning stages, Turley was concerned that Harbortown would not attract families with children, because it is part of the Memphis school district, which, like practically every urban school district in America, is considered substandard. He offered a "baby bonus" of $1,200 credit per child against a lot purchase, and by 1994, sixty kids were living on the island. Turley built a grammar school to accommodate them and planned an addition for the seventh and eighth grades in the summer of 1995.

It is a five-minute walk across the bridge from Harbortown to downtown Memphis. (Unlike many other bridges in America, which make no provision for people, the Harbortown Bridge has eight-foot-wide pedestrian rights-of-way on both sides.) It's easy for people who live in Harbortown to walk over it to work, or to the Pinch Historic District and Beale Street, home of the blues and birthplace of rock and roll. It's just as easy for Memphians to come over to Harbortown from the city. The bridge obviously functions as a psychological barrier between downtown and the island. It's not a gate but it affords no other land access in and out of Harbortown's neighborhoods.

The price of houses in Harbortown, even with their lack of front lawns, all that dreaded density, and proximity to the problems of the inner city, is 10 percent higher than comparable suburban houses in the city's sprawling eastern hinterlands. That vague slouching beast, *the market*, apparently likes what it sees. The lessons of Harbortown are infecting the thinking of planning officials in the region, who are now able to view a three-dimensional model of ideas that contradict all their cherished dogmas. Turley says that some of the traffic engineers who first hassled him about the street dimensions are now claiming credit for Harbortown's streets, and proudly pointing them out to other developers as the right way to do things.

Notwithstanding the success of his project, Henry Turley laments the condition of American cities in general, and of Memphis in particular, where he grew up and where his family lived for four generations: "I see a phenomenon that's not unique to Memphis, the abandonment of the historic city. I see a re-segregation of people. It's immediate and palpable and visceral. I see decisions bein' made out of fear and negativity. It's not pleasing. I was compelled to do good work because I was endeavorin' to overcome the prejudices of my time."

A DEBACLE IN BROOKLYN

Anybody who complains about "greenfield development," and the nation's general failure to fix up existing towns and cities, should pay heed to the saga of the Atlantic Center. This story illustrates the kind of idiocy that urban redevelopers are up against.

In 1986, a young developer named Jonathan Rose, scion of a New York real estate fortune, was concerned about socially responsible development and attempted to redevelop a 24-acre bombed-out area in the heart of Brooklyn, but was defeated by the environmental movement. The Atlantic terminal, as the area was known, was one of the most complex transportation nodes in America. A dozen subway lines, the Long Island railroad, and nine bus routes converge there. But by the late 1980s, the only buildings standing on this large parcel were a meat-packing plant condemned by the city twenty years earlier, a gas station, and a shabby corrugated steel structure used to temporarily shelter the stairs to various underground trains.

Rose engaged San Francisco architect and planner Peter Calthorpe to devise the master plan, and New York's firm of Skidmore Owings and Merrill to design some of the commercial buildings. Atlantic Center, as the project was named, would be a classic, urban, mixed-use development, incorporating 2.7 million square feet of office space, 200,000 square feet of retail, and 688 apartments, 90 percent of them subsidized for middle- and low-income families. The apartments were designed as four-story low-rises, all in harmony with the surrounding nineteenth-century brownstone. They were optimally arranged to define public space, creating several mini-parks and courtyards. Day-care centers, recycling, and solar energy were additional elements of the project.

Then-mayor Edward Koch was solidly behind the project, since it was expected to provide 2,500 jobs in financial services, plus a slew of social benefits, not the least of which was lots of tax revenue where for decades there had been zilch. Koch also felt that the project would be viewed as a much-needed model for a nation full of trashed cities that had seemingly forgotten how to renew themselves.

Koch personally walked the project through the city's Byzantine permitting process, because he was anxious to get it underway. Corporate jobs were hemorrhaging out of the city into the suburbs. New Jersey was undergoing a fantastic boom in suburban office construction, and city-based companies were falling over each other to move out there. Under the circumstances, the Atlantic Center won quick and unanimous approval from the city. But then, developer Rose was slapped with a series of lawsuits.

What proved to be the fatal lawsuit was brought by a community action group. At issue was something called "secondary displacement." In a nutshell, secondary displacement alleged that by improving a 24-acre wasteland, the developer's actions had the effect of improving real estate values in adjoining neighborhoods, *and that this was a bad thing because rents would rise and poor people would be forced to move out.*

Its theoretical merit aside for a moment, the allegation had no basis in fact, because adjacent Fort Greene was a neighborhood where 80 percent of the residents owned their own brownstones. Besides, Fort Greene itself had already been gentrified in the 1970s, and practically all the remaining rental housing there was either rent controlled or rent stabilized. As a philosophical matter, what could have been more absurd than fighting urban redevelopment on the grounds that it *improved* neighborhoods?

The lawsuit dragged on for years because of New York City's clogged court dockets and a weird law that required judges to pass cases on to other judges if they ran longer than eleven months. Rose eventually won, but the suit was appealed, and this time an environmental organization, the National Resources Defense Council (NRDC), filed an *amicus* brief. By a strange coincidence, Jonathan Rose had been a longtime supporter of the NRDC. He was appalled at their action. So, in an attempt to reason with them, he met with NRDC President John Adams at the Council's Manhattan headquarters.

"What they sued on this time," Rose recalled painfully, "was not secondary displacement, but *the methodology by which we had studied it!* I said, 'Look, guys, the effect of your suit is that it's going to make the air quality worse in New Jersey, because you're going to move 2,500 jobs there, and those people are going to have to drive to work instead of taking public transit.' And that's when the guy [John Adams] said to me, 'That's not our airshed.'"

John Adams refused to comment, despite numerous calls to his subordinates at NRDC.

Eventually, drained financially, fatigued by years of effort, worn out by lawyers, hurt by the withdrawal of anchor tenants who got sick of waiting for buildings to go up, and disheartened by the unraveling of complex fi-nancing schedules, Jonathan Rose threw in the towel on the Atlantic Center.

This episode illustrates something dangerously defective in the current ideology of environmentalism. If environmental groups such as the NRDC don't support the re-use of existing towns and cities, then all their efforts to save the wild places and the wild things that live there will fail. It is as important to understand the design of the human habitat as it is to understand the ecology of a wetland. People belong somewhere. How will they live? In coherent towns and cities, or smeared all over the countryside? What could be more foolish and self-defeating than a position which essentially states that urban redevelopment is a wicked thing and that we shouldn't do it?

FORGOTTEN NEW ENGLAND, OR NEW ENGLAND FORGOTTEN

On the shoulder of Cape Cod, sixty-five miles from Boston, lies the township of Mashpee. Though it is surrounded by classic New England villages—and a lot of newer stuff—Mashpee itself never had a town center. It had never been more than pitch-pine scrub dotted by a few cranberry bogs. During the early 1960s, it got a 2,000-acre second-home housing pod built around a golf course, and a shopping center to service the pod, but as the years went by, further development passed over Mashpee for more populous Barnstable, Hyannis, and Falmouth. During the seventies and eighties—a rip-roaring time for sprawl-building elsewhere on the Cape—the Wampanoag Indian Council brought a lawsuit challenging land title to a substantial portion of Mashpee, which froze development there for years, though the town eventually won the suit.

But Mashpee officials were horrified by what sprawl had done to its neighbors in the meantime, so they concocted a new master plan to protect themselves. It was a classic NIMBY document, calling for large-lot residential zoning as the supposed antidote to sprawl. Essentially, it was a tool for making any more tract housing impossible to build. Yet, it lacked a positive vision of a desirable living arrangement, because for all their horror at the surrounding sprawl, the town officials were completely bogged down in the conventional thinking of their time. They could picture sprawl, and they could picture virgin pine scrub, and that was the limit of their imaginations, because mixing houses with other stuff was *verboten* in their worldview. The only other thing the master plan did was permit a little more commercial development on land around the intersection of highways 151 and 28, which was a traffic rotary, along with a new town office, library, police station, and a church.

Now, it happened that there was an existing shopping center right off that rotary. In 1968, the Chace family of Providence developed the New Seabury shopping center as a commercial "amenity" for the 2,000-acre golf course housing. By 1984, the shopping center was getting shabby. Coincidentally, Buff Chace, then in his mid-thirties, was taking a larger role in the family land development business. He wanted to do something about the aging shopping center—besides making it bigger and giving it a cosmetic makeover. He enlisted family friend Douglas Storrs, an environmental planner then living in Vermont, to help come up with a plan. They visited other historic towns on the Cape and elsewhere in New England, using measuring tapes to figure out the dimensions of things. They inventoried the features that they liked: the human scale, the street trees, the village greens, the building types. What they finally decided to do was try to turn the dreary old shopping center into something that Mashpee never had: a true town center based on a traditional New England village.

The plan they conceived was to infill the parking lots with new buildings and create an intersection of two new commercial streets off the highway where there had not been streets before. They wanted to add a second story above the stores for apartments or offices, and to create more sense of solidity—since, as a rule, traditional New England towns are not composed of one-story buildings. They purchased 275 adjoining acres with the idea that, in the future, a coherent network of new streets with houses and greens and other civic buildings could somehow be integrated around the redesigned shopping center—and also to keep big box stores and other predators from putting up some terrible *dreck* in the vicinity. Like Henry Turley down in Memphis, Chace and Storrs were also arriving at the TND idea on their own, in a vacuum.

It took a laborious eleven months of twice-a-week meetings to get the necessary approvals from the planning board for the first phase of Mashpee Commons, as the project was called. This involved the creation of Market and Steeple streets, the two new streets that would form a commercial intersection of a town center. The various officials involved were not happy with the street design. The rights-of-way were too narrow, they worried about firetrucks turning the corners, blah blah blah, the usual stuff. To get around their objections, Chace and Storrs designated Market and Steeple streets "access roads to parking lots," rather than public streets, and they were approved. They were granted a special permit to put second stories on the old shopping strip buildings, which included permission for 100 apartments or offices. Otherwise, the zoning was not changed. At once, they built four new buildings to infill the parking lots and renovated two of the old ones.

Meanwhile, Chace and Storrs had a piece of land in Florida they wanted to do something with. It was now 1987. Having seen pictures of Seaside in the magazines, they called Andres Duany and Elizabeth Plater-Zyberk for some advice about developing the parcel. They met at the architects' Miami office. Naturally, Chace and Storrs mentioned their Mashpee project, and showed them some crude drawings. Suddenly, Andres and Lizz were all worked up. They didn't want to talk about the Florida land anymore. What excited the architects was that Mashpee Commons was something like Seaside done backward. At Seaside they had started with the houses, hoping to add the commercial town center later. Here at Mashpee, the town center was getting built first with the intention of putting houses around it later. This was fortuitous because Andres and Lizz had been asked to design dozens of Traditional Neighborhood Developments after Seaside, and the notion of town centers was scaring bankers to death. The bankers couldn't wrap their minds around the concept. *You want to put shops and stuff in the middle of a housing development?* Mixed use was totally alien to them. More to the point, they wouldn't lend money for projects like that.

Even at Seaside, the great iconic model of the TND, the commercial core was lagging behind. All Seaside's town center contained in 1987 was a corner grocery, a restaurant, and a post office. The houses, with their small lots and short setbacks were cake compared to doing the civic portion of the ensemble. People were starting to complain that the TND concept wasn't what it was cracked up to be. Especially outside the professions of architecture and land development, where ordinary folk had no idea of the kind of obstacles presented by zoning laws and planning boards and conventional thinking. So, Duany and Plater-Zyberk were delirious to find this case where the town center was phase one. It was an answer to their prayers.

Chace and Storrs were swept up in DPZ's enthusiasm. In short order, Duany and Plater-Zyberk flew up to Cape Cod, scoped out the property, and held a charrette. As usual, the charrette involved the government officials from the town level on up, traffic engineers, citizens, and other interested parties. The result was a very handsome full-blown master plan to replicate a New England town in New England. The only hitch was that to get it built required that the town replace its existing zoning with a TND ordinance. In reality, the rehabilitated shopping center was still zoned C-1 (i.e., a 40,000-square-foot lot with 20 percent "coverage," and 200 feet of highway "frontage"). The land under a proposed neighborhood of attached townhouses was also zoned C-1. And the land under a proposed neighborhood of single-family houses to be built at a density of eight to the acre, was zoned R-2, meaning two-acre lots. The bottom line was that nothing else could be built at Mashpee except the sort of suburban sprawl that the zoning specified. And despite the fact that the charrette had produced verbal agreements about how to proceed, the town officials lacked the will to make the necessary changes in the zoning laws.

Something else happened in the meantime. By the early 1990s, the citizens of Cape Cod became so panicked by the cancerous spread of suburban sprawl that they instituted the Cape Cod Commission, whose job was to figure out what to do about it. The first act of the commission was a temporary moratorium on building anything at all on Cape Cod. It was an act of desperation, but reasonable under the circumstances. Cape Cod was rapidly being ruined. Eventually, though, instead of replacing their stupid zoning with a new set of building regulations aimed at producing compact development (traditional towns and villages), the Cape Cod Commission merely became an additional layer of bureaucracy on top of the local planning boards using the old zoning. The Cape Cod Commission, like the Mashpee planning board earlier, was unable to *conceive* of an alternative to suburban sprawl or no development at all. The Cape Cod Commission could not imagine a traditional New England village as a model for development. The Cape Cod Commission couldn't imagine Cape Cod. So the end result is a destructive template left in place (zoning), with extra procedural bullshit layered on top of it (the commission) to make sure that nothing gets built under the bad template.

The inability of Cape Cod officials to recognize the traditional New England town as a viable model for development speaks pathetically for a general failure of imagination across the nation as a whole. After all, New England has traditionally thought itself the most enlightened region of the country. Harvard, Yale, and MIT are there. They presumably know something about their own history. Many of them actually live in fine old neighborhoods and towns: Beacon Hill, Marblehead, Ipswich. They have theme parks entirely devoted to historic settlements (Sturbridge Village and Plymouth Plantation). If they can't figure out how to build the human habitat in a region so rich with historical models, how the hell can we expect the citizens of Lorain County, Ohio, or Maricopa County, Arizona, to do it right?

Mashpee Commons has been stalled ever since. Market and Steeple streets were built. There are offices over the sixty stores there, not apartments, because people will not want to live in apartments over the stores *until* there is a surrounding community they can be a part of, complete with public gathering places, yet the public consensus, as expressed through the layers of government, won't allow that to happen. The property for the adjoining neighborhoods is still there, waiting until the town planning board and the traffic engineers and the Cape Cod Commission get their heads screwed on. Nowadays, Chace and Storrs put most of their energy into the task of rehabilitating nearby Providence in Rhode Island. Contrary to many people's hopes, Mashpee did not become another Seaside.

"We beat our heads against the wall too long and too hard," Storrs told me. "Right now, Mashpee is a good-looking shopping center, but it's not a true town."

REHABILITATING MAIN STREET

Main Street in Corning, New York (pop. 13,000), isn't even called Main Street, but rather Market Street. Compared to other small towns across America—their local retail economies sucked dry by predatory chain stores—Corning's Market Street is a surprisingly healthy Main Street. There's a reason for it.

Corning is the headquarters of Corning Glass, a healthy Fortune 500 company. While other American manufacturers have floundered in the face of foreign competition, Corning shrewdly parlayed its expertise in housewares and optics to the making of high-tech components for computer electronics. It's all just so much silicon. Corning Inc. has been the dominant influence in town since the 1860s, when Brooklyn Flint Glassworks transplanted itself there and changed its name. The town is located in Steuben County, New York's "southern tier." Three rivers converge there: the Tioga, the Cohocton, and the Chemung, a tributary of the Susquehanna, which makes a direct water route to Chesapeake Bay and its major port, Baltimore.

I first visited Corning back in 1967 during a rather bleary sojourn to a state university drama festival sponsored by the glass company, where I performed in a play (we won a prize) and drank too much. The town used to boast that its forty-four bars gave it the highest proportion of drinking establishments per capita in the state. This seemed rakish and sporting to a nineteen-year-old sophomore. Market Street at that time was a dingy ten-block stretch of gin mills and beer joints geared to factory workers from the glass works.

Anyway, in 1972, Hurricane Agnes wandered in from the Atlantic Ocean. The winds were no big deal by the time it arrived inland, but the storm dumped so much rain on the southern tier that the three rivers over-flowed their banks and nearly swept away the town. People had to live in federal disaster relief trailers for months. Businesses went under. For all the trouble and heartbreak it caused, though, the flood was a blessing in disguise.

Just before the hurricane, a bunch of civic groups had begun an effort to make Corning's downtown a nicer place. The glass company itself was increasingly concerned about the quality of life there because it proved to be a big negative for executive recruitment. This was in addition to its geographic isolation—more than five hours by car from New York City. Capable middle-aged men with families, who could afford to pick and choose among employers, would fly in to interview for a job and get the creeps just driving around town. The company realized it would have to play an active role in making the town a more appealing place in which to live, or settle for second-rate executives.

The hurricane damage happened to bring in lots of federal and state disaster money, which, on top of Corning Glass's resources made for quite a civic war chest. The company and the town quickly formed a cluster of non-profit agencies and corporations to take charge of the town's rehabilitation. On the downside, one of the first things this partnership did was to take a federal Urban Development block grant and bulldoze five of Market Street's ten blocks to build a Modernist civic center. This unfortunate blunder turned out to be one of the more ludicrous exercises of its kind, and I shall describe its features shortly. But better things also happened:

They made a commitment to restore the five remaining blocks of Market Street and set up a separate agency to accomplish it. They used some of the disaster money to install granite curbs, brick sidewalks, and orderly rows of fast-growing locust trees on the five remaining old blocks. They created a nicely scaled, brick-paved public square around a clock tower in the center of Market Street's east-west axis, and renovated the buildings around the square. They redesigned the parking program, including a new multilevel parking structure behind Market Street. They made realistic plans to create a riverfront park in place of an abandoned railroad right of way. And finally they made a commitment to move Corning Inc's corporate headquarters from the far side of the Chemung River to a site one block off the public square—virtually in the center of town.

The Market Street Restoration Agency has taken these remaining five blocks of the old downtown and done a very sensitive job of bringing them back to life. The agency got Market Street onto the National Register of Historic Places in 1974, though it was still a mess, and not just because of the flood. As virtually elsewhere, Market Street's buildings had suffered cosmetic makeover treatments over the decades. Everything from volcanic tufa rock to self-illuminating glass panels (a Corning Inc. experiment) had been used to clad a very nice ensemble of nineteenth century brick buildings. The agency's approach was circumspect. They worked to keep a few of the best of these re-do jobs—for instance, some 1940s art deco glass storefronts—while the most atrocious stuff went in the dumpster. The result was a street that successfully avoids the pitfalls of theme park sentimentality and treats the recent past respectfully—as though it happened.

The Market Street Restoration Agency can regulate signs, but beyond that they must rely on incentives and persuasion to keep the facade standards above the current American norm. It does this effectively by serving as a conduit for money from the other non-profit agencies set up by Corning Glass and the city, and by offering free design service for facade improvements. In effect, this means the building owners get free architectural services and subsidized renovations. When I revisited the town in 1995—some twenty-seven years after my sophomoric binge at the drama festival—the director of the restoration agency was an architect named Elise Johnson-Schmidt, who had an impressive record of experience in historic preservation, including work on the renovation of the ceiling of New York's Grand Central Station.

Corning's Market Street is a successful downtown shopping street—the closest mall is fifteen miles away—with an impressive mix of retailers. In 1995, there was a drugstore, a book shop, more than one bank, a newsroom, a tailor, a shoe store, a sporting goods shop, a home furnishings store, an electric guitar shop, two electronics emporiums, several lunch spots, an ice cream parlor, a jewelry store, an art supplies store, a couple of realtors, travel agencies, several fancy restaurants, a Chinese takeout, and a U.S. Army recruitment office. There were a handful of glass boutiques, art galleries, and antique shops, too, but altogether the retail mix was about as authentic as any Main Street can be these days. It was markedly better, for example, than Santa Monica's Fourth Street pedestrian mall, which is almost entirely composed of touristy boutiques and eating establishments. The achievement at Corning's Market Street, therefore, is the modest and subtle one of having re-created a genuine small-town business district. It doesn't seem like such an achievement until you travel around and see that most of the Main Streets in the northeast United States are abandoned.

The Corning Corporation eventually did build its headquarters on that site adjacent to Centerway Square. It opened for business in 1993. It is a big hunk of corporate architecture in red brick and tinted glass with that vaguely sinister Hollywood look—like a well-dressed government assassin in sunglasses. The building was designed by Kevin Roche, one of America's leading prestige designers of such things. Whatever its merits or defects as a work of architecture, at least it stands in close proximity to the heart of town. It sends 600 employees scurrying out to Market Street in search of meals every day, and no doubt quite a few of them drop into the bookstore and the sporting goods shop. The company has shown good faith in the town and the town shows it. It is a lucky town.

Now, for the Modernist Civic Center. It was built hastily in the aftermath of the flood, and shows it. The components were a new city hall, a new library, a new hotel, a union hall, a social services building, and, as its centerpiece, an outdoor ice rink. The opportunity to assemble such a collection of civic buildings all at one time is very rare for any size town, and the botch they made of it beautifully illustrates the idiocies of Modernist planning—especially as contrasted with the old Market Street restoration.

The first thing you notice is that the Civic Center's pedestrian way—a continuation of Market Street without the cars—is slightly off axis. Whether they did this deliberately to make the pedestrian way look sporty, or by accident, is unclear, but the two thoroughfares don't line up. The Civic Center is completely confused as to what is the front and what is the back of its buildings. It ends up having no front. As you proceed down the pedestrian way, there are no shops. All you get are blank walls. Amazingly, the hotel decided to locate its restaurant Fry-o-later exhaust fan so that it blows directly onto the pedestrian path, literally eight feet from your head as you stroll by. The hotel's main air conditioning compressor unit also stands there, emitting a deafening whine. Benches are deployed right beside the noisy unit, as though a sane person might actually sit there for the pleasure of destroying his hearing. The mall entrance to the social services building is permanently locked, and the little plaza in front of the door has sprouted weeds. A dinky clock tower made out of flimsy steel trusswork (not to be confused with the one in Centerway Square), contains a broken clock, which would be hard to read even if it were working because instead of hands, it has dots that move around the face, and it also has dots instead of numbers—it's abstract art! To the side of the clock, there is a fountain (or "water feature," as the landscape architects say in their *Star Trek* lingo) which is also broken (it was June when I was there). The brick pavers all along the pedestrian path have spalled and cracked. The library presents two kinds of blank walls to the pedestrian: plain cement, and plate-glass windows lined with venetian blinds. Ornamental planting beds, installed to give some relief from the blank walls, have sprouted sumac bushes, a common weed in upstate New York, and a sign that nobody takes care of the beds. City hall tried to dress up its blank glass wall entrance with an enormous mural of cartoon human figures. The crowded mural contrasts eerily with the deserted pedestrian way. The ice rink, built between city hall and the library, lies under a high steel shed roof, a few feet below grade, affording nice views of skaters from the sidelines. Unfortunately, no one in the one-story library would be able to see the skaters from that angle, and city hall didn't have any windows on the rink side of the building. Also unfortunately, the rink's coolant system broke down in 1994, and the rink itself had to be refitted at considerable expense.

Altogether, the Corning civic center was a very instructive example of Murphy's Law—whatever could have gone wrong, did go wrong. It was a wonderful model of what *not* to do. It also made the old end of Market Street look great. It illustrates that the principles of traditional civic art actually produce a much better everyday environment, at far less cost, than the abstractions of Modernism.

TRIBAL WARFARE

In 1993, the little village of Chatham, New York (pop. 2,000), in the old Dutch highlands east of the Hudson River, not far from the Massachusetts line, found itself in a quandary. Two major developments were proposed. Both posed serious questions for the village. The implications frightened them.

Chatham had been through many periods of growth and decline. It grew after the Revolutionary War; it declined when the Erie Canal opened. It grew again with the coming of the railroads; it sagged again with the coming of the motorcar. It has endured through most of the twentieth century in a state of marginal stability verging on somnambulism. Today, the town has a small plastics manufacturing company, another small factory that makes cardboard, and a Blue Seal Feed agricultural depot. It has a modest Main Street with a dozen stores that are supported in part by the shadowy presence of a second-home economy, which sends weekending city dwellers swarming in from the surrounding hills for the Sunday papers, a leaf rake, or a bag of croissants. Columbia County holds its annual fair in Chatham—another big draw for the Martha Stewart Country Weekend crowd. Main Street has an old one-screen movie theater, beloved by all, and it shows first-run pictures for an amazing $2.50. There's a very nice bookshop. The village even possesses, perhaps through some bureaucratic oversight by NYNEX, a downtown pay phone that will place your call for a nickel.

Chatham is a settlement of some charm and also some grit. It has an impressive inventory of nineteenth century mansions, and several streets of mid-twentieth century suburban-style bunkers. The highway, the railroad, and Stony Creek all run through the same valley, which makes it seem a bit cramped. In 1878, 100 trains came through town every day, including nine mails. Passenger service has now stopped entirely. (AMTRAK runs one pathetic passenger train a day from Albany to Boston, but it no longer stops at Chatham, just passes through.) Ten freights rattle through every day, affecting traffic. The handsome granite and wood train station is boarded up, with decrepitating eaves, and burdocks sprouting on the old baggage dock. The train tracks bisect the Main Street diagonally in an awkward way, and a dusty marshalling yard owned by CONRAIL occupies five derelict acres at the center of town.

The two projects proposed in 1993 were these: first, a mixed-use scheme that would have put a small supermarket and some apartments in the CONRAIL yard; and second, a strip mall with a large supermarket on the southern fringe of the village. Though the villagers dimly sensed a threat to their Main Street, the strip mall had an air of inevitability about it, especially insofar as it was allowable by "special use permit" under the village's zoning. The rail yard project upset the villagers more, because it was right downtown and it excited the NIMBY syndrome. There was also a lot of anxiety about the old train station, which stood on the property. The strip mall was proposed by a local resident named Greg Bervy. The rail yard project was proposed by an "outsider" named Ed Hoe, who actually lived five miles away in Spencertown, N.Y. So perplexed were the mayor and the Village Board of Trustees, that they hired a professional town planner to advise them.

Joel Russell, then forty-three, was the professional. He worked out of an office in Dutchess County, the next county to the south. He had the physical demeanor and the bearded face of a nineteenth-century country doctor, say, a character out of a Chekov play. Russell came out of Harvard in the late sixties, then got a master's degree in urban affairs at Boston University. He had serious musical aspirations (clarinet), but eventually abandoned them to get a law degree, also at Boston U. For a while, he worked in the Boston office of the architects Skidmore Owings and Merrill on transportation issues. In the late seventies and early eighties, he veered off to New Hampshire to work on alternative energy projects. When the Reagan administration ended grants for these things, he moved to the Hudson Valley and helped found the Dutchess [County] Land Conservancy, an organization devoted to protecting rural land from suburban development.

By and by, Russell came to realize that rural land could not be protected unless the human habitat was assembled correctly in towns and villages. He saw how zoning laws militated against the creation of towns and villages. He brought a lawyer's eye to understanding the deliberate obfuscations of typical zoning ordinances, which make them incomprehensible to normal citizens. Like Henry Turley down in Tennessee, and Jack Lucks in

Ohio, Russell recognized that traditional town planning was the best way to create functional places worth caring about. His convictions were bolstered by unhappy memories of growing up in the suburbs.

"I was born in the city of Hartford," he said. "My family moved to a new ranch house in 1954. Four years later, they built their dream house in an upper middle-class suburb, and I grew to detest it. We had a half acre, and we were one of the first houses in the subdivision. It was on an abandoned golf course that had started to grow back. It was an interesting landscape. Every spring a new crop of old golf balls would come out of the ground. I watched with great sadness as this landscape turned into wall-to-wall suburbs, and all the beautiful trees that had been part of the golf course came down."

In 1988, Russell quit the land trust and began practicing as a free-lance town planning consultant. "It was focusing only on one side of the problem, the open space and the countryside," he said. "I couldn't see working on that set of issues in isolation." Outside government bureaucracies, there were very few independent professional town planners in the United States, and fewer with law degrees. Townships and municipalities had been accustomed for fifty years to buying zoning "kits" right off the shelf from companies that sold generic zoning ordinances. If you wonder why the suburbs of Tacoma, Washington, are identical to those of Scranton, Pennsylvania, seek no further.

One of Russell's first jobs out on his own was to redesign the zoning of a mostly rural township named Hillsdale in Columbia County, near Chatham. The rural development and village design guidelines he devised for Hillsdale were so good that the New York Planning Federation quickly published them as their model for rural land use planning before Hillsdale even voted to approve them.

The Chatham charrette was held in the "cafetorium" of the elementary school on a drizzly weekend in November of 1993. Two hundred and fourteen citizens showed up—more than 10 percent of the village. On Friday night, Russell put on a slide show. Using two projectors side by side, he'd show an image of a mall parking lot on the left and the image of Main Street on the right, then a street of houses with porches on small lots, and a suburban bunker on a huge lot, and so on in that vein. In events of this kind, Americans instinctively recognize what is good and what is crap—even if the crap looks like their own home or their workplace. What's more, there's the thrill of having much of their longtime displeasure and anxiety over their surroundings made comprehensible *for the first time*. The slide show enabled the villagers to understand that their deep suspicions and yearnings had some validity.

Therefore, on Saturday, when the assembly broke into small groups, they were able to discuss more clearly why their own laws and codes did not produce the kind of environment they wished to live in. They began to see, for instance, that their zoning didn't permit small lots, so they couldn't extend their traditional street pattern when new houses were needed. They began to see that their desire for ultra-convenient parking was at odds with a walkable downtown. They learned that one of the reasons they had a "parking problem" on Main Street was that business owners and employees parked in front of their own shops instead of behind the buildings, where there was plenty of space. They realized that the public realm in the village had been short-shrifted—they longed for a village green, and they saw that there was plenty of derelict property downtown to create one. The final day, Sunday, under Russell's guidance, they assembled a list of fifteen goals for the village's future development. Some of them were fluffier than others—for instance, *Improve aesthetics of the village* as opposed to the more forthright *Protect existing trees and plant new ones along streets.*

This was the middle of the process. Russell was under contract to write a new master plan. He knew quite well that the master plan was only an elaborate wish list, and that the more crucial question lay in its implementation—namely, whether the village would go further and actually do something about its zoning laws. In the meantime, a big fight erupted over one of the two proposed developments. Russell was inclined to favor Ed Hoe's proposed development for the rail yard because the project came with some apartments, the multi-acre site was right next to Main Street, and the supermarket would have sent some customers to the nearby local shops. "I thought it was okay, as long as he could do it without blowing a hole in the downtown fabric," Russell said. He was disposed unfavorably to Greg Bervy's strip mall proposal because it was not physically integral with the existing village, and would have posed a serious economic threat to all of Main Street's businesses.

Ed Hoe was a boyish-looking forty-one-year-old former hippie potter turned real estate developer, originally from Poughkeepsie, who now believes he made his big mistake by wearing a suit and tie to the planning board meeting where he pitched his proposal for the rail yard. Unfortunately, he had also earned the enmity of a local businesswoman on an earlier occasion for backing out of what would have been a bad business deal on a Main Street building, based on financial information he got from her about five minutes before signing the papers. The local businesswoman, in turn, had earned the enmity of a civic group called "Preserve and Improve Chatham" (PIC) for buying Chatham's old and beloved general store and turning it into a dollar mart. She and the editor of the weekly Chatham *Courier*, another woman, broke off from PIC and formed their own group called the Chatham Business Alliance (CBA). They also started a historical society together. The society's mission was to turn the old train station into a museum.

Now, as part of Ed Hoe's proposal for the rail yard, he offered to give the old station to the village free of charge—with the stipulation that repairs on the building get underway within a year or ownership would revert to him. The reason was that the wooden roof of the station was falling apart, and it demanded immediate attention. This stipulation inflamed Ed Hoe's enemies. The newspaper began a campaign of obloquy against him on the grounds, among other offenses, that he was an outsider. It also lashed out at Russell's charrette, calling it "a charade."

Soon, the battle over the train station blossomed into all-out tribal warfare between an odd alliance of, on one side, the newspaper, the historical society, assorted NIMBYs, and the volunteer firemen (the natives), and, on the other side, the city weekenders, and the less-than-lifetime residents (the perceived pointy-headed, used-to-be-hippies, intellectual outsiders). Ultimately, Ed Hoe became so disgusted with the situation that he threw in the towel, sorry that he ever proposed anything in the first place. Greg Bervy, the local boy, breezed through the village zoning board and got his special permit to build the strip mall at the south end of town.

Despite the imprecations aimed at him by the newspaper, Joel Russell stayed more or less in the middle of all this, marveling at the spitefulness of small-town politics. "I had a long talk with the fire chief and he didn't pull any punches about it," Russell said a few months later. "He doesn't like Ed Hoe because Ed Hoe is *not one of us*. He's not really against development on that site. He's against Ed Hoe developing on that site. He'd like to pass a zoning law that says, *If you're from here, you can do anything you like with your land; if you're not from here, get the hell out of town.* I asked [the fire chief] how come you guys are allied with the historical society, and he just sort of laughed and said it probably wouldn't be a bad idea to just bulldoze the old train station."

A year later, the acrimony had died down. Ed Hoe was long gone. Russell's master plan was done, and the village came up with a little more grant money from the New York Planning Federation so that he could revise their zoning codes, though he would have preferred to replace them altogether. Russell actually had a hard time physically assembling the existing codes. Chatham's last major revision had been in 1979. Since then, they'd made small incremental changes and inserted them on loose-leaf notebook paper into the Village Board's filing cabinet—so there was, in effect, only one copy of the damn thing.

The changes Russell eventually drafted were these: allowing more mixed use in and around the village core, requiring tree planting, pedestrian connections (i.e., sidewalks), and meaningful open-space set-asides, reducing parking space requirements for business property owners, strengthening historic preservation requirements, creating build-to lines more consistent with a traditional village, and prohibiting future highway strip developments. Russell wanted to take the document a step further by including illustrated design guidelines, and drafting the stuff left over from the old days into plain English, but the village didn't want to spend any more money to do that.

As of autumn, 1995, the village had adopted the master plan, but not yet voted to formally adopt Joel Russell's zoning changes. They were waiting for the document to come back from a publisher of legal codes.

In the meantime, Greg Bervy's strip mall was up-and-running on the south end of the village, with a Grand Union supermarket anchoring it and five other retail shops competing with Main Street.

Joel Russell went on to bigger jobs the following year, rewriting codes for the town of Brunswick, Maine, and Beaufort County, South Carolina.

The roof of the Chatham train station is still crumbling.

THE GREENFIELDS OF DEVELOPMENT

Many people, including some partisans of the New Urbanism, are uncomfortable with the creation of new towns from the ground up on previously undeveloped land, even if they turn out to be great places like

Seaside. This has earned the movement the epithet *The New Suburbanism*. I think there is something to their complaint philosophically: greenfield development seems, at least, wasteful and redundant. Without decent public transit, people are still stuck with their cars whenever they travel outside the TND. But the alternative to greenfield TND development, the rehabilitation of existing towns and cities with traditional civic fabric, is very difficult to bring off most places these days, as must be evident in the examples cited above. This being the case, should New Urbanists sit on their hands until the gasoline runs out?

It seems to me that we badly need three-dimensional models of good development, and Seaside is not enough. We need them in other regions of the country, where many people will be able to walk through them, and bankers will see how they perform in the market, and builders and planning board members will see for themselves that there actually is a better way of doing things than suburban sprawl. If it takes a few thousand acres of good rural land to get these models built, I believe it will be worth it. Anyway, for every acre of greenfield TNDs currently being built, we're still getting a thousand acres of conventional housing pods and malls every year. So it's not as though the cancer of sprawl is about to stop even if the New Urbanists were to cease their activities altogether.

At least a score of New Urbanist greenfield developments have been approved the past few years, and are in various stages of completion now. They share some common, unanticipated problems, not necessarily of their own making.

"What the New Urbanists have down pat is the design part. They know how to do the charrettes, the plans, the beautiful renderings that initially sell the vision of a new neighborhood or village," says Peter Katz, author of a book on the subject.* "What's been more problematic is getting those visions implemented in a manner that resembles the design team's intent. At every turn, builders, regulators, citizens, even the project's own developer try to dismantle the plan and the codes, especially if it restricts them in any way."

Probably the biggest impediment has turned out to be the banking establishment. The banks simply do not recognize any form of development beside conventional suburban sprawl to be a legitimate investment. The

The New Urbanism, by Peter Katz (New York: McGraw-Hill, 1994).

Savings and Loan crisis, and the sharp-fanged descent of federal regulators, made loan officers pathologically timid. They have only grudgingly lent money for New Urbanist projects, and then only for the housing component, because they don't believe that mixed use buildings—i.e., apartments and offices over stores—have any market. This may be changing, slowly and painfully. Despite turmoil in the banking industry, the national real estate slump of the early 1990s, and the financial problems of individual developers, New Urbanist projects performed exceptionally well. The houses have sold readily, and for demonstrably higher prices than comparably sized houses in nearby pod developments. So bankers now have proof that there is something about these communities that the market seems to like—even if they don't understand it themselves.

Two developments that merit a look as interesting cases in point are Duany and Plater-Zyberk's Kentlands, in the Maryland suburbs outside Washington, D.C., and Peter Calthorpe's Laguna West, outside Sacramento, California. They were ambitious projects of similar scale which encountered similar problems with different outcomes. Both Kentlands and Laguna West got under way during the worst real estate recession in memory, and in two of the hardest hit markets. Both of them had developers who tanked out, though even under foreclosure construction and sales went forward.

Kentlands lies embedded in one of the worst suburban crudscapes in America, like a Fabergé egg in a county landfill. This is the so-called technology corridor between Rockville and Gaithersburg along I-270, one Radiant City office park after another, pod-upon-pod of income-targeted houseburgers, strip after numbing strip of chain stores, fry pits, and multiplexes. It's like Southern California, only arguably worse, because from the 1960s to the 1990s the traffic engineers have managed to ratchet up the scale of everything—the commercial boulevards are wider, the intersections vaster, the setbacks ever deeper, the juniper-covered berms ever larger. Except for a few tatters of remnant farmland, this is a tragic landscape of postwar zoning with all its predictable horrors.

Kentlands was assembled on one of these tatters, the 356-acre Kent farm, incorporating the existing farm buildings. It would finally include 1,700 dwellings—apartments, rowhouses, and freestanding houses—and a population of about 5,000 living in five distinct neighborhoods, each with a civic focal point. For instance, the first neighborhood built was focused on a circular green around which were disposed such civic buildings as the elementary school, a church, a day-care center, and a small store. Another neighborhood was to be centered on a town pool and tennis court complex, another called Midtown was to be a mixed-use "main street" of shops, offices, and apartments, and so on. Unlike Seaside, Kentlands was a year-round community.

In the DPZ manner, Kentlands was designed to have small lots, narrow tree-lined streets, public parks and greens, and a mix of housing types. Accessory apartments were permitted throughout, and some houses even came with rental units over the detached garage as a form of economic infrastructure. There was an urban code, which regulated the street design, lot sizes, building types, and the built-to lines, and an architectural code that regulated materials, roof pitches, dormers, porches, and windows. Adjoining Kentlands, and an integral part of the project, was a big shopping regional center on a corner between two humongous existing highways. Duany and Plater-Zyberk had deliberately designed the shopping center so that at some future time the parking lots could be infilled with buildings and streets, a la Masphee Commons.

The charrette, which involved officials of Montgomery County and the town of Gaithersburg, was a nightmare of bargaining and compromise. All sorts of strange little design quarrels cropped up. For instance, the Gaithersburg School District was in control of the architecture of the elementary school. They wanted to put the loading dock right on the front of the building. Duany had a shit fit over it. Finally, he got them to agree to put a Greek temple portico on the front—as long as the developer paid for it—and it was eventually built that way. There were many fights over the street dimensions and grades. But on the whole, DPZ's design survived remarkably intact. Construction began in 1989, just in time for the recession.

As a consequence of the recession, and of associated shenanigans in the financial markets, including the leveraged buyouts of certain department store chains, the deal for the adjoining shopping center component of Kentlands fell apart. As a further result, Kentland's developer, Joseph Alfandre, lost control of the whole project, which was taken over by the Chevy Chase Bank, its main lender. That is, the bank *became* the developer by default. To put it mildly, banks lack certain expertise in that end of the business. This could have been a fatal catastrophe, except that DPZ had built in some very shrewd protective mechanisms. The Kentland

TND codes had the force of law. The TND ordinance *was* the zoning for those 356 acres. The Gaithersburg town government had passed it into law after the charrette. So, to do anything differently than the DPZ plan called for would require variances—a neat reversal of the usual scenario where zoning reigns. The variances would be impossible to get because DPZ had left a "town architect" in place as an employee of the homeowners' association. He had a spacious office in the center of the place with a staff of three, and he was there every day, like an architectural policeman, walking around, watching the houses go up, chatting up the guys with the pneumatic nailing guns. His job was to make sure the codes were followed, for example, to make sure that the individual builders didn't start putting garage doors on the fronts of houses. The town architect had an ever-growing constituency, because virtually every home buyer who moved into the place understood that he was paying a premium price for a higher standard of civic design, and that homebuyer, more than anybody, didn't want to see it compromised. So the five neighborhoods got built very much as they were planned on paper. The pool and tennis complex got built, with a shingle-style clubhouse that looked like something out of McKim, Meade, and White, circa 1904—a strikingly handsome building. The codes limited individual builders to a few dozen houses each, to avoid the tedious uniformity of the typical suburban pod.

By late 1995, Kentlands' housing component was about 95 percent built out. It looked great. People I talked to who lived there felt happy and fortunate. It was such a pleasant environment that residents of surrounding pods would *drive* into Kentlands to do their jogging, or just walk around (the surrounding pods had refused to connect their streets with those of Kentlands). The school and the day-care center were open, and the church built "on spec" had been sold quickly to a congregation. The resale value of houses in Kentlands remained relatively high compared to the rest of the D.C. suburbs, in which anxiety over government downsizing was being expressed in a chronically depressed real estate market.

The biggest disappointment about Kentlands was the district designated "Midtown," which was to be Kentlands' commercial core. The Chevy Chase bank lacked the confidence that such a mixed-use development could succeed as originally designed. They made some feeble attempts to get it under way, but they were determined to job the whole thing out to a single developer, to build Midtown all at once, like a mall. They also got greedy, and tried to reconfigure it as a regional entertainment destination, with a multiplex theater and so on, instead of the local retail center it was originally intended to be. The plan would have required a 700-car parking structure. The homeowner's association objected to this transparent effort to create a mini-theme park in the middle of their community. What the bank failed to consider was the more modest solution of platting the district into individual building lots and selling them off to willing buyers who would be required under the codes to build the mixed-use fabric of Midtown one building at a time—the way towns organically are built. This seemed beyond them. Consequently, as of late 1995, Midtown still does not exist.

Laguna West, eleven miles south of Sacramento, designed by Peter Calthorpe of San Francisco, was more ambitious than Kentlands at twice the size. It was to be the western showplace of the New Urbanism. It was a TOD (Transit Oriented Development) in Calthorpe's parlance, as opposed to a TND (Traditional Neighborhood Development) in DPZ's language. The transit in this case was to be a light rail line emanating out of a regional system centered on Sacramento. Laguna West looked great in the drawings. It was more baroquely formal in physical plan than Kentlands, which had some romantic Olmstedian overtones. The plan called for an urban core of apartments, stores, offices, and civic buildings focused around the transit stop with the density decreasing to a more overtly suburban pattern as it radiated outward. Laguna West got under way about the same time as Kentlands, and developer Phil Angelides met a similar fate as Kentlands' Joseph Alfandre: he lost control of the project to the banks.

The result at Laguna West has been very disappointing so far. The part that went into construction first was the outer ring of suburban houses. The "design guidelines" intended to regulate the build-out were not incorporated into the local zoning in the form of an ordinance. They had been loosely adopted by the developer without any provisions for enforcement. Unlike Kentlands, there was no town architect in place to supervise the daily goings-on. With the developer out of the picture, the banks took over Laguna West and, panicked by the large sums of money at stake, reverted, wherever possible, to the depressing conventions of standard California shlock development. They relaxed the codes, letting the builders do whatever they wanted. Lot sizes increased. Garage doors were brought back up to the street facade. Service alleys were eliminated. Sound walls—

a California specialty—were erected along the most formal avenue. The construction was undertaken by some of the nation's biggest home-building companies, who would not tolerate being restricted to a low number of lots. The result of that was a numbing uniformity of house types and floor plans. The project incorporated a 65-acre artificial lake as a central public amenity. In the original plan, about half the waterfront was designated a public promenade. When the banks took over, part of the public frontage was sold off for private homes. Pretty soon, it was hard to tell Laguna West from any ordinary California upscale housing development.

Little of the dense mixed-use town center exists except a church (built "on spec" and purchased by a Greek Orthodox congregation), the town hall, which is currently used as the project's sales office, a day-care center, and a town green. The light rail connection to the state capital, which was a centerpiece of the original design, remains a fantasy. Two major corporations, Apple Computers and JVC Electronics, were induced to build offices across the highway from Laguna West. It is certainly conceivable that their presence will revive the project. It is too early to write it off as a failure. It is a large project, and the piece that might ultimately tell the story—the transit oriented core—remains unfinished.

No one has been more frustrated with the current outcome of Laguna West than its designer, Peter Calthorpe. The experience convinced him that the future of urban design lay not in the undeveloped greenfields but in filling up the empty spaces in existing towns and cities, especially in the American West, where the urban pattern is sparse and lacks focus. Calthorpe also decided that comprehensive regional planning policy was imperative. "We're stuck between national solutions that are too generic, bureaucratic, and large," he said, "and local solutions too isolated, anemic, and reactionary. The answer lies in between, in creating regional strategies."

In an attempt to prove this point, Calthorpe signed on as consultant to the Portland, Oregon, Metropolitan Planning Agency (Metro). Metro was the best regional body of its kind in the country, because it had enforcement power, and because it had instituted an urban growth boundary (UBG) to limit future sprawl outside the city of Portland.* The problem with Metro all along, however, has been a lack of standards for the stuff be-

*I discussed Portland at length in *The Geography of Nowhere* (pp. 200–207).

ing built *inside* the UBG, within which a dozen incorporated towns all had their own single-use zoning codes of the type that produced little more than low-grade sprawl. Calthorpe's mission in the 2040 Plan, as it was called, was to replace that obsolete template with new codes that would promote the growth of mixed-use dense town centers, and to establish a level of agreement about the nature and quality of this new pattern between all the towns of the region. To date the 2040 Plan is still creeping slowly through an arduous approval process, and it remains to be seen whether the obstacle of governmental inertia—to which even the excellent Metro agency is subject—can be overcome.

DOING IT ALL WRONG

A greater threat to the New Urbanism than ambitious stumbles like Laguna West are the half-baked knockoffs and rip-offs that are proliferating across the country, using the rhetoric about *community* as a sales gimmick without delivering any real civic amenity. This kind of fraud is pretty easy to pull off in a nation full of people who long to live in real communities, but who have only the dimmest idea of what that means in terms of physical design.

Among the worst frauds I saw in two years of traveling around the country was a huge, five-thousand-acre development outside Columbus, Ohio, financed by Leslie Wexner, the zillionaire casual clothes mogul, owner of such shopping mall stalwarts as The Gap, The Limited, and Banana Republic, whose company headquarters stands a few miles away. (Actually, the great black glass corporate structure doesn't exactly stand, but rather slouches horizontally on a hillside, like the insectile *Alien* of filmdom.) Anyway, Wexner's big development was called New Albany, after a nearby crossroads village.

Alas, Wexner's development *was* poorly planned and ill-conceived. It was, in fact, nothing more than an ultra-fancy golf course pod. (The development's coat of arms was a pair of seven irons crossed on an escutcheon.) The street network relied heavily on the cul-de-sac. Instead of pedestrian crossing signs on the streets, the signs depicted little golf carts. The only retail establishment in the whole place was the pro shop. The houses themselves were gigantic "Georgian Palladian" hulks based on Virginia Tidewater plantation mansions—only with three- and four-car garages. They looked like Toad Hall. In one part of the development, they had cobbled together several such behemoths in a cluster on a cul-de-sac to create "attached housing." The streets had preposterous Anglophile names such as *Bottomly Crescent* and *Ethret Round.* One cluster of houses— supposedly a "neighborhood"—was dubbed, laughably, *Upper Clivedon.*

Since the streets were no better than any typical upscale mini-mansion pod, the public realm of the development defaulted to the golf course, with the super-ultra fancy Country Club as its centerpiece. There was a slight catch, however. Membership in the club was clearly stated to be "by invitation only" in the promotional literature. That is, one did not automatically become a member by buying a house on Bottomly Crescent. So, if the Board of Directors happened not to like the way you wore your hat, well, maybe that was just tough noogies. .

Americans are so lost when it comes to the real issues of community and place that it seems they can be gulled by just about any lame come-on. The comers-on themselves seem equally confused. If New Albany was the most mendacious fraud I encountered out in the heartland, a development called Seawind in Palm Beach County, Florida, was the most pathetic. They were trying to promote it with the poem that follows.

A MANNER OF LIVING

A place of peace
and one of people.
Moments, memories, the flight of an eagle.

Greens and blues
and the breezes to weave them
around and about and through
the communities that breath [sic] them.

Voices, vistas,
a canvas of textures.
That choice of place where we come together.

We have become a very abstract people indeed.

CHAPTER 7

A MERCIFULLY BRIEF CHAPTER ON A FRIGHTENING, TEDIOUS, BUT IMPORTANT SUBJECT

O U R system of property taxes may be the single most insidious, pathogenic factor contributing to the geography of nowhere. It is almost impossible to discuss. It involves numbers and formulae resembling mathematics, from which many otherwise healthy adults shrink in tearful bewilderment. It implies the confiscation of one's earnings and chattels (i.e., one's security and well-being), which provokes a mindless terror that no mere talk can overcome. The impenetrable jargon of economists does not make it any more inviting—they don't call it the dismal science for nothing. So, we complain about taxes, and vote for candidates who promise vaguely to make them lower (and are eternally disappointed by them), but we leave the details to presumed experts because taxes are too painful and baffling to think about. This being said, I will undertake to discuss the undiscussable.

Our system of property taxes punishes anyone who puts up a decent building made of durable materials. It rewards those who let existing buildings go to hell. It favors speculators who sit on vacant or underutilized land in the hearts of our cities and towns. In doing so it creates an artificial scarcity of land on the free market, which drives up the price of land in general, and encourages ever more scattered development, i.e., suburban sprawl. In tandem with zoning, the taxing of buildings rather than land itself promotes such wasteful practices as putting up cheap one-story burger joints in huge parking lots on prime city land. It is one of the biggest impediments to the free market creation of affordable housing. As a consequence of all these things it is a drag on economic productivity and employment.

This happens because we tax buildings much more heavily than the land under them. These buildings are visited by an official assessor who determines their value. The higher the building's value, the higher the tax. Under this system, a rational person has every reason to put up crappy buildings that will not be highly assessed, or he has every reason to let his property run down, or build nothing at all. This is a major reason for the current desolation of American towns and cities.

The alternative to this is to tax land itself and not the buildings on it. The criteria for assessing the value of land minus buildings is based on its location or site. If it is one block away from Main Street, for instance, it is considered to have high site value because it is very close to other things that people like to be near: public utilities, the post office, civic amenities such as parks, museums, libraries, schools, other businesses and other services, and so on. The theory behind this is that in human society land derives value from both explicit public investment (sewers, water lines, streets), and from the aggregate of private human activities that go on around it. This is termed *socially created value*. Owners of prime real estate derive large benefits from socially created value and therefore should be taxed on that basis rather than on the basis of whether they choose to use or squander those benefits—for example, whether they chose to use it in the form of a vacant lot or a seven-story hotel. I will try to make it clear why our current system favors the vacant lot and discourages the hotel.

Viewed over the millennia one sees a strong tendency toward centrality in human settlement. People like to be around other people for safety, comfort, and excitement, and business enjoys certain advantages where there are other businesses. This is both the essence of civilization as a social construct, and of its physical manifestation in towns and cities.

Through history the site value of land close to the center has always been high. In our century, motorized transport and single-use zoning have undermined this tendency but by no means extirpated it. (Indeed, it is my view that Americans are suffering deeply from the centerlessness of suburbia.) Even in the face of these forces, land close to the center remains desirable. It still has high site value and high market value. Such land near the center, enjoying high socially created value, should therefore be said to have a higher taxable site value than land farther out, *regardless of the buildings on it*.

Living in America today, one would scarcely believe this. But even places as desolate as downtown Detroit have high site value—apart from all the disincentives operating to discourage the current landowners (including the city) from doing anything useful with the property. If nothing else, this land retains proximity to major streets, public services, and geographic amenities like waterfrontage, and we recognize its potential high utility.

In America today, much downtown land stands vacant, or contains decrepit buildings, or is underused in the form of parking lots. This land is being held in speculation. Someone is making a bet that at some point in the future it can be sold for lots more money than he paid for it. Land speculation is a form of hoarding. It contributes nothing to the life of the community. It takes prime land off the market and puts it in long-term cold storage, creating an artificial scarcity, which drives up the price of the land that *is* on the market. This behavior is supported by low taxes on the land itself.

Under our current system, a vacant downtown city lot is taxed much lower than a lot with a thirty-eight-story office tower on it. The owner can afford to pay lower taxes year after year, perhaps even for decades. This is called the *holding cost*. It is in the interest of such a speculator to allow whatever buildings that exist on his property to decay. Not only do his property taxes stay low, but he can enjoy the added benefits of depreciation on his income taxes as well. (Buildings depreciate, land does not.) It is a common misconception, by the way, that slumlords make their money on rents. Rather, they make their money on windfall profits when the city finally condemns their buildings and has to pay market value for the land according to the law of eminent domain—the market value being artificially jacked up by the condition of artificial scarcity created by the very slumlord/speculator/hoarders who benefit from it. What a wicked racket, huh?

Under the system I have just described, a downtown city lot with no buildings on it may have low taxes levied against it, though the market value of the land alone might be a million dollars.

Under the alternative system of site-value taxation, the owner of that million-dollar city lot would have to pay a much higher tax, a tax commensurate with the land's site value, regardless of what kind of buildings stand on it. Thus, his holding cost is increased, perhaps to the degree that he is presented with two courses of action besides just sitting there doing nothing with the land except waiting for it to get more valuable. These courses of action are as follows: he can put a building on the land that will produce enough wealth to cover the higher taxes and generate additional profit besides—let's say a hotel, which would employ lots of people and make the city nicer (increasing the socially created value of other nearby properties); or, if he lacks the ambition or ability to do something useful with it, he can sell the land to a willing buyer. This gives somebody else, perhaps with more ambition or imagination, the chance to do something useful (and profitable! and socially beneficial!) with the land.

If all landowners in a city were faced with such a choice of actions, many parking lots would go on the real estate market in short order. A higher tax would probably reduce the pool of potential buyers, lowering demand. Increased supply and decreased demand implies the lowering of price. Speculative holding would be discouraged and, with no tax on new buildings, city lots would more likely be put to some productive purpose.

There is a third course of action: the land owner could default on his higher land taxes, in which case the city would take over the property and auction it off as soon as possible to the highest bidder, who would then be faced with the same choices as spelled out above.

The criticism has been put forth that such a tax system would promote super-high densities in cities, with an excessive building of skyscrapers. Actually, the opposite tendency is true: the current system of taxing buildings rather than land perversely encourages skyscraper construction by keeping so much land off the market in speculative cold storage that the price of available parcels rises to fantastic and artificially high levels. Therefore, when a building is contemplated, only a skyscraper will justify in rents the huge cost of the land underneath it, usually with tax abatements thrown in to sweeten the deal.

Under an alternative system of site-value taxing, much more land would come onto the market as a result of higher taxes, but the price of lots would fall, due to increased supply and reduced demand. One could say that the up-front cost of purchasing land would be much lower, while the long-term holding cost would be higher. With buildings not taxed, many more land owners would seek to build profitable structures. But the demand for office and apartment space would then be diluted over many more pieces of property, discouraging excessively huge buildings on any single parcel as economically impractical. In any case, regulating the mass and height of buildings is one of the legitimate functions of city planning. Many cities already have height restrictions on buildings, including Washington, D.C., Paris, and Berlin.

One of the more likely results of such a system would be buildings of much higher quality and generosity, for example, apartments with higher ceilings, larger rooms, and attractive entrances. As anyone knows who ever lived in New York City, the luxuriousness of middle-class apartments dating from the early decades of the twentieth century seems incredible.* In contrast, many East Side co-ops built in recent decades have apartments with small rooms and dinky eight-foot ceilings. The latter buildings were designed primarily for tax depreciation and secondarily for the comfort of their inhabitants.

The effect of our current system of taxing buildings is one of the prime causes of our affordable housing crisis. Because it rewards decay and punishes new, high-quality construction close to the center, almost no middle-class housing has been built since early in the twentieth century. Also, under the current system, high taxes on buildings tend to be shifted to renters. This is precisely what caused the perverse conditions at the end of World War Two in which the rent for Ralph Kramden's apartment was higher than the monthly mortgage payment of a house in Levittown, leading ultimately to the complete abandonment of the city by the middle class.

Under the alternative system of taxing land, not buildings, much more

---

*My mother, who lives in a seventeen-story Manhattan apartment built in the 1920s, has a working fireplace in her living room.

middle-class-market housing could be profitably built in cities, increasing the supply and lowering rental prices, as landlords compete for tenants. Since the site-value tax would have to be paid whether the land was used productively or not, there would be much more incentive for owners to build rentable housing at the highest densities allowable under the city codes. With a healthy supply of apartments, the market would bid down rents while increasing the standards of quality in rental housing stock as landlords compete to fill their buildings. Almost all economists agree that a tax on land alone stays with the land and cannot be passed along to renters.

Because site-value taxation encourages building, it also promotes the increase of *socially created value*, since the more activity and vitality there is in a given neighborhood, the more desirable it becomes to live and work there. Site-value taxation therefore creates a sum of value greater than the value of individual pieces in a given neighborhood. In the long run, this additional activity will make land more valuable, increasing the city tax base.

Since in the natural order of things affordable housing is housing that is older, and because some owners take better care of their property than others, eventually middle-class housing becomes the housing of the lower classes. It need not be decrepit, only less desirable. Because our current system encourages decrepitation, that is precisely what the poor get for housing.

Fear has been voiced that site-value taxation would be harmful to farmers, who generally own large amounts of land. In point of fact, 90 percent of land values are in cities. Site-value taxation would encourage more compact town and city development, and would take the development pressure (demand) off property in the hinterlands. There would also be less tendency to run highways, sewer lines, and other public "improvements" out to rural lands and their site value would be proportionally much lower, which would be reflected in lower taxes paid by farmers. Where farms stand close to existing towns, or perhaps newly formed centers, their site value would reflect that proximity and the farmer could profit from it. Most states have "agricultural district" rules that provide tax mitigation for farmers. Under the current property tax system—which promotes speculation in farmland—they *need* that mitigation desperately. Under the regime of suburban sprawl, a great deal more farmland is currently being lost than would be lost under an alternative site value tax system.

In recent decades, it has become accepted practice for farmers to "cash out" at retirement by selling their farms for housing developments and shopping malls. This has come to seem a sort of entitlement in my part of the world. Obviously every generation of farmers to come won't be able to enjoy a million-dollar bonus on retirement, for in a few generations there would be no farmers and no farmland left. Therefore, the cashing-out syndrome must be viewed as one of the social aberrations caused by our current system. Sooner or later it must stop. Site-value taxation would tend to keep farmland in farming.

While the beneficial effects of site-value property taxation may be obvious, the mere thought of higher taxes on land might be an inducement to reflex vomiting on the part of citizens who are apt to be deeply suspicious and fearful of any proposed change in the status quo. One of the added benefits of site-value taxation is that it tends to be much fairer, clearer, and simpler to administrate than all other forms of taxation. The overwhelming number of poor people own no land whatsoever, the middle class generally own only the land under their homes, and the rest of the land privately held *in towns and cities* is owned by the relatively wealthy, including corporations.

It is reasonable that a person (or a company) should pay taxes in relation to his ability to pay, but the amount ought to be in some relation to benefits derived. Owners of valuable land benefit from socially created value based on the location of their land, so under a system of site-value taxation the relation between tax paid and benefits received would be clear and proportional. Under our current system of taxing buildings rather than land, taxes may be (and often are) out of proportion with the benefits received, which a normal person would rightfully construe as unfair. For instance, a homeowner whose assessment is increased because he decides to fix up his old house derives no increased benefit in municipal services. Why should he be penalized for taking care of his building? This sort of policy can only make citizens cynical. The site value of land, on the other hand, is relatively simple to assess, compared with the value of buildings, which are often unique. Benefits derived from the location of property alone are typically obvious. Site-value taxation therefore has both the appearance and the reality of greater fairness. Land can't be hidden—you can't stash it in a secret Panamanian bank account.

The idea of taxing land and not buildings comes from the nineteenth century political reformer Henry George (1839–1897). His life coincided with the rise of industrial cities in America, and his ideas were an attempt to remedy some of the unprecedented social distortions that accompanied it. George observed the paradox that poverty seemed to surpass the increased societal wealth generated by industry, and his taxing notions were an attempt to rectify that inequity without resort to the kind of Robin Hood economics embodied by socialism. George ran for Mayor of New York City in 1886 and came in second in a three-way race—losing to the Tammany Hall machine candidate A. S. Hewitt, and beating Republican Theodore Roosevelt. He ran again in 1897 but died suddenly of a cerebral hemorrhage during the political campaign at age fifty-eight.

It is important to recognize that Henry George lived in a period when cities grew and changed drastically and the cost of operating them went up astronomically. Vast new sewer and water systems were installed for the first time. Great bridges went up. Parks were created. Skyscrapers appeared for the first time in human history. The population of cities ballooned with a flood of immigrants. The cost of police and administration went up. Citizens in general were being asked to pay much more for the costs of running society. The income tax would become law a few years after George's premature death, but he was deeply involved in the debates that surrounded its creation, and he did not favor it. George saw that many of the common methods for raising taxes, including excise and sales taxes, and the proposed income tax, constituted a levy on productive activity, whereas a tax on land constituted a levy on unearned increases in socially created value from a natural resource with a fixed supply. He saw further that the huge unearned increment of wealth generated by the socially created value of cities accrued to a limited and concentrated segment of society who were contributing little in return to the cost of running this evermore-complex city-based society.

It must also be remembered that the rapid rise of industrial capitalism generated enormous public resentment which was often expressed in political violence and in many different revolutionary movements aimed at overthrowing the entire system. The last thing Henry George could be described as is a Marxist. His ideas essayed to improve the ability of a capitalist society to function. He did not aim to abolish wealth or punish the wealthy classes. He did not seek to abolish democracy or establish a *dicta-torship of the proletariat*. He viewed the grotesque social imbalances of the machine age and saw that they could be reasonably rectified within the bounds of the existing economic and political system.

George died the year after Henry Ford introduced the motorcar, and he obviously did not live to see suburban sprawl. But his ideas have remained influential both here and in other industrial nations. I dare say he would have viewed suburban sprawl as just another set of social distortions in-evitably produced by industry working in tandem with government's ten-dency to tax productive activity. George recognized that a tax on productive activity tends to erode its base. For instance, a tax on income decreases people's ability to buy things and use services, meaning it de-creases productivity, the incentive to earn, and employment in general. A tax on good buildings tends to promote the decay of all buildings.

Now, the question arises: if the Georgist tax idea is so great, why hasn't it been tried? The answer is that it is being tried right now in a score of American cities, in Australia, and New Zealand. The most notable exper-iments are taking place in Pittsburgh, and in Harrisburg, the capital of Pennsylvania. The system they are using is a modified Georgist approach called two-tiered taxing. Two-tiered taxing is a gradualist method. It taxes land proportionately more than buildings, and over time the proportion continues to shift from buildings to land. The reason the old system of tax-ing buildings is not overthrown altogether is due to the reasonable fear that a sharp drop in land prices resulting from so much property coming onto the real estate market might destabilize a local economy, causing, in effect, a local depression.

Pittsburgh instituted a rather timid two-tiered property taxing as long ago as 1913. The steel barons had big estates within the city limits, in-cluding private deer parks, and they were contributing proportionally lit-tle in taxes. So the city ratcheted up the tax on site value just a little. Unfortunately, the change was very slight—so as not to anger the steel barons—and the city instituted this system at the dawn of the suburban era, just as the automobile was about to open the urban hinterlands for de-velopment. The upshot was that Pittsburgh toodled along for the next sixty years, like most other cities, without much apparent benefit from the two-tiered tax system, with its middle class decanting to new suburbs in large numbers. The exodus also had to do with the fact that Pittsburgh was an extraordinarily unpleasant city, even by American standards, renowned for its soot, smog, and noise. However, the precedent had been established for a modified Georgist tax system. It just lay dormant for a long time.

Beginning in the 1970s, the steel business began to close down in Pittsburgh—which is to say the floor dropped out of its economy. In 1979, as a kind of desperation measure, the city took another look at its old two-tiered property tax system and decided to increase the tax significantly on site value while lowering the tax on buildings. Results were impressive. For the three-year period afterward, building permits issued in the city increased 293 percent compared to the national average. The city then shot itself in the foot by instituting a local wage tax (a tax on productivity), which provided new incentives for residents to move to the suburbs. But on the whole so far, the two-tiered tax system has had salutary results in that city. It has enabled Pittsburgh to make the difficult transition away from the steel industry to an economy based on hospitals and medical services. With the steel mills gone, soot and smog are a thing of the past, and Pittsburgh is now consistently ranked among the nation's most livable cities.

Harrisburg began a shift to site value taxation in 1977. It had lost nearly half its population since 1950. The downtown was dead. It was declared one of the most distressed cities in America. Under two-tiered taxing, it has made an impressive comeback. In 1994 the city issued the highest number of building permits for any year in its history. The number of businesses on the mercantile tax roles has risen from 1,908 in 1981 to 4,541 as of 1994. In 1994 and 1995 Harrisburg was considered to be among the top twenty-five American cities for affordable housing. The last tax increase of any kind was voted in 1987.

Other towns experimenting with a modified Georgist tax system are Scranton, Aliquippa, Newscastle, Titusville, McKeesport, and Clairton. In 1995, an extremely distressed Mohawk River factory town named Amsterdam in upstate New York adopted this system out of desperation. It is too early to see results there.

Historically, the city with the purest Georgist tax system was Edmonton, Canada, which, in 1904, instituted a plan that totally exempted buildings from tax consideration. Edmonton was then a brand-new city, growing up at exactly the time when elevator buildings were becoming technically feasible. Consequently, Edmonton quickly developed a dense downtown core, considered by many to be an exemplary exercise in civic design. Unfortunately, in 1918, to mitigate the expense of fighting World War One, the city slapped a 60 percent tax on the value of buildings, instead of simply increasing the tax on site value.

Experiments in Australia indicate that a modified Georgist approach in Sydney is already showing beneficial land-use results, compared to Melbourne, where a substantial tax on buildings is still in effect.

It is too early to say that site-value taxing has proved unequivocally to be superior to existing systems, but the evidence points in that direction. Many of the problems of industrial cities and automobile suburbs are still new to us. Our frantic attempts to cover the costs of running these organisms of habitation, with their vast infrastructure, has led to self-defeating behavior that is poorly understood. Many of our efforts to cope have produced unfortunate unintended consequences, such as the abandonment of cities by the middle class, which has produced further unanticipated repercussions, such as the social pathology of the inner-city poor, and the spiritual impoverishment of suburbia. All of these things have grossly inflated the cost of running society, which we ever more desperately try to cover first with higher taxes, and then by spending money that doesn't exist—the national debt—on social services and other mitigations. It is clear that we've reached a limit in our ability to generate either more taxes by current means, or more debt by any means. Reform of our property tax system along the lines advocated by Henry George is a straightforward means for restoring the economic health of our ailing towns and cities—no smoke, no mirrors, no voodoo.

REMODELING HELL

O N a November afternoon in South Florida, the sun beat down so re-morselessly that parked cars turned into mini-crematoria, and you could have blackened red snapper on a manhole cover. The general ambience anywhere outdoors was that of pulling a gym sock over your head—re-minding the casual observer that civilization had not been possible in this part of the country before the advent of air conditioning. I had come to the land of neon flamingos to consort with some of the characters who are leading the movement to change the way we construct the human habitat in America. It was one of life's many paradoxes that so much new talent in architecture and town planning was being concentrated in such a terrible place.

That blazing day, I drove up I-95 north of Miami with one of the more unlikely heroes in this war of paradigms, Dan Cary. Cary, a big, rangy chain-smoker in his early forties, with boyishly tousled silver hair, wearing jeans, a rumpled cotton tartan shirt unbuttoned to mid-chest, and a silver

Navajo bracelet on his wrist, had literally walked out of the Florida swamps and blundered into a career in town planning. His personal journey seemed emblematic of his generation's struggle to save the earth from the human race and to save the human race from itself.

As a biology major at the University of Miami in the 1970s, Cary had spent years in the Everglades studying birds, getting around in an airboat that he built himself. Sometimes he'd flip the craft and would have to walk out.

"It happened three or four times," he recalled, crammed behind the wheel of his Ford Taurus like a large meat-eating bird confined in a steel cage, the ghastly vistas of North Miami shimmering before us in the heat. "You're left knee-deep in mud and waist-deep in water, and sawgrass going up the rest of the way. Your heart's pounding 90 miles-per-hour from the work of lifting your feet out of this mud. One time I walked out and thought *It's a good thing I didn't wear my gun because I would have shot myself.* You'd make the Tamiami Trail [Route 41] just about dark, or later, and then there was the challenge of swimming the canal, which was open water full of alligators and snakes, to the road. You'd stand there and see your truck on the other side, and you'd be kind of looking, watching the water, to see if there *was* anything. Then you'd have to decide whether to swim like hell as fast as possible, or go slowly, quietly. I always opted for the slow, quiet, steady crawl. The alternative was to sit there all night."

Next, Cary spent two years at a research station in the rain forest of Ecuador classifying hummingbirds by blood proteins (often dining on large tropical rodents). Then he made "a crazy deviation" into business.

"I'd had this incredible life in the jungle, doing all these bizarre things that people would think was a lot of fun, but I never made any money," he said. "So I went into insurance, of all things, through a family friend, worked for two years, and made quite a bit of money. It was a horrible experience. Everybody should do sales for two years."

Eventually, Cary returned to the University of Miami as a grad student in ornithology. His masters thesis was a study of a snail-eating raptor called the Everglades Kite. On the side, he worked as a consultant for a new jetport that Dade County proposed to build near the edge of the Everglades, basically just sitting out in the sawgrass watching birds at $125 a day. The jetport never got built.

In the early 1980s, he hired on with a regional planning council up the coast, doing more wildlife impact studies. His sheer dogged competency resulted in rapid promotion. Soon he was reviewing entire developments by all the arcane bureaucratic criteria that had come to replace civic art in our time. By and by, his boss quit. The board interviewed him for the top job. Thinking he lacked the necessary credentials, and had no real chance for the position anyway, Cary told the board exactly what he thought: that development in South Florida was atrocious and completely out of control, that all the lovely golf-course condo clusters so dear to their hearts were environmental and social disasters, and that the miserable strip malls that passed for "towns" in their part of the world would embarrass a race of palmetto bugs. To Cary's amazement, he got the job.

From 1985 to 1994, Cary ran the Treasure Coast Regional Planning Council, one of eleven such state-chartered councils. Its jurisdiction covered four counties in the coastline conurbation that emanates north out of Palm Beach (Indian River, St. Lucia, Martin, and Palm Beach counties). It already contained the worst kind of postwar suburban crud development imaginable, a 60-mile-long corridor straddling old U.S. Highway 1 lined by strip malls, car dealerships, franchise fry pits, gated retirement home subdivisions, and all the other equipment of *the world's highest standard of living*. The scale of it was really something to behold. In some respects it was even worse than northern New Jersey, or Los Angeles, the prototypes of highway strip development. The buildings were farther apart, set back farther from the highway, with immense parking lots. And the relentless flatness of the Floridian landscape, its lack of topographic features, only added to the sensation of being lost in a surrealist painting, a panorama of strange, cartoonish objects (the buildings) all verging into a single vanishing point along an abstract horizon. This was not a landscape that made you feel all warm and cuddly. You felt like an ant, broiling in the sun, about to be squashed under a giant's boot heel.

There was almost nothing old here. A "historical" building might date from the 1920s, the period of the first big Florida land boom, and there were darn few of them left. Of these, almost none were assembled in any groupings that implied urban design. This meant that there was next to nothing in the way of good models for traditional town planning. This absence of visible, palpable history in Florida was a particular problem for Dan Cary, because history still reverberated through his own memory. He had grown up in a very special American place, the village of Ripley, outside a town named Chautauqua in Western New York State. The Chautauqua of his boyhood represented a superior human habitat—and not in nostalgic terms but as a matter of strict human *ecology*.

"Chautauqua was eight miles over the hill from us," Cary recalled as we plied farther north on I-95, past the unspeakable low-rise smarm of the nether Lauderdales. "It was probably the most perfect of small towns. It started out as a camp meeting place where they'd bring people in and show them how to teach Sunday school. Then it branched out into a place that taught the classics to rural America—Plato and Virgil. It was designed on a grid. Over time those tents built on wooden platforms were replaced by cottages and hotels. The town really took off around 1900, the classic period of town planning in America. It was lucky to have a rich supply of public buildings—churches, auditoriums, lecture halls—and each of them was done beautifully. The town green was perfect in terms of structure. It was roughly 200 feet by 600: about 3 acres. On one end was the library, the opposite end was the Colonnade, a commercial structure below with a grocery store and all, and the town offices above. On another side was this long, incredibly beautiful building called the Refectory, which was basically a fast-food place, but looked great. They used to make and sell ice cream there, and hamburgers. Next to that was a big-columned post office, which had a bookstore underneath in the basement. On the corners were Victorian wooden commercial buildings. Opposite the post office was the St. Elmo Hotel, wooden, four-story, which also had some shops and restaurants on the ground floor. And next to it were a series of single-family houses, the doctor's house, all nicely done."

"This apparently made quite an impression on you," I remarked.

"Yeah," Cary said. "In two ways. One was Chautauqua itself. But another was the huge difference between my life in New York and my life later on in Florida. The only way of living I'd known was in these pre-automobile-based towns where a large portion of the population didn't need a car, where you had neighborhood schools, where there was this sense of community and roots, where there was no crime. And then you come to this *nowhere* of South Florida where you don't have any friends, where everybody's constantly moving around, where the communities—if you can call them that—aren't made to live in for long periods of time. It disgusted me."

At the Treasure Coast Regional Planning Council, Cary's job was to review big development proposals over 1,000 acres, the usual autocentric garbage. Most of it made him sick, even if he couldn't say exactly why. Cary had instincts, but no set of principles to define what his instincts prompted in him, no authorities to turn to. Furthermore, Cary observed, the whole officialdom of the planning profession—of which he was now a member—seemed to function as little more than an enabling mechanism for the cement industry, approving any project that would result in the maximum use of cement. The planning profession had, in effect, given up on *the art of planning* long ago.

"I began to realize that these places we were building were really pretty sick," Cary said. "I knew that there was something wrong, and I knew it had to do with their lack of completeness. I couldn't put my finger on it."

Around that time, he noticed an article in a traffic magazine written by Andres Duany and Elizabeth Plater-Zyberk. It changed his life.

THE DPZ SHOW

Andres and Lizz, in addition to their work as architects and town planners, were functioning as missionaries to the design professions and the building trades, trumpeting the rediscovery of civic art and its implications for some of the nation's most depressing social problems. And they were infectiously optimistic, even facing the tremendous wall of institutionalized inertia that stood between their vision of the future and the self-satisfied, unsustainable, third-rate reality of Mall City, USA.

Andres, was a showman, tirelessly traveling the country, giving lectures at universities and museums, and leading charrettes, ridiculing current practice to the delight of even those whose communities he held up to ridicule. He was at once charming and merciless. He'd show slides of familiar suburban stuff and dissect it as though it were a freshly killed rat.

" . . . see all the little zigs and zags in these rooflines?" he'd say, pointing to a slide of some jive-plastic condominium cluster. "They're supposed to make everybody feel special, but all they really do is to make everybody feel exactly the same."

He logged hundreds of thousands of air miles a year. His schedule was terrifying in its complexity. For example: Miami to Kingston, Jamaica, to Toronto, to Providence, back to Miami, all in a week's time, with performances and professional meetings at each stop. Still, he seemed to thrive on this insane level of activity. In 1994 alone, I ran into him in Providence, Los Angeles, Cambridge, Miami, and Seaside. He relished his role

ELIZABETH PLATER-ZYBERK AND ANDRES DUANY,
ARCHITECTS AND TOWN PLANNERS.

as the provocateur and sometimes even blew his stack with especially obdurate audiences.

Lizz counterweighted Andres's flammable persona with a cool, fierce intelligence that could capably seize command in a roomful of bickering
males in the full efflorescence of testosterone-drenched egomania, and
lead the whole gang of them by the nose to concord and unity like so many
bulls, leopards, and rams out of an Edward Hicks's *Peaceable Kingdom*. (She
had been born and raised in Hicks's Pennsylvania.) She was assailed with
offers of academic deanships and professorial chairs, but regularly turned
them down so as not to disrupt the Mission.*

*In the spring of 1995, she finally caved in and took on the Deanship of the University
of Miami's graduate program in architecture and town planning.

Andres, a military history buff, had lately embarked on a strategy that he called "Capturing the Transmitters." It was based on the model of modern guerrilla warfare, specifically, Castro's takeover of Cuba, the island from which the Duany family had fled when Andres was nine years old. Capturing the Transmitters meant rewriting manuals that architects, planners, and civil engineers routinely turned to for specifications whenever they undertook to design something.

Let's say an architect is engaged by a "developer" to design a "housing development." He pulls off the bookshelf a big heavy tome called *Architectural Graphic Standards*. It gives him all the specifications for such a project. The whole thing is predetermined, like the directions for laying out a basketball court—if basketball were played in cars. The book says that the streets in such a configuration must be 90 feet wide—just like a county highway (so motorists won't bump into each other). The houses are to be set back 75 feet from the front lot line, the rooftops must be no more than thirty feet high, and so on. It's a recipe for the usual sterile suburban housing tract. Like some other working people, architects, and civil engineers are tempted to take shortcuts. The *Architectural Graphic Standards* book, as a manual of shortcuts, did all the thinking for them. Architects got away with it because following the instructions resulted in a design that (a) conformed exactly to generic zoning codes and made it through the permitting process with a minimum of fuss, and (b) resulted in a product for which people seemed willing to pay, regardless of its actual quality.

Andres Duany's great insight in this matter was to realize that while it was nearly impossible to persuade people to design things better, even if they stood to profit from it, they would happily follow instructions just to save themselves from the pain of thinking. Therefore, he reasoned, simply change the instructions. When he called around and volunteered his services in "updating" various transmitters, by golly, the transmitters welcomed him with open arms. It turned out that the publishers of such manuals were just as lazy as the people who used them, and if an architect of international reputation volunteered his services, well, so much the better.

"On the whole, our experience has been that we knock on the door and they open it," Andres told me. "At the very least they say, 'Do an appendix' or 'Do an addition to the standard volume.'"

He enjoyed notable success with *Architectural Graphic Standards*. When they opened the door he completely rewrote their codes for suburban development. Duany's version turned out to be a model TND ordinance, to be used in place of zoning. The TND ordinance was a manual for assembling a mixed-use traditional neighborhood, complete with stores, affordable apartments, narrow, tree-lined streets, service alleys, public squares, and other socially beneficial, economically sensible, aesthetically pleasing details that hadn't been used in the United States since Calvin Coolidge's day. He suggested that the publishers throw out the old pages from the 1980s, and they did. He'd captured the transmitter. Meanwhile, Andres had one of his colleagues, Rick Chellman, a civil engineer from New Hampshire, rewrite the official "Green Book" of the Institute of Traffic Engineers, another influential book of technical shortcuts.

Andres and Lizz operated out of an industrial building on a back street in the Little Havana neighborhood of Miami. They had done a streamlined neo-classical rehab job on the place. The exterior was sand-colored stucco. The front entrance was dramatically set into a peristyle draped with exterior curtains. It looked vaguely Etruscan. Inside, about twenty young associates and assistants toiled in a set of high-ceilinged bays wainscoted in tongue-and-groove cypress wood. The atmosphere was cool and tranquil. Sometimes Andres's mom worked the reception desk. His younger brother, Douglas, a Harvard-trained landscape architect, also worked there, wrapped in a blanket to ward off the air-conditioning. A dachshund named Teddy (Roosevelt), beloved and pampered by the principals (loathed and sometimes goaded by the staff), tyrannized the office, yapping whenever he was ignored for three minutes, and hopping about the tops of desks and conference tables, oblivious to the meticulously hand-drawn elevations that lay unscrolled there.

The company lunchroom was a Cuban diner called the Casablanca, a few blocks down the street, where one partook of fried plantain chips, *Morros y Christianos*, heroic portions of roast pork, and of course, Cuban coffee, which had an effect on the brain somewhat greater than Methadrine and a little less than voodoo. The whole office staff was addicted to the stuff. They kept an espresso machine in the back room and drank it all day long out of little plastic cups of the sort that nurses use to dispense medication. The first time I saw Andres knocking back a shot of the sepia liquid, I couldn't help saying, "Excuse me, but how come everybody's drinking soy sauce around here?"

GETTING WITH THE PROGRAM

"What happened was—I'll never forget it—there was this traffic magazine with Andres and Lizz's picture on it," Dan Cary continued as we drove past the illegible glut of commerce along U.S. 1 in Deerfield Beach, north of Lauderdale. "I picked it up and read maybe two inches of it. I didn't even get down the first column. I just said, I've got to talk to this guy. So, I picked up a phone on the spot and called him because I had this big 1,000-acre project in St. Lucie County that I wanted to be done like a real place, a real community. It had enough land. There was no excuse *not* to build a real place. But I didn't know how to do it.

"This was in 1986, just after I became director [of the Treasure Coast Regional Planning Council]. We'd had the huge job of writing a regional comprehensive plan dumped on our shoulders. It had to deal with everything from children and the elderly to the normal classic issues of roads, infrastructure, protecting the environment. It had social stuff in it, too, about eliminating crime, lowering divorce rates, and I remember arguing with the legislature when this came out. My board told them, 'We're not gonna write this. We don't know anything about divorce and crime. We know about drainage, the environment, and endangered species. Go see the social service people about that other shit.'

"But the legislature mandated that we do it, so I actually started going to meetings with the social service people and talking to them. I wrote this plan and it really opened my eyes. I started seeing connections between affordable housing and unemployment and the structure of communities. I thought about my own life and how different it had been, how we had dealt with all these problems in small-town America without artificial supports, how Grandma lived with us—she wasn't trucked out to some facility somewhere. It forced me to see that, in fact, physical planning was related to social things. It was about the same time that this 1,000-acre project came along. Then I saw that magazine with the article by Andres and Lizz, and realized that somebody knew how to put these things together. . . ."

BRIEF DIGRESSION: A UFO LANDS IN BOCA RATON

By now, Cary and I had arrived at one of the more unusual places in South Florida: Mizner Park. Named in honor of the late architect and developer Addison Mizner, who had designed some of the better things in Florida in the 1920s, Mizner Park was a brand-new 30-acre chunk of truly urban fabric embedded in the incoherent sprawl of Boca Raton like an emerald in a slag heap. To the casual observer, it looked to be a three-block fragment of some modern vaguely Mediterranean city—a place you might recognize but whose name you've forgotten. A boulevard divided by a broad parklike median planted with palm trees ran between multistoried pastel-colored urban buildings that contained shops on the ground floor and offices and apartments above. You could plausibly sleep, work, shop, eat, visit the periodontist, and find amusement there without getting into a car. Naturally, the design of Mizner Park was completely incongruous with the featureless low-rise rubbish everywhere around it. It was as though a UFO in the shape of three city blocks had landed there.

Mizner Park came into being because a fifteen-year-old shopping center occupying the site had *died*. It had lost too many tenants to pay for its own operation and had gone bankrupt. The city of Boca Raton had acquired

MIZNER PLACE, BOCA RATON, FLORIDA

A REAL-ESTATE DEVELOPMENT IN THE FORM OF AN INTEGRAL TOWN, MIZNER PLACE LANDED AMID THE STRIP-MALL WASTELANDS OF BOCA RATON LIKE A UFO. (PETER KATZ)

the property in lieu of taxes—but it seemed more a liability than a financial asset. Dead shopping centers were increasingly a problem around the
United States, as it became apparent that certain types of buildings were
designed to be thrown away. In fact, shopping centers hardly qualified as
buildings in the historical sense of the word. Rather, they were merchandise distribution machines that came in boxes that *resembled* buildings.
The actual disposal process itself was problematical. It wasn't as though
you could load the damn thing in the back of a truck and cart if off to the
city dump.

The dead shopping center syndrome became particularly aggravated in
the 1980s, when the U.S. government deregulated the banks then known
as savings and loan associations. Under the relaxed rules, the directors of
S&Ls could profit hugely off any cockamamie real estate venture, whether
it succeeded or not. Whenever a given deal was inked—before a single
spadeful of earth was turned—the S&L would award itself "points" for being the lender. These points would be translated into instant premiums or
bonuses paid to the bank's officers. The developers would likewise award
themselves big bonus fees off the top. The development would get built—
let's say a strip mall. Whether it succeeded or failed in normal terms meant
little to the bankers or the developers, who had already hit the jackpot.
The worst thing that could happen was that the bank would fail or the development company might go bankrupt. In either case, the principals
would have long since transferred their personal fortunes to the Cayman
Islands, Panama, or Switzerland, where all the U.S. Treasury agents who
ever lived could not pry loose a single deposit slip. Meanwhile, the money
actually invested (i.e., lost) had existed in the form of federally insured
bank deposits, so the individual depositors didn't lose either. Why should
they care how the banks pissed away their deposits, as long as they got
their money back from the U.S. Treasury? In the end, the estimated half-
trillion-dollar aggregate losses of all bankrupt S&Ls were merely chalked
up to "the deficit," that chimerical many-numbered beast that stalks the
TV airwaves at election time.

Florida, in particular, had suffered a hangover from the worst excesses of
1980s-style finance because deregulated banks walked hand-in-hand with
money laundering operations needed to sanitize the vast sums of drug loot
that saturated the state's economy. One of the best ways to launder drug
money was through commercial real estate investment. The physical

residue of all these financial shenanigans were the vacant shopping centers that now littered the Florida roadscape. Shopping centers were the models of choice for such funny money investment schemes because they were no-brainers. The design was strictly off the shelf—that is, cheap—and official approvals were guaranteed in short order, because one of the few things that local planning boards understood and fervently believed in were shopping centers. To local politicians, shopping centers represented "growth," the best kind of growth, promising whopping increases in sales and property tax income—unlike housing developments, which were net losers from the revenue point of view because more goshdarn kids meant more goshdarn schools at $10 million a pop. And, of course, funny money had other traditional ways of lubricating the political skids.

Mizner Park was certainly unlike anything built in Palm Beach County for three generations. It arose in this man-made wasteland like a wonderful mirage, replacing the dead shopping center in 1991. It was the brainchild of a well-connected real estate lawyer with artistic aspirations named Charles Seimon who had long wanted to reproduce in Florida an urban space modeled on Rome's Piazza Navona. These days, lawyers could get things built much more effectively than architects or just plain Rich-Guys-with-a-Vision, and Seimon did a bang-up job. He engineered a "marriage" between a big commercial developer and the city of Boca Raton which made sure that Mizner Park got designed, approved, and built in eighteen months—a remarkably speedy outcome as big projects go. He also obtained millions of dollars in Community Redevelopment Agency funds to pay for the landscaped boulevard that was the project's centerpiece. There were various ways of interpreting this deal. But in the least cynical view, the taxpayers picked up the tab for the creation of a decently embellished public space, which is, perhaps, as things should be. At least the public got something for its money that it can use and enjoy. And, in fact, the public swarmed to it. It became an enormously popular place to hang out. Finally, one had to simply admire Mizner Park as a piece of civic art. It was a good model. It made Florida a better place by one small increment. It was also a financial success. Occupancy of the commercial space stood at 96 percent in 1994, and every last apartment was rented.*

*Sustainable Development, a report prepared by the Economic & Planning Systems Company, Berkeley, Ca., January 1994.

In his role as director of the Regional Planning Council, Dan Cary had served as a facilitator for Mizner Park, making sure that the plans passed swiftly through the permitting and approval process. He was proud of it and what it augured for Florida's future. We left his car in a parking structure located behind one of the large urban buildings and headed across the handsome boulevard into a new seafood joint where you could watch people walking up and down the sidewalk—an unusual experience in Florida. Over crab sandwiches he resumed the story of his evolution from a wildlife ecologist to a town planner.

An Enlightenment

" . . . Andres and Lizz were the first people I ran into who knew what the hell they were talking about," Cary continued. "Andres realized early on that I needed to read, so I could use the terminology. He gave me a stack of books and I really got an education. After I got it, every time one of my planner types would leave, I started replacing them with people out of the School of Architecture [of the University of Miami]. What's evolved is that we have the paradigm in mind, which is the TND, and we try to focus every goddam thing we do from redevelopment to infill to new development in that direction.

"The power I had was that people always had to be polite to me. It's incredible power, but I'm kept in check by a board. I can't be arbitrary and capricious. But when you have the power to make a recommendation on a big real estate project, you're granted a certain respect, and people have to listen. We'd get these developers and start putting on slide shows—basically, give them a six-hour lecture in my office. We'd literally wear these guys down, the point being to convince them before they put pen to paper that they had to do things right.

"One time, this guy had about a hundred acres and proposed to just randomly plop these condominiums around a lake—everywhere else it was all parking lot. This was going to be middle-income housing for families with children. And I said, 'Jesus, where's the playground?' Finally, I blew up at him, in front of all these engineers, architects, and other people at the table. I started swearing at the guy, saying, 'Would you fucking move *your* family into this house?' His mouth drops open. 'No, you wouldn't. It sucks. And if *you* wouldn't live in it, what are you doing proposing to build it? This is shit. You can draw all you want, but by God I'm going to deny the approvals!' They walked out of the room and never came back. Disappeared.

"There's some things I'd go down in flames for," Cary continued. "It's taken until the last couple of years, time to learn enough myself, and convince myself to have the guts to stick my neck out. The biggest inhibition for me was that for the last twenty years so much shit was built here on a regular basis. So, it becomes awkward after you've approved ten terrible projects to go to the board and say, 'Uh, we're not going to do this anymore.' Because they're sitting there thinking, 'Well, how is this different from the last ten projects we approved?'

"The reality is that Florida is dead if we don't stop impacting all we have left. And people don't understand how important Florida is relative to other parts of the U.S. A big chunk of the bird population migrates down here. South Florida is actually *crowded* with birds during the winter. Sometimes there will be hundreds of robins in your yard, grabbing every little bit of food they can find. It's so crowded that Florida is like a bottleneck in the food supply. If you've ever watched migrations coming back from South America, you realize how important that food is. We used to go down to the Dry Tortugas, sixty miles west of Key West—the first land that a bird migrating out of Mexico sees. Warblers will rain down on that island, starving. They can't make it to the mainland, they're so hungry. It's difficult biologically to prove that it's Florida's fault that the North American migratory bird population is dwindling. But there's a certain logic to it when you understand the mechanism and see what's happening. We've already wiped out more habitat than we can afford. We have to start living more compactly.

"You've got to understand: I was having a great time sitting out in a blind out in the Everglades. It was a real romantic thing to do, watching birds. But I got to the point where I frankly felt that was kind of selfish, because what was scaring the hell out of me at night was automobile use and pollution and rain forest loss and major things that could collapse the whole ecosystem. If you're an ecologist, you're pre-adapted to do planning, because all ecology is about interactions between things. I think the TND is a very ecologically holistic way for man to live as part of the ecosystem. It's very adaptable to any development situation: infill, redevelopment, or starting from scratch. It's almost a panacea for a lot of social problems that

Florida is facing, and it gets at the environmental problems that have been too long ignored. If all developments had the average density of about ten units per acre [i.e., the density of a traditional American town], most of the environmental impacts that we cry about wouldn't have occurred."

SOFT MUD

The next time I saw Dan Cary was nine months later in Los Angeles. The occasion was the second meeting of the Congress for the New Urbanism (CNU), which was being held in Los Angeles. Not any old part of L.A., but the newly refurbished core of *downtown* L.A., which proved to be one of the most unfortunate examples of anti-urban design conceivable— a horrible clump of gigantic blank-faced glass office towers, most of which contained absolutely nothing at their ground floors but vacant walls of polished stone. No stores, no windows, nothing. It was like walking through an endless athletic club shower room from which the shower heads had been mysteriously omitted. And of course, only months after the big L.A. earthquake of 1994, with aftershocks still tweaking the city daily, about the last place you wanted to be was standing under those colossal glass towers. At night, the area was absolutely desolate. New York's financial district at night was a fiesta in comparison. It was such a terrible place that I had anxiety attacks every time I left the hotel.

Dan Cary was a charter member of the CNU, and he was there. But he was obviously going through some episode of inner torment. His usual good humor had deserted him. He seemed distracted, mentally thousands of miles away. At first I thought downtown L.A. was affecting him as badly as it did me. We had lunch at a Mexican place outside the skyscraper zone and he smoked about half a pack of cigarettes while alluding to some unspecified professional worries. A few months later, I learned what he'd been going through.

The Florida legislature had clipped the wings of its eleven regional planning councils—largely because of Dan Cary's activities over on the Treasure Coast, his insistence on a new set of planning standards that neither developers, nor local officials, nor state bureaucrats understood. He'd pissed off too many people. He was an impediment to "growth." The main thing the legislature did was to remove the council's ability to use the

courts to stall bad projects. In effect, it stripped the councils of the one enforcement tool that gave them any power. This had left Cary in an untenable position. Now he could only *recommend* that developers do the right
thing, which meant, of course, that 99.9 percent of the time they would do
the wrong thing, because all they understood was dipshit tract housing and
golf course condominiums and strip malls. So, Cary had been quietly suffering for months, wondering whether to quit his post, and where to go if
he did. He had a wife and two kids to consider. He also had an abiding
commitment to making Florida a better place.

Around the time of the second CNU out in L.A., something had come
up. A young lawyer named Sam Poole, with a B.S. in forestry and a master's degree in planning, had been appointed to head a state agency called
the South Florida Water Management District. Water had become to
South Florida what air quality was to Southern California: an overriding
consideration for economic development. The agency's mission was to
protect the groundwater of South Florida, which happened to include the
Everglades, most of the Lake Okeechobee drainage region, and the coastal
megalopolis that sprawled from Key Largo through Miami and Lauderdale
clear up to Vero Beach.

By the 1990s, the groundwater situation in Florida had reached a stage
of continual low-grade crisis. Decades of ambitious canal-building and
drainage schemes promulgated by the Army Corps of Engineers to boost
agriculture had screwed up the Everglades. The enormous swamp no
longer recharged itself seasonally and the whole ecosystem was in danger.
Lake Okeechobee was shrinking, too, for similar reasons, plus the pressure
of suburban sprawl development moving inland from the coast. Florida
Bay, the great shrimp hatchery between the Everglades and the Keys, was
ruined in turn by algae blooms caused by agricultural runoff.

Agriculture in South Florida—which is mostly carried on at industrial
scale—is more like hydroponics than dirt farming. The planting medium
is basically sand, to which you must add large amounts of water, fertilizer,
pesticides and herbicides, which then percolate into the ground. Underlying the thin sandy crust lies a porous layer of spongy limestone called the
Biscayne Aquifer. Scientists had lately begun to realize what a fragile un-
derlayment it was. The only thing that kept seawater out of the aquifer was
the fresh water that fell as rain and continually cycled through the com-

plex wetland system of which the Everglades was a part. This process had kept the limestone saturated and hence protected from the sea. The expensive engineering and diversion feats of the twentieth century had compromised that hydraulic equation. So had the mishmash of urban and suburban development since 1945, including the drilling of hundreds of thousands of residential wells with their accompanying septic systems. Finally, there was the specter of global warming, to which Florida was especially vulnerable. If ocean levels rose a few feet, much of South Florida would simply vanish under the Gulf Stream, the state was that low and that flat. The highest spot in South Florida was the old garbage dump in Palm Beach County, a malodorous heap that stood along the Florida Turnpike with methane ventilation pipes sticking out of it as though it were a half-buried, giant, stinking porcupine from hell. In fact, South Florida would be economically devastated by even a modest global warming event, at the low end of what scientists predicted, because even if the state didn't drown completely, a small rise in the ocean level would salinate the groundwater along the coast, where 90 percent of the population lived, destroying the residential water supply for millions of people and thus making normal life impossible.

The South Florida Water Management District had a staff of 1,600, a third of whom were scientific and professional personnel—biologists, geologists, hydrologists, and civil engineers. Its human resources made the Treasure Coast Planning Council look like a senior seminar in comparison. All the agency lacked was a flashy acronym. Some government wits had tagged it with the acronym SoFMD—pronounced *Soft Mud*.

Now, it happened that in the late 1980s and early 90s Sam Poole had worked with Andres Duany and Lizz Plater-Zyberk as a real estate lawyer on a number of TND projects around Florida. He had also played a part in writing a TND ordinance for Dade County, a kind of alternative planning code put in place in anticipation of Dade County's inability to sustain further sprawl, the catch being that it was still *optional*. Poole, therefore, was intimately acquainted with Duany and Plater-Zyberk's point of view and with the most minute technical aspects of their town planning principles. He came on board the South Florida Water Management District in August 1994, and one of the first things he did was to hire Dan Cary as chief of the agency's planning division.

RETURN TO HELL

When I saw Dan Cary again that fall he was tanned, relaxed, twenty pounds slimmer, and leading a charrette that involved 200 or so citizens of Martin County, just up the coast from Palm Beach. The mission of the charrette was to begin drawing up a new comprehensive land use plan that would allow development (or "growth" in the popular idiom), while it protected extensive wetlands. The charrette was being sponsored by the Martin County government, the Treasure Coast Regional Planning Council, and South Florida Water Management. The design team hired to actually conduct the charrette was the firm of Dover/Kohl of South Miami. Victor Dover and Joe Kohl were two guys barely into their thirties who had one of the hottest architecture and town planning practices in the United States. They had been close friends as undergraduates at the Virginia Polytechnical Institute, and gone to Miami as a team to study under Lizz Plater-Zyberk at the University of Miami. After graduate school there, they'd gone to work for Duany/Plater-Zyberk, and finally struck out on their own.

Dover and Kohl had pioneered a computer imaging technique that enabled them to compose pictures of what places might look like under differing scenarios. For instance, they'd photograph some sloppy-ass suburban boulevard with the fry pits and the drive-in banks, then *enhance* it to show what it would look like built out to the maximum extent allowable under the current codes, following all the setback, square footage, and usage rules. Invariably it would look frightening: *Blade Runner Meets Hackensack*. People would goggle at the picture and shriek during the slide shows. Or, Victor and Joe could show the same sloppy-ass boulevard built out under a more thoughtful design code, say, one that called for sidewalks, and arcaded facades, and orderly rows of street trees, and congruent building masses. And all of a sudden the picture would look something like Royale Street in the French Quarter of New Orleans—a real human place as opposed to Android Boulevard. The audience would go "oooh" and "aaah."

The computer image proved to be a great tool for educating the general public. What had previously taken prolonged efforts at verbal persuasion and cajoling and browbeating—with little success—could now be accomplished in a few minutes. The pictures eloquently stated what had previously been obscured by the technical jargon of traffic engineers and the economic scare tactics employed by politicians and their pals. It turned out that ordinary people had a remarkable ability to recognize a human habitat of high quality, and to agree about its character. They all wanted human scale, more intimate streets, the orderly rows of trees, building facades with dignity, and corner stores. They wanted real towns, real neighborhoods. When they saw a picture of it they invariably responded warmly.

The Martin County charrette was held in a junior high school off Highway A-1-A in the town of Stuart. Stuart lay exactly halfway between the Mousketropolis of Orlando and Miami. It was far enough away from both of them to have escaped mega-development until the 1980s—but then it got walloped with some of the worst stuff imaginable: supermarket parking lots that could have easily handled jet aircraft, setbacks so monstrous that you literally couldn't see the stores across the highway because of the curvature of the earth. The cultural climate was getting so warped that new housing subdivisions were being marketed with a political spin. One development advertised on a billboard along the Dixie Highway (U.S. 1) was named "Danforth—Family Values." A local resident informed me that the name honored the former vice-president J. Danforth Quayle, though he had had nothing to do with the venture. Danforth proved to be a cul-de-sac subdivision arranged around a man-made lake shaped in a cartoon figure of a man. It was heartbreaking to see how clueless Americans really were about the central vacancy in their lives.

The charrette opened with a Friday night public meeting in the school's spacious cafeteria. Declarations of greetings and good will were tendered, statements of goals avouched, and the battery of edifying slides by Dover/Kohl presented to horrify and tantalize the citizenry. The underlying message was: *your county is a horror and here's a better way*. It got everybody fired up with hope and enthusiasm, and the participants went home to their trundle beds in the condo clusters with visions of civic life dancing in their heads. Saturday morning, coffee and tons of free donuts were served. Stoked on caffeine and sugar, the citizens formed into groups of half a dozen around cafeteria tables. With paper and colored pens they drew plans of specific improvements they imagined in their surroundings. Having been through dozens of charrettes, Dan Cary was not surprised to see that the overwhelming majority of local folks envisaged compact, traditional neighborhoods and Main Street type business districts. The purpose of this exercise was not so much to ascertain this—it was predictable—but to reinforce in the citizens' own minds that the stuff they wanted differed from what they were actually getting.

During this day-long session I had a conversation with one of the major players, a land developer named John Lindstroth, fifty-two, a blond athletic former Navy pilot from Minnesota who had lived in Florida for twenty-three years and claimed to have built "one-third of West Palm Beach." Lindstroth, a fascinating bundle of contradictions, who said his favorite place to live was New York City, owned a tract of several thousand as-yet-undeveloped acres in Martin County. The day's doings had put him in a rather foul humor and he denounced the Traditional Neighborhood Planning ideas that Dover/Kohl and Dan Cary seemed to be pushing. Lindstroth had heard it all before. He said the ideas were "elitist," that they might go over in Washington "where people were willing to live like lemmings," and where there were "a lot of low child-bearing couples," but that in South Florida "the single-family subdivision is preferable—everybody aspires to it!" He said that by pushing neo-traditionalism, its promoters would "disenfranchise a generation of their hope." Thus operates the "conservative" mind in our age. It can't abide tradition.

After lunch, the public presented their ideas on stage, group by group. There was a bit more good fellowship and self-congratulation and then the public was more or less dismissed for the week. Dover/Kohl and ten members of its design team, along with Dan Cary of Soft Mud and Ramon Trias, an architect with the Treasure Coast Planning Council, retreated to the basement of the building, where a battery of computers and drafting tables had been set up. Here the grunt work of actually making some sense of Martin County took place in the spirit of a college hell week. They would toil eighteen-hour days, breaking only for meals and sleep at a cheap chain hotel on U.S. 1, until the following Friday night, when a final presentation to the citizens was scheduled.

AFTER ANDREW—A SIDE TRIP

While the charrette team labored in the school basement, I made a trip way down to South Dade County, below Miami, the area that had been pulverized by Hurricane Andrew in the early morning of August 24, 1992. I was curious to see what had happened in the two years since Andrew. For all its horror and devastation, the storm had presented Floridians with a rare opportunity to reassemble one of the most sprawling inchoherent suburbs in the whole country. The damage was so complete that there was the sense of starting with a practically blank slate, and that brought a lot of idealism to the task of reconstruction. Among the volunteers who offered their professional services was Lizz Plater-Zyberk. On surveying the damage, she warned that the region had "the potential of becoming the first large-scale suburban slum in the United States."

In monetary terms, Andrew was the costliest natural disaster in U.S. history: $12 billion in property damage. Only fifty people lost their lives, but 250,000 were left homeless. Officials estimated it would take every man, woman, and child in Dade County thirty years to generate an equivalent amount of trash to match the debris caused by Andrew in a few hours.

South Dade's economy was military and agricultural. Homestead Air Force Base had been subject to rumors of possible closure in the early nineties, but Andrew put to rest any doubt by pounding the installation into a scrapheap. The farm economy was diversified in terms of products—everything from string beans to citrus to ornamental shrubs—but not in terms of scale, which was generally immense, with oceanic individual fields, a type of agriculture that required lots of hired help. So the population of South Dade included many fruit and vegetable pickers. The fruit pickers tended to be African-American, and they were accustomed to following fruit harvests north every year, proceeding from the orange groves around home, through the Georgia peach crop in summer, to the apple orchards of upstate New York in the fall. Fruit picking didn't pay too badly, and one could do it standing up. A skilled picker could make over a hundred dollars a day.* Many of them owned houses in South Dade and made enough money to endure intervals of forced leisure between harvests. The vegetable pickers, in contrast, tended to be Hispanic newcomers, many of them in the U.S. illegally. They were paid chump change compared to the fruit pickers, and their work was backbreaking stoop-labor. Many of them did not migrate at all, but stayed in South Dade around the seasons, switching crops, from lettuce, to peas, to beans.

Heat shimmered off the Dixie Highway as I motored south toward the town of Homestead. A country music station on the car radio played

---

*The author worked as a *checker* in an upstate New York orchard during the harvest of 1977. The crew hailed from South Florida. They'd been working the same orchard for years. They were paid by the bushel and my job was to certify the exact amounts they picked. I did this by roving the lanes of the orchard, checking large wooden bins.

"There Ain't No Future in the Past." Twenty minutes out of Miami one began to notice signs of Andrew's visitation: the skeletons of Norfolk pines, the trunks of decapitated palm trees stuck in the sand like giant lollipop sticks, the abandoned concrete trailer pads, brushpiles the size of eskers, the shattered strip malls turned flea markets, and vacant lots where gas stations and convenience stores had seemingly been sucked out of the universe.

Maybe the punishing heat affected one's mood, but it was hard to imagine a more oppressive landscape. The horizon itself slumped with hopelessness and every road ran a straight path out to its own vanishing point in the distant haze, like a small, desperate life disappearing into oblivion. Martin County seemed intimate in scale by comparison. The lines of trees between the vast crop fields didn't even help much, because they were so battered and deformed. A desert would have possessed more simple grandeur. The tableaux vivants and human artifacts presented a uniformity of squalid desolation. Prison gang-workers crouched in drainage ditches along the collector roads, halfheartedly whacking at sprays of sawgrass as they glowered at passersby. The houses, both old and new, were of a type conceivably worse than trailers. They had all the charm of packing crates and none of the structural integrity. Sunstroked, half-starved dogs slept in the dusty intersections of subdivisions composed of such houses. For some bizarre Cartesian reason, the street numbering system of Miami had been extended a good thirty miles from the city, so that a given street sign declared, for instance, that you were on the corner of "SW 187 Court and SW 318 Terrace." One tried to imagine the psychological effect this would have on children—or a teenage girl trying to explain to a date how to get to her house.

At SW 380th Street in the town of Florida City I came across a federal emergency housing center. It contained scores of identical gray trailers set on concrete blocks. The complex, set smack in a barren agricultural field at least a mile across, like an island in a sea of dust, was enclosed by a brutal steel fence. The trailers were all tattooed with stenciled figures: A-163, A-164, and so on, in the obsessive-compulsive spirit of federal officialdom. A guardhouse stood at the entrance to the Andrew Center, as the place was named. The security guard on duty did not speak English and looked barely twenty years old. I tried to explain that I was writing a book, held up my steno pad and pantomimed writing. He soon gave up trying to understand and waved me through. Three of the trailers near the guardhouse were given over to offices. Both the substance abuse office and the outreach program were closed at 11:30 A.M. on a Tuesday. A woman answered the door at the complex's general administration trailer, but said only that they were closed for lunch and then furtively shut the door in my face.

The rest of the trailers appeared still fully occupied more than two years after the hurricane. Here and there residents tried to customize their dwellings with tiny gardens and pink cement swans. There was no grocery store, or anything like a commissary on the premises, nowhere to buy a quart of milk or a newspaper, but the many old cars parked everywhere indicated that even these displaced poor were expected to participate in the nation's compulsory motoring program. They could apparently afford cars but not housing—a stark illustration of America's official social priorities.

The architects and planners who descended on South Dade in the aftermath of Andrew had the idea that they could create town centers where there had been none. They were struck, more than anything, by the profound disorienting quality of the place. Of course, the auto suburbs of America are generally characterized as lacking *a sense of place*, but after Andrew, twenty-year residents couldn't even find their way home after a trip to the federal disaster aid field office. Such mundane landmarks as *the pink trailer on the corner* were gone. Out of this chaos the architects wanted to create real traditional neighborhoods, even if the housing had to be cheap. They wanted walkable shopping streets and civic landmarks, town halls that looked like town halls, with formal squares in front. In fact, as mentioned earlier, Dade County already had a TND ordinance in effect—Duany, Plater-Zyberk, and Sam Poole had seen to that. Unfortunately, it wasn't mandatory. It existed side by side with the old sprawl codes, as an option, if you *felt* like doing it. Well, that wasn't the only problem after Andrew.

"People just wanted to get on with their lives," said Raul Listra, one of the volunteers who, two years later, was running the planning department of posh Key Biscayne. "We were sketching town squares and beautiful monuments for guys whose houses had just blown away except for the front porch and the back wall, guys who this was the worst thing that ever happened to them. What we were pushing seemed like a luxury."

Some people were begging to have their houses condemned, thinking they'd get more money from their insurance company. Others without insurance were begging *not* to have their houses condemned because they would lose everything including the only place they had to live.

"One guy got shafted because he took precautions and boarded up his house so the damage was minimal," Listra said. "Meanwhile, his neighbor's house blew down and he made out just great."

The insurance companies finally refused to pay for anything but exact duplicates of what was demolished *exactly where it had been before.* That pretty much put the shnitz on the architects' hopes and dreams for real town centers and walkable neighborhoods. Lizz Plater-Zyberk had been attending public meetings twice a week for a year and a half in South Dade as a volunteer. What she had to show for it was the design for a modest complex mixing a homeless shelter, inter-generational housing, battered women's transitional housing, and an elementary school, surrounding a small public square—kind of a community of the dysfunctional. It was an elegant plan on paper, but it was only a plan, an idea. Nobody had agreed to go forward and build the thing. Otherwise, new strip malls rose out of the rubble of the old malls out on the Dixie Highway and new trailers replaced the blown away trailers, and it was not possible to say that anything had really improved in South Dade County after Andrew except that there was measurably less stuff there than before.

I drove back to Miami the way I'd come down, past ruined car washes with their tin roofs peeled back like the lids of canned nacho dip, past billboards where advertisements for movies only out a few weeks were already faded in the blistering sun. Ronnie Milsap sang a song on the country station that went, "I'm a prisoner of the highway, imprisoned by the freedom of the road." At Coral Gables an ad came on saying, "Ever see a skin-diving monkey? You can at Monkey Jungle!" and I knew that I was back in civilization.

Sub-epilogue: Ten days later, tropical storm Gordon suckerpunched South Dade. Gordon never reached hurricane strength in terms of wind velocity, but it dumped record gouts of rain on the area, ruining 35,000 acres of crops valued at over $65,000,000. Andrew had struck a few weeks before fall planting when there was nothing in the ground. Gordon's floods came a few weeks before the fall harvest.

THE FINALE

Back up in Stuart, Dan Cary, Victor Dover, Joe Kohl and the crew had been drawing all week in the church basement. The drawings had been converted into slides. Two hundred and fifty citizens of Martin County waited noisily upstairs in the cafeteria to see if the charrette team had made any sense of the place they called home. Whatever excitement the team members felt about the final presentation was somewhat modified by the fact that they were cross-eyed with fatigue.

You could hear the lost nights of sleep in Dan Cary's raspy voice, but he managed the proceedings masterfully.

"I want to emphasize that we're just putting some ideas down, not telling you what to do," he reassured the audience, and then showed slides of Martin County utterly transformed. There was a good deal of oohing and aahing, and a little grumbling, but on the whole they seemed to like what they saw: a network of coherent traditional towns surrounded by undeveloped wetlands and river corridors. What the plan called for in terms of policy was infilling the existing communities, like Hobe Sound, which actually had a pretty good modified orthogonal street grid, designed in the 1920s (of course), that never got built out to anywhere near its potential. At the same time, Cary tried to explain as nicely as possible that the supermarket strip malls that already existed were pieces of shit that would have to be replaced fairly soon anyway, and they might as well put the gosh-darn shopping in the right place, near where folks lived. Cary managed artfully to never use the term *suburbia* or *sprawl* during the presentation. Rather, he would call it "modern style development," or "development of the type we've gotten in the past twenty-five years."

The centerpiece of the plan was an "Eco-village" that Cary had designed himself. It was intended as a jumping-off station for tourists to explore the wetland and river system on horseback and canoes. It included a hotel, a conference pavilion built in the manner of an open-air Seminole chikee, a horse barn complex, all integrated into a 350-lot mixed-use, mixed-housing TND—in other words, a town—which had room to grow larger and denser as long as it observed a few simple rules of urbanism.

The sketches were very elegant. The drawings looked like everybody's fantasy of a classic American town, though the buildings had an appropriately Floridian Spanish neo-classical gravity. The urbanism itself—the arrangement of the buildings in relation to one another and the kind of civic spaces they defined—was straight out of classic John Nolen and Raymond Unwin. It was also Chautauqua, all over again.

The citizens were invited to comment. There was the predictable carping about parking, parking, parking. Cary explained that on-street parking would accommodate most of the cars, and that the whole point of TND design was to create places in which *not* owning a car was a plausible option. One elderly gentleman rose unsteadily to his feet, shook his fist at the ceiling, and cried, "A pox on growth! Why can't we just keep it more human here!" This generated some applause as well as laughter. Another senior got up and said, "I don't see any commercial in all these pitchurs. We need jobs!"

To which Cary replied, "Uh, sir, those attractive buildings we showed you *were* the commercial: shops, workplaces, offices. You're just not used to seeing commercial structures that don't look terrible."

It was altogether a very interesting exercise in subtlety. And perhaps nothing was as subtle as Cary's answer to an indignant citizen who uttered the standard pseudo-patriotic rot about people having inalienable rights to develop private property however they wanted to without the government sticking its big blah blah blah. And Cary just tossed off the reply, "Well, sir, this isn't an area rich in water." Because this remark, which perhaps 98 percent of the audience didn't even register, really defined the future terms of the argument. Which was that the South Florida Water Management District would simply not permit much more *development of the type we've gotten in the past twenty-five years.* Until now, hardly anybody in state government had the balls to take on the development industry, and Dan Cary's remark was the first public shot in what was liable to become an epic struggle. Unlike South Dade, where nobody had been in place to enforce any design standards after Andrew, a line was being drawn in the sand here. To say there wasn't enough water here might have struck more people as absurd, if they'd been listening, because half of Martin County was wetland. The real issue was whether that water could be siphoned off for more golf course hazards or lawns or carwashes, and the answer, if you listened carefully, was basically "no."

Politically, it was already a hot potato. The Martin County charrette took place during the last week of the 1994 election campaign. It happened that Democratic Governor Lawton Chiles was in a very tight race with Republican Jeb Bush, son of the former president. The first day of the charrette, Bush had publicly declared his intention to fire the board members of Soft Mud who had hired Sam Poole and the rest of the "anti-development" gang he said was running the agency. So Dan Cary had been speaking with some intimation that he might not occupy this sensitive position a few months down the line. As a matter of personal sentiment, it was hard to tell whether Dan Cary was tired of fighting against morons, or just plain tired from staying up for seventy-two hours straight, or both. But at the age of forty-four, in a complacent republic in an ominous period of history, he seemed like someone who had reached a point when he was absolutely determined to stand or fall on principle.

You had to say this much for Jeb Bush: at least he could smell what was in the wind.

The trouble was, he lost the election.

CHAPTER 9

A CITY IN THE COUNTRY

O N E raw spring night a few years ago, I went to a meeting of a local organization called the Open Space Project. I was a casual member of the organization, meaning I had contributed twenty-five bucks every year to what seemed like a worthy cause, but I had not been active in its affairs. In fact, I wasn't quite sure what its aims were, beyond a general concern for the vanishing rural landscape that surrounds Saratoga Springs, New York, and related issues of parks and greenspaces inside the city proper. Inasmuch as I was writing a book about things like that (*The Geography of Nowhere*), I felt obliged to become more involved, so that blustery spring night I ventured out to the meeting.

It was held in the chapel of a deconsecrated church. The interior dimensions of the old place were expansive and delightful, with a soaring ceiling, subtle lighting, and fine nineteenth-century wainscotting—none of the usual prisonlike cinderblock walls, claustrophobic drop ceilings, and ghoulish fluorescent lights one associates with civic meeting places these days.

I've lived in this town nearly twenty years, and recognized most of the twenty-five or so members by their faces. Of these, I was casual friends with perhaps fifteen—meaning we'd stop and chat on the street—and good buddies with five—meaning we did things together like play tennis or have dinner. After a certain amount of routine business, they settled down to discuss a lively issue: what to do about the six-acre superblock that had been the site of the magnificent Grand Union Hotel (see Chapter 4, *Charm*), which was demolished in 1953 and replaced by a trashy strip mall that included as standard equipment a gigantic parking lot. The strip mall building itself was now reaching the end of its *design life*, as the engineers say. It is hard to overstate what a piece of junk the structure is. When you go into the liquor store on a rainy day, there are so many tarpaulins rigged to the ceiling, with plastic tubes directing leaks into five-gallon joint compound buckets, that the store looks like some kind of weird indoor maple sugaring operation. In short, the strip mall was dying. Its owners were an out-of-town realty company who seemed determined to do nothing with the property. Actually, the rumor was they were waiting for gambling to be legalized so they could put up a casino.

The task underway at the meeting that night—to come up with ideas for using the property occupied by the decrepit strip mall—was an activity that is lately called a *thought exercise*. That is, the Open Space Project had neither any proprietary stake in the land, nor any official advisory role vis-a-vis its owners. This was strictly a brainstorming session by a group of concerned citizens. One reason that it was particularly interesting was that quite a few committee members were design professionals. There were at least two practicing architects present, four landscape architects, one N.Y. State planning official, one professor of urban planning from a first-rate technical school (Rensselaer Polytechnic Institute), not to mention the official city planner of Saratoga Springs. Of the remaining members, many were professionally involved with land development, real estate sales, property law, land trusts, or environmental agencies.

Now, I must set the scene with one final bit of information. The parcel occupied by the strip mall, its huge parking lot, happened to be right across our main street from the most important formal greenspace in town: Congress Park. This eleven-acre park had been designed by Frederick Law Olmsted, the man responsible for New York City's Central Park, Brooklyn's Prospect Park, Boston's "Emerald Necklace," and numerous other beloved greenspaces. Despite some casual butchery over the years, Congress Park was still recognizably an excellent civic open space. It contained a series of duck ponds, a formal Italian garden, several greenswards and shady groves, a band shell, two fountains (one with a sculpture by Augustus Saint-Gaudens), several mineral spring pavilions, and finally, in the center, the old Canfield Casino, a fine, dignified Italianate brick structure which was now the city's museum.

The Open Space Committee members hashed over this entire matter for a couple of hours, and the result of all their brainstorming—supported by a wealth of technical knowledge and professional experience—was that the best use for the six-acre strip mall property would be a park. An *open space*.

Huh? Excuse me . . . ? Did I hear that correctly? A park? Right across the street from an existing eleven-acre park designed by Olmsted? Was I

BROADWAY, SARATOGA SPRINGS, NEW YORK

THE FORMER SITE AND ENVIRONS OF THE GRAND UNION HOTEL IN SARATOGA SPRINGS: (A) DECREPIT STRIP MALL (B) PARKING LOT (C) WEEDS (D) THREE-STORY BUILDING (E) FOUR-STORY BUILDING (F) CONGRESS PARK BY FREDERICK LAW OLMSTED AND (G) OLD TROLLEY STATION.

dreaming? Was this some kind of nightmare that writers are supposed to have when they're struggling to produce a book?

No, I wasn't dreaming. I heard it right, and now you hear it right. Their solution to the problem was to put a new city park across the street from an old city park. Not to continue the urban pattern of Broadway, the city's main street, namely multistory, mixed-use buildings brought out to the sidewalk edge with retail on the ground floor and offices and apartments above. That one was so obvious that a nine-year-old kid from Düsseldorf could have figured it out in five minutes flat. Nor to propose a grand institutional building like a library for this important site, nor a center for the performing arts. Nor to break up the six-acre superblock—an anomaly of history—by cutting some adjoining streets through it, and therefore creating a finer grain of city fabric for decades to come. Nor even, for goodness sake, to put a major hotel there, like the magnificent one that had occupied that site for a hundred years until 1953, and made that block the spiritual heart of the city. None of these things. Instead, a park across the street from a park.

This incident made a deep impression on me. Hey, why fib? It blew my mind. If the town's best-intentioned citizens, supposed experts in their fields, could not solve a fundamental problem of civic design that should have been child's play, then who could? As a design problem, it didn't come close to the artistic difficulties of detailing streets in the auto age, or creating dignified building facades under the formal constraints of handicapped codes, or the manifold intricacies of public transportation.

In fact, the record of civic planning efforts during my two decades in town had been pretty dismal. As late as the mid-1980s, we were still dropping new suburban-style strip malls all over downtown, with parking lots right on the street edge, ruining Broadway's "feeder streets." These were the only things that *could* be built under the city's zoning regulations. Saratoga Springs was otherwise becoming a patchwork of vacant lots. If you looked at an aerial photograph, fully two-thirds of the existing downtown fabric (not including the streets) was occupied by empty pavement. This condition was leading to civic death. We'd turned a rich, dense, finely grained, classic American small-town business district into a single commercial corridor—Broadway—and made all the other streets running off it either functionally irrelevant or too ugly and forbidding to walk on.

Most of the parking lots occupied blocks that were leveled under the federally subsidized urban renewal programs of the 1960s and 1970s. This was sold to the public with the promise that old, decrepit buildings would be replaced by better new ones—a promise that was broken. Some of the old buildings were, frankly, worthless and deserved demolition. Many were not. They could have been rehabbed and put back to good use. Many featured the kind of nineteenth-century craftsmanship that cannot be replicated in our time, when merely competent masons command thirty bucks an hour and real craftsmen are out of the question, assuming any can be found at all.

The outcome of two decades of urban renewal was that almost nothing of enduring value got built. Evidently, the city valued parking lots above all other things. To aggravate matters, the city's unbelievably stupid building regulations made it virtually impossible to build anything new in harmony with the traditional character of the town. Probably the worst rule was a formula that mandated x-number of parking spaces per the given amount of a proposed new building's square footage. For instance, if you contemplated a 10,000-square-foot row building consistent with the existing fabric, the rule would require you to come up with something like thirty-five parking slots. This formula was flatly inconsistent with the laws of physics as they're currently understood. Two things can't occupy one space at the same time—a parking structure and a row building.

The truth was, under this rule, and several others, you could not build anything downtown unless you put up precisely the sort of building that would kill downtown: convenience stores surrounded by parking, franchise fry-pits, strip malls, and always, *always*, one-story buildings. In my two decades living in Saratoga, there had been two major fires on Broadway as well. These lots were quickly put into service for car parking, though they created "missing teeth" along our main street. One overall trend was clear: the folks in charge were doing everything possible to turn Saratoga into the antithesis of what it *had been*, the place that people like myself had chosen to live in, the place that tourists from New Jersey came to visit on three-day weekends: the classic American town.

I left that meeting of the Open Space Project in a fog of despair tinged with amazement, and had to resort to analgesic beverages to get over the shock of what I'd witnessed. In the weeks that followed, I had occasion to ponder the incident. It seemed to me that the Open Space Project had basically been undone by language. The very name of their organization had channeled all thinking along a predetermined route leading to an inevitable outcome: their mission was to create open space, regardless of any other civic design considerations. A park across the street from a park made perfect sense. I naturally wondered what would have to happen to change this unfortunate sort of thinking.

THE PREPOSTEROUS AND APPALLING SAGA OF EXIT 14

In the winter of 1994, a year or so after that outlandish evening, a white-haired, grandfatherly, out-of-town developer named Thomas Deveno, who had made a bundle on suburban development in southern Saratoga County, applied to the city of Saratoga Springs for permission to build an office park on the fringe of town. In order to obtain a permit, he first had to apply for a zoning variance, which complicated matters. The parcel in question was 13.5 acres off Exit 14 of Interstate 87 (the major auto route between New York City and Montreal), slightly east of town. There are three exits for Saratoga Springs: Exit 13, which dumps people 2 miles south of downtown; Exit 14, which brings people downtown past the city's fabled racetrack along Union Avenue; and Exit 15, 2 miles north of downtown, where all the malls and WalMart clones rose up out of the cornfields in recent years.

The Deveno land was a sensitive site, because through a peculiar set of circumstances, Exit 14 remained pristine. No suburban smarm, no Burger King, no gas stations, *nothing* had been built near any of its off-ramps. One corner of the cloverleaf was bordered by an artist's colony called Yaddo, which occupied the mansion of a former estate and over a hundred acres of gardens, forest, and ponds. The two corners on the far side of I-87 were wetland and not buildable under current New York State environmental rules. At the time of the proposal, Deveno's property contained nothing more than a defunct horseback riding academy which amounted to a couple of derelict barns.

His land was zoned 2-acre residential, meaning the minimum-size house lot allowed was 2 acres. This posed some rather severe practical problems. The proximity of the noisy highway would have severely devalued any big fancy houses built there—making them not worth building—and a few tiny, cheap houses on 2-acre lots didn't make sense either from the speculative builder's point of view, so nothing had been built there.

Many small cities like Saratoga have established large-lot residential greenbelts on the fringe of their towns as a supposed buffer zone against commercial development. Except as a political expedient, this has turned out to be a lamebrained solution. Houses on 2-acre lots ruin rural land, especially farmland, just as effectively as fifty-unit housing pods. The supposed "greenspace" they create has no civic meaning nor any rural significance—it's too big to mow and too small to plow. This failure of greenbelts to solve the growth problem calls into question many of the notions on which *open space* advocates have based their thinking. More ominously, large-lot zoning promotes "leapfrog development." It makes land farther out from the greenbelt more attractive to developers and cheaper to finance. Hence it generates even more sprawl, more car traffic, longer commutes, and more places with no character and no future. Anyway, because his land was part of the 2-acre lot greenbelt, Mr. Deveno needed a variance to build what he had in mind on that particular site, and to get it, he had to enter the frightful realm of city real estate politics, including its bureaucratic chamber of horrors, the Planning Board.

What he had in mind was a 45,000-square-foot office building surrounded by parking lots. In the drawings it looked dismal. It was so submediocre, in fact, that the architects proposed to plant a screen of trees and shrubs along the road to hide it, so people wouldn't have to look at the damn thing, and they had paid for elaborate sets of renderings to illustrate how inoffensive it would be. Making this argument right off the bat suggests that they knew very well what a piece of *dreck* the building really was.

Actually, the matter of the building's appearance was a tactical ruse. It was supposed to deflect attention away from the more serious issue, which was: *where do office buildings really belong in our town?* By deliberately playing up the "aesthetic" issue (and its supposed mitigation), the Deveno team thought it could control the terms of the debate and ram the proposal through. Deveno's attorney, a bulldog of an Irishman named Michael J. Toohey, had shepherded many such land development proposals through the chamber of horrors, and was famed in the region for his winning record in these battles.

There was one additional, scintillating complication. Deveno tried to sweeten the deal for the public by inveigling a school called Adirondack

Community College (ACC), which had its main campus in neighboring Warren County, to lease a *separate* 15,000-square-foot building on the site for use as their night school. Deveno would build it just for the school. So the proposed project was no mere office park. It would be the new *home* of *a great educational institution!* How could decent citizens object to such a civic ornament?

In fact, for years ACC had been using a downtown Catholic school for the handful of night classes it offered in Saratoga. It had been paying the school $38,000 a year in rent. Under Deveno's plan, they would pay $200,000 a year in rent. For the same amount of money ACC could have financed the purchase and renovation of a building downtown, and owned it free and clear in a few years, or even put up a piece of brand-new architectural garbage such as Deveno proposed to build for them out of the goodness of his heart. The odor of dead carp hung over this strange partnership from the very start. It seemed a blatant and clumsy attempt to bribe the public's good will. But it backfired badly and ended up making ACC officials look like a bunch of shills at a snake oil show.

The planning board scheduled a series of hearings, with the general public invited to comment for two minutes each after the formal presentations. The turnout was impressive, the hearing room in city hall packed with concerned citizens. Leading the opposition was the Open Space Project.

Local politics bear a brief historical digression. Saratoga never really went through the Great Depression, or the New Deal, which was its antidote. So the forces that elsewhere molded the modern Democratic party into a "progressive" organization had no impact here. The Democrats remained a stunted, larval, ineffectual opposition to the dominant Republicans. The town itself was functionally depression-proof. In the 1930s Saratoga was the nation's gambling capital (Las Vegas then was a mere desert tank town) and gambling came to be controlled by organized crime, which also controlled the liquor supply during prohibition. Under the businesslike leadership of Charles "Lucky" Luciano, the dominant gang of each major U.S. city was assigned a piece of the action. The action consisted of a set of posh casino-nightclubs dispersed on the rural outskirts of town, made possible, of course, by the new phenomenon of the motorcar. The New York mob ran the Brook Club, the Chicago mob ran the Piping Rock Club, and so on. Gambling was expressly illegal under New York law, but Luciano owned Saratoga's reigning Republican machine, and he also

generously supplemented the plebeian salaries of certain state police officials in nearby Albany. So, nobody got raided, nobody even worried about
the possibility of getting raided, everybody made lots of money, from Mr.
Luciano, as he was always addressed, down to the lowliest newsboy, and
Saratoga partied on. The Depression was something that happened in
newsreels to other people in another America.

Gambling was extinguished here in the early 1950s as a result of Senator Estes Kefauver's committee hearings on organized crime in America,
which shed an unflattering light on Saratoga in particular as the mob's favorite watering hole. By then, Benjamin "Bugsy" Siegal had built the
Flamingo Hotel out in Nevada. With Las Vegas up and running, Saratoga
sank into decline. The Republicans stayed in charge of city hall by sheer
inertia, except for a loopy period in the mid-1970s, when Watergate interrupted the long political coma. The Democratic party has otherwise remained an ineffectual opposition, while the Republicans have evolved
from factotums of the mob to an efficient local land development machine
made up of lawyers, bankers, realtors, and speculators, dedicated to maximizing their short-term profits at the expense of the town's future.

At the outset of Thomas Deveno's ordeal in the chamber of horrors, the
local Republicans, who completely dominate the Planning Board and the
City Council, unintentionally showed their true colors. They complained
loudly in the newspaper that opponents to the Deveno project were dangerous "radicals," while claiming they were prudent "conservatives." This
was a fascinating inversion of the most obvious point at issue. The truth
was, Republican conservatives were the ones most eager to radically compromise the town's traditional character, while the so-called radicals were
the ones most determined to conserve it.

The opposition mounted against Deveno's Exit 14 project was the first
big protest against a Saratoga land development deal in anybody's memory.
The battle had a salutary clarifying effect on the "growth" issue. As it
heated up, the Open Space Project people finally got it through their
heads that they would never be able to save any *open space* unless they figured out where development *ought to go*, which implied some attention to
real town planning. They began to realize that not all open space is the
same, or of equal significance—that there's a difference between a farm, a
vacant lot, a city park, and the weedpatch in the center of a freeway off-
ramp. The Deveno proposal allowed them to understand that if so-called

office parks were not desirable on the fringe of town, there must be a more appropriate place for offices to exist. Offices were a necessity, after all. Even the Open Space Project had one.

They concluded that downtown was precisely the appropriate place for such activity. This led the Project to start thinking about all the other implications of what downtown stood for, indeed to the question of civic life in general, and finally to the amazing discovery that there was a link between the physical form of town and the quality of life it fostered. They'd come a long way, intellectually, since that brainstorming session in the old church. The town Democrats, in turn, joined the opposition to Exit 14. They seemed grateful to have discovered a local issue they could sink their gums into. The discovery that it was possible to be against stupid developments without being against economic "growth" seemed to rejuvenate them.

When attorney Michael J. Toohey unveiled the artist's renderings of the Deveno office park at the opening round in a packed city hall hearing room, nobody was fooled. The immediate response was: *if this is such a wonderful building, why do you want to hide it behind all these trees?* Toohey huddled with his troops. They'd hoped to neutralize the opposition's main beef: that the buildings themselves were eyesores. Scores of opponents rose to take their two minutes at the microphone denouncing the project on other grounds and the hearing dragged on until nearly midnight, leaving both factions cross-eyed with fatigue and consternation.

The Republicans proved to be utterly clueless about civic life issues, and completely unprepared to discuss them intelligently. They hadn't really thought about such things, ever. These were the same folks, you understand, who were forever yapping about traditional and family values, yet to save their lives they couldn't recognize the traditional principles of civic design that made their town what it was. They were traditionalists with no notions of tradition. The members of the Planning Board in particular knew less about traditional town planning than they knew about thoroughbred handicapping, Chinese cuisine, or personal injury law. Their ignorance on the subject proved to be spectacular. In a letter to the editor of the paper, one Republican shill made the hilarious assertion that the proposed office park at Exit 14 was a good thing because it would keep "four hundred fewer people [from] crowding our streets every evening." As though that were a problem. Quite the contrary, the town's main street was dead after six P.M. from October to May, and the local shop owners were despondent over it.

With their initial strategy derailed, the Deveno team resorted to tactical boredom. They turned the debate to issues like ambient lighting, site grading, water runoff, sewer capacity, and other matters which (1) made it seem as though the project was a done deal, with all but a few technicalities ironed out, and (2) enabled the process to drag out weeks longer with elaborate recitations of statistics and impressive displays of charts, proving how splendidly they had handled these matters, all aimed at boring to death any opponents who dared to show up for the additional hearings. But the opposition kept showing up in force week after week. They continued to speak out against the project on grounds other than environmental technicalities. And they doggedly refocused the debate on the more important issues, against which Deveno's representatives still offered no credible arguments—other than how great it would be to have a community college's extension night school at Exit 14, and what a pity it would be if the city threw away the fabulous tax revenue it would generate. Finally, with much ceremony and a great buildup of false suspense—because the outcome was a foregone conclusion—the planning board voted in favor of the development (to a chorus of catcalls). However, there was a big catch.

The catch was that this did not quite amount to official approval. It amounted only to a *recommendation* to the city council that the council vote for approval, because only the council could pass the necessary amendments to the city's master plan that would permit the development to go forward. So, now the whole extravaganza had to be replayed in the Council. Between the planning board hearings and the council vote, many strange and wondrous complications arose.

First, the Yaddo Foundation—the renowned artist's colony whose property was closest to Deveno's site—filed a formal objection to the development, on the grounds that it didn't appear to be mainly "educational," as the Deveno forces kept claiming. Actually, both factions had been wondering where Yaddo stood all this time. It was assumed that they didn't want to get involved because the foundation annually received sizable contributions from many local Republican bigwigs. And as soon as their objection was made public, it was also whispered that some of their financial support was ceremoniously withdrawn, as though a warning.

However, Yaddo's official protest changed the terms under which the council could approve a rezoning in this case. The city council is composed of the mayor and four city commissioners, all elected separately. Because of some recondite point of the city charter triggered by Yaddo's protest, the project now required approval from four out of five council members instead of a simple majority vote. The sole Democrat on the council, Public Works Commissioner Thomas McTygue, had sworn publicly to vote against Deveno's proposal. The mayor and two other commissioners were considered definitely favorable to it. Commissioner of Public Safety Lewis J. Benton refused to hint at his position. He was a Republican, but his silence made everybody nervous.

Anyway, in a stunning tactical gambit engineered to seize victory, Deveno's lawyer, Michael J. Toohey, announced in the newspaper that they were scrapping the plan for the 45,000-square-foot commercial office building, and would *only* put up the building for ACC's night school. "Now the entire project will be educational," Toohey said.

It seemed rather crazy on the face of it, as though Deveno's sole mission in life now was to provide Saratoga (where he didn't even live) with a few continuing ed classes from a second-rate junior college headquartered in the next county. But then, when pressed by the reporter, Toohey would not rule out the possibility of bringing back the office building proposal for reconsideration at a later date. So, his smooth move was easily unmasked for the clever ploy it was. Yet, events got weirder.

It was revealed in the paper that one of the five city council members, Finance Commissioner J. Michael O'Connell, was employed by the Adirondack Community College as a part-time teacher, suggesting possible conflict of interest. City Attorney Peter Tulin, a Republican, publicly advised O'Connell that, while an actual conflict of interest was arguable, the *perceived* conflict was sufficient grounds for the commissioner to excuse himself from voting on the matter. O'Connell ruefully took Tulin's advice and told the newspaper that he would not vote on the Deveno project. This seemed to seal its fate. With O'Connell publicly pledged to abstain, and McTygue dead set against it, there could not be any four-out-of-five vote on the council for approval. The simple arithmetic crackled across town and cries of jubilation rang out. Naturally, they proved to be premature.

The resourceful Republicans had rooted out some functionary in the State Secretary of State's department in Albany—a department staffed by dreary creatures like Bartleby the Scrivner copying state documents onto vellum sheets in ink made from lampblacking in dim little cubicles, a department so obscure that it hadn't made a peep about *anything* since the administration of Samuel J. Tilden—who issued an "opinion" that O'Connell should be allowed to vote because "he was not a direct party to the lease" between Deveno and ACC. Commissioner O'Connell responded via the newspaper, saying rather cryptically, "I made my statement a week ago [about not voting], and I stand by that—*but anything can happen* between now and April 11." That was when the vote was scheduled. The interpretation of O'Connell's baffling remark by just about everyone was that he stood by his remarks, subject to a possible change of mind about where he stood.

In connection with the issue of O'Connell's voting status, the President of ACC sent a letter to the city which stated that the college was not in any formal way an "involved" agency in the Deveno proposal, and that, in fact, no signed lease existed between the college and Deveno, the implication being that O'Connell ought to feel ethically free to vote on the matter. This was *very* interesting news, indeed, because ACC's Dean of Administration had sat in the front row beside Thomas Deveno *throughout every planning board hearing,* all but holding the developer's hand. She had even addressed the board on one occasion, in her official capacity, to support the project and to defend the school's honor in being part of it. Of course, the President's letter also begged the question of what that functionary in the Secretary of State's office had been referring to when he declared that Commissioner O'Connell was not a party to a lease between ACC and Deveno. What lease? Perhaps what he meant, but didn't manage to articulate, was that O'Connell couldn't have been a party to an agreement that didn't exist. Ah, well, the wheels of the law grind exceedingly fine. Once more, the odor of decomposing carp wafted over town.

Finally the great occasion arrived when the city council was called upon to vote on a proposed change in the master plan, concerning the zoning status of 13.5 acres owned by Mr. Thomas Deveno, who sought approval at this time to build a classroom facility for a community college—and possibly another commercial building in the future, maybe, he and his representatives weren't quite sure, it was hard to say. . . . The council held its meeting in the city's fairly new (1991) convention center to accommodate the large crowd expected to turn out for the spectacle.

Among the opening remarks by the council members, Commissioner O'Connell verified his own recent apparently prophetic utterance that "anything could happen" by declaring that he had, in fact, changed his mind and would vote on the matter at hand. Boos, hisses, whistles and objurgations filled the acoustically imperfect post-modern hall, with its cheap plastic furniture and *no frills* ambience. O'Connell added through the din that he would resign his job with the college as soon as it opened for business on the proposed site. "Giving up my job to establish a local educational facility is not just the right thing to do," O'Connell read from a prepared statement, "it is the *only* right thing to do." Well, anything *could* happen. Winged monkeys could fly out of his butt before the night was over. Deng Tsao Ping could show up with three hundred fifty orders of mu shu pork. Who can ever say what the future holds. . . ? A crestfallen public, astonished by O'Connell's effrontery, grumbled through an hour of procedural rigmarole, presaging a vote that now seemed hopeless.

Michael J. Toohey, suddenly fortified by the scent of victory (or was it eau du carp?), launched into his final arguments with a brio he hadn't displayed since the early rounds of the wearisome struggle. The public then denounced the project one last time, taking their abject, ritualistic turns at the microphone in the evident face of defeat. A call went out for the fateful vote. That was when Commissioner Lewis J. Benton seemingly awoke from some anguished private nightmare and asked Toohey for a guarantee that the land in question would always be solely dedicated to educational use. Toohey squirmed with incredulity and sweated into his dark, rather natty, spring-weight suit. A guarantee? Like, in writing? Well, yes, Benton said, and he formally moved that further discussion, or indeed a vote, be tabled until such a guarantee could be drawn up by the city attorney, pondered over by all concerned, and . . .

Groans now welled up over the huge room while the council members themselves swapped anxious glances—all except Commissioner McTygue, the Democrat, the one certain "no" vote, who concentrated fiercely on some doodle he was drawing. The mayor, a patrician lady of a certain age named A. C. Dake, tried to pawn off the nasty question raised by Benton on city attorney Tulin, as though any impromptu ruling he might make on the spot would allow the rest of them to escape responsibility for further delay. Yet, to general amazement, Michael J. Toohey cleared his throat and ventured that such a guarantee really wasn't in the cards, with the implication that . . . *well, didn't the commissioner understand, for crissake, that Mr. Deveno reserved the right to reapply for more commercial development on the property sometime in the future, like maybe six months from now, who can say?* In other words, *get with the program, Lew!*

"You mean you want to go ahead and vote on this right now?" Benton asked Toohey.

"Correct," Toohey replied.

"All right," Benton said, shrugging his shoulders, and a few moments later cast his vote *against* the Deveno proposal. Mayor Dake made a big show of counting and recounting all five votes as though some arithmetical error might be discovered to explain the peculiar outcome, three to two, not good enough for approval.

Everybody else in the enormous room, both pro and con, was too stunned to shout, whisper, cheer, groan, snort, weep, or express any emotion. They sat poised to wait for some evil procedural mistake to assert itself, with consequent further delay, resurrection of false hopes, and then a last vengeful sword thrust to the opposition's soft, squishy, pathetic, suspiciously effeminate, under-oxygenated, eternally bleeding liberal hearts—with some sadistic cackling a la Richard Widmark in *Kiss of Death* to attend the fall of everlasting darkness.

It didn't work out that way. The vote stayed at three to two and Thomas Deveno's proposed zoning change was denied. That was simply the end of it. In the stunned silence, Commissioner Benton bustled off into the spring vapors of night before any of his political cronies could smack him on the head and say, *Hey, whaddaya, ya stupit . . .*

The victory was real and sweet, and the forces of good prevailed over the forces of wickedness. The town received an interesting lesson in the principles of civic art and the meaning of civic life, the Open Space Project donned the heroic mantle of righteousness, and the goshdarn office park didn't get built at Exit 14.

Some interesting twitches of an epiloguenous nature ensued. First, the mayor, in some fugue state of retribution, nominated Commissioner J. Michael O'Connell for the board of the Saratoga Springs Historic Preservation Society. The board promptly and emphatically rejected the nominee without explanation.

Next, attorney Michael J. Toohey announced in the newspaper that his client, Thomas Deveno, was "drawing up plans" for a half dozen single-

family homes to be built on his property just off Exit 14—which he is entitled, by zoning, to do—and where the lucky homeowners would, presumably, be lulled to slumber each night by the white noise of
tractor-trailers plying Interstate 87 a few yards from their bedroom windows.

To date, not a spadeful of earth has been turned over in that venture.

In the spring of 1995, Mayor A. C. Dake announced her intention not
to seek another term. The Republicans subsequently nominated Finance
Commissioner J. Michael O'Connell, who was duly elected mayor by a
slender 400-vote margin in November 1995.

FARMER

I'VE known Steve Gilman casually since I settled in this part of upstate New York twenty years ago. For a long time, he had a farm in White Creek, near the Vermont line. He worked as a carpenter around Saratoga and he'd show up on the social scene now and again. We were about the same age, and it seemed to me that we carried similar cultural baggage out of the 1960s. Steve has worn his hair in a ponytail all these years. Now it's gone gray. He's six-foot-two, and hard work has kept him at the same 162 pounds he attained as a senior in high school. I thought of him as a sort of unreconstructed hippie back-to-the-lander, and he later agreed in so many words that he saw himself that way too.

Steve comes from a family of lawyers over in Bennington, Vermont. There was a certain expectation that he would follow his father down that path, so he became a political science major at Union College in Schenectady in the late 1960s, but dropped out in his senior year to be an anti-Vietnam War activist. Among other things, he picketed then-Defense

Secretary Robert McNamara's vacation house in Aspen, Colorado. His voice, rather high and strained for such a tall man, sounds as though he had screamed his lungs out at one too many peace rallies and never fully recovered. In 1970, he returned to Union College for his bachelor's degree. But law was not what he wanted to do with his life, so after graduation he went back to the Bennington area, married a girl who was a potter, and bought the spread in White Creek, just over the New York line.

Eight or ten years ago, Steve started showing up regularly at the twice-a-week farmer's market in Saratoga, and it became evident that organic farming was overtaking carpentry as his vocation. He sold herbs and vegetables at the market and he was also supplying some local restaurants. But with its steep, rocky hills, his property in White Creek was better suited to grazing animals than to crop farming. He was never able to get more than five acres under cultivation, though he practiced an intense form of raised-bed agriculture. By the late 1980s, his first marriage unraveled. They'd had no children. He and his ex-wife sold the farm in White Creek and Steve went looking for better land closer to town.

"A realtor would send me computer printouts of what was coming onto the market," he said. "I'd check them out with soil maps—which are available in any county office. You can also tell the condition of the soil by what grows on it. For instance, if it's wild strawberries, you know it's acid. I finally found land that I wanted in December of eighty-eight. It was on Ruckytucks Road, which was still dirt then. I thought, *That's real pretty in there*. I got permission to take soil samples. There were these little frozen ponds all over, which worried me a little. I shot a few grades with a hand level to determine that there was enough slope so you could make water drain. I knew the soil type was basically clay, which means drainage problems. There were obvious springs coming up."

On the positive side, the land had only been used as a night pasture for dairy cows for the preceding fifty years. Field corn hadn't been grown there, with all its pesticide and herbicide inputs, the residues of which could have prevented the growth of broadleaf crop plants for years into the future, and also killed the living soil-building microorganisms that are the key to successful organic farming.

"I did a little test myself with oats," he went on. "Put them in a cup of that soil. It's a real good indicator crop, very sensitive. If they don't come up, you know there's some kind of herbicide residue."

The oats germinated. Finally, he got down to negotiating with the owner in a room at the realtor's office.

"The owner was a former farmer who liked the idea of a farmer buying his land. But he took one look at me and said, 'Oh, you just want to grow pot!' So, then, in front of all these other people, I said, 'We're gonna take a blood test, right now. You bring somebody in. And you're gonna take one too. You're not even going to find alcohol in my veins.' And boom, we closed the deal."

In the spring of 1989, Steve commenced a year-long campaign to improve the drainage and get the weeds under control. The property was 47.06 acres. Twenty-five of this was in woods. The rest was the old night pasture. He invested $12,000 in rented earth-moving equipment, dug an irrigation pond, deepened a seasonal stream that ran down the center of the pasture, so it would drain more effectively, and dug a new drainage ditch around the perimeter. He sowed cover crops to begin the laborious process of lightening the clay soil. In the course of things, he met a woman named Sherrie Mickel, who worked as a librarian at a nearby university, and married her. They lived in a 14-foot camping trailer while Steve began building a house, and they conceived a child, a girl they would name Maeve.

A LOOMING NATIONAL CATASTROPHE

Two percent of the American population are now engaged in farming, and therefore in feeding all the rest of us, plus a significant number of people in other countries who depend on food we export. Increasingly, and especially west of the Appalachian Mountains, this farming is being done on enormous consolidated spreads of several thousand acres by corporatized entities rather than families. More ominous, however, is the current method of American farming. The model is industrial: you put x-amount of material plus technology in, and get a predictable amount of salable product out. Inputs and outputs, they call them. Seeds, pesticides, herbicides, fertilizer, gasoline are inputs. Corn, soybeans, and wheat are typical outputs. This is agribusiness, as opposed to agriculture. So, what's wrong with it? There's no apparent shortage of Wonder Bread or Hostess Twinkies.

In practice, the model is much closer to strip-mining than farming. It is an extractive and destructive process. It produces short-term gain in exchange for long-term losses. It is destroying the basis of farming, which is the soil.

Let's look for a moment at the American heartland. When settlers arrived in the Midwest, they found a geological legacy of topsoil six feet deep in places. It was unbelievably good, rich, deep topsoil by any standard in the world. This territory had existed as grass-covered plains since the last ice age, undisturbed by any significant human cultivation. For eons, the plains had renewed and enriched themselves through natural cycles of growth, death, and prairie fire, fertilized by stupendous herds of wild quadrupeds. Cereal grains, which are grasses biologically, were perfectly suited to it. So this area, which today includes the states of Illinois, Wisconsin, Minnesota, Iowa, Nebraska, Missouri, Oklahoma, Kansas, parts of the Dakotas, Texas, and Montana (as well as Canada's provinces of Manitoba and Saskatchewan) became the breadbasket of the Western world.

The weather in this region is very severe. Wind sweeps easily over the flat terrain. Rainfall often occurs in the form of intense storms, punctuated by long dry spells—and just as often these storms bring with them destructive tornadoes, lightning, hail, and flooding. Before farming, the thick roots of prairie grasses held together prairie soils in the face of these meteorological assaults.

The mechanization of farming that followed World War One introduced practices that allowed farmers to increase their scale of operation by orders of magnitude and at the same time promoted a much larger scale of regular soil erosion. The dust bowl of the 1930s was a symptom of these aggressive, mechanized farming practices, combined with a drought of several years duration. It made an impression on our national psyche with frightening duststorms, much-photographed rural desolation, and catastrophic social consequences, but the soils of the American breadbasket have continued to erode steadily, if less dramatically, ever since.

Today, that once-six-foot-deep layer of topsoil has been reduced in places to less than six inches. The other 66 inches have either washed into the Missouri–Mississippi River drainage or blown away. It is estimated that nowadays topsoil losses exceed the weight of grain harvested by five times in Iowa. This erosion is taking place largely because of our methods of cultivation, and the mechanical needs of the gigantic pieces of equipment used to cultivate cereals, especially corn. Herbicides keep the soil between the cornstalks bare and exposed. Additionally, herbicides and pesticides kill any of the living organisms that organically hold soil together. Every time it rains, the water and topsoil form a thick slurry that turns the rivers of the Midwest a rich ocher color, like house paint. Eventually it ends up as new swampland down in Cajun country.

The once-magnificent soils of the American grain belt have been reduced to mere growing mediums, with little nutrient value of their own. We compensate for the absence of nutrients with more and more chemical fertilizers. We do not compensate for the deadness of the soil, its lack of beneficial microorganisms. Erosion is the long-term price we pay for that. The short-term winner has been agribusiness: the chemical and oil companies. A crop may be destroyed by a hailstorm in June, but Monsanto has already been paid for the inputs it sold the farmer in April—his pesticides and herbicides. Fertilizers are made largely of petroleum by-products.

California's Central Valley, agribusiness's other Eden, has somewhat different soil problems, but the cause is similar: unsustainable methods and inappropriate scale. The Central Valley is as big as all of Massachusetts and Connecticut. Pacific-borne winter storms pass over it and dump all of their moisture in the Sierras as snow. The Sierra sends the huge runoff of its winter snows into two major rivers—the Sacramento to the north, and the San Joaquin to the south. These two rivers eventually converge in San Pablo Bay, near San Francisco. Since 1900, their tributaries have been dammed in order to provide flood control, and diverted into aqueducts to water both the cropland of the Central Valley and the huge suburban sprawl agglomerations assembled in the Los Angeles Basin and around the San Francisco Bay area. This has led to evermore bitter quarreling between the thirsty, ever-growing cities and the lettuce growers and peach producers of the Valley. The quarrel has been settled temporarily in favor of the cities, whose happiness is considered to be more important economically these days. Meanwhile, California farmers are beginning to see some scary, unexpected consequences of an agribusiness based on continual irrigation, the salinization of the soil.

As I drove from San Francisco to L. A. down Interstate 5 in June of 1994, past little burgs called Raisin and Richgrove, I frequently saw barren farm fields hundreds of acres in size with a weird, dirty-white crust on them, as though they'd been sprinkled with volcanic ash. These were salt precipitates caused by decades of continual irrigation. Crops could no longer be grown there, and there was no technical remedy for the problem.

Nearly all irrigation water, whatever its source, contains traces of salt. More troublesome is that many chemical fertilizers contain compounds of chlorine. Those molecules not used by plants can decay into free chlorine ions that recombine into other compounds, of which sodium chloride is one. So year by year there is a slow but constant increase in the buildup of salts. These salts invade the water table. Over decades, the salinity of underground water can become increasingly concentrated. Where drainage is poor, the water table lies close to the root level of crops, and some crops are subjected directly to salt water. Water also has a tendency to wick up to the surface by capillary action. In hot, arid places, like California's Central Valley, there is naturally a higher evaporation rate. As salinated water wicks back to the surface and evaporates, the salt precipitates out of it and eventually forms a crust on the surface.

This is not just a problem peculiar to California in the 1990s. Worldwide today, fully one-third of continually irrigated land is being ruined by salinization. Great civilizations of the past have faded to insignificance because salinization ruined their croplands. From 2100 B.C. to 1700 B.C., the Sumerian empire's crop yields fell by 75 percent in lands irrigated by the Tigris and Euphrates, and the cities that depended on them withered away. The prospects for California's croplands are similarly dire.

The destruction of soil is one part of our agricultural predicament. A related problem is our reliance on food that is trucked thousands of miles from where it is grown to where it is eaten. A Caesar salad might be made of ingredients that have traveled at least 1,500 miles to get to your table. Our ability to continue this behavior is based on the belief that we will always have cheap gasoline and be able to maintain our highways at their current high "level of service," as the traffic engineers say. Both of these assumptions stand on quicksand.

In order for a given system to break down, it is not necessary for *all* the parts of the system to fail. It is not even necessary for one of the parts to fail completely. All that is necessary is for one of the parts to fail partially. The larger the scale of a system, the less adaptable it is to change, and the more vulnerable it will be to the partial failure of one part.

If the price of gasoline were to go up $1 a gallon next week—a catastrophic increase by American standards, but still half the average current European price, and therefore "cheap" by world standards—fresh vegetables might become luxury items in the United States. Or the profit would be eliminated for the farmer, or the trucker, or the supermarket chain. Today, a trucker hauling a load of muskmelons leaves Fresno with a reasonable expectation that he will arrive in Philadelphia some 48 hours later with his perishable cargo. What if Interstate 80 between Des Moines and Mendota isn't in very good shape because the U.S. government and the states of Iowa and Illinois happen to be short of funds in the year 2006? What if many stretches of the Interstate Highway System operate at a diminished "level of service"? Without that *reasonable expectation* of delivery, the trucking business becomes a high-risk venture. These prospects portend an end to business as usual. U. S. agriculture is currently at risk in several parts of the system. The distance between Fresno and Philadelphia is not apt to get any shorter.

Another consequence of our current farming practices is that we've put out of business whole communities that once supported agriculture locally. It's estimated that farming has a multiplying effect of seven dollars to one on related business that supports farming: feed and seed, equipment, food processing, hardware stores, even cafes. This also represents the social capital of people employed in various businesses, which once constituted local communities in the form of American small towns. Their common equipment was a retail infrastructure owned and operated by local merchants—who, incidentally, also comprised a middle class that took care of the town's civic institutions. All over the United States, but in the Midwest particularly, agricultural towns have been killed off almost as completely as the buffalo a hundred years ago, largely a result of the consolidation of family farms into huge corporate farms. There are simply less customers. Instead of selling twenty-three small tractors a year, an equipment dealer can now sell only one gigantic combine. What good is a cafe if there's no group to socialize with? Obviously, it becomes hard to remain in business on those terms. Similarly, the national chain retail stores, like WalMarts and Kmarts, have put to death a whole local merchant class using an out-of-scale method of distribution and sales that is the analog of giant-scale farming.

All these things—soil erosion and degradation, inappropriate scale of operation, inordinate distances of transport, destruction of local communities—lead to one pretty obvious conclusion: that the agriculture of the future will probably have to be conducted closer to where we live, at a smaller scale, and by more thoughtful and careful methods.

This is especially true in the Northeast, where, since 1945, local agriculture on the fringe of towns and cities has been sacrificed for the tawdry blandishments of a suburban sprawl economy that offered huge short-term profits in "land development." New Jersey—now held up to ridicule as the embodiment of everything that can go wrong with a place—was called *the Garden State* because its many farms supplied the New York metropolitan area with most of its fresh vegetables. Table vegetables were commonly grown off-season in commercial hothouses as well. Today, we routinely get lettuce and tomatoes from Florida and California all year round, while formerly rural New Jersey has become a nightmare landscape of freeways, malls, and jive-plastic commuter dormitories.

In upstate New York, where I live, farmers grew more durable food crops like onions, potatoes, and apples. The Hudson River made it relatively easy and cheap to ship these crops to the New York City market. The area just east of Saratoga was well-suited to seed crop cultivation, because the gentle, folded hills afforded isolation for genetically different strains of seed vegetables. The seeds were sorted and packaged here, too, in a handsome Victorian factory that still stands in the nearby village of Cambridge, N.Y. (artists' studios now occupy the decaying bays). Seeds were a big business and employed many people who were not engaged in farming. This area, by the way, is where Anna Mary Robertson ("Grandma") Moses lived and painted, if that gives you some idea of the landscape.

To most people around here farming means dairying. But local agriculture in this part of the country was far more diversified in the past. Only with the coming of electricity, the automated milking machine, and the refrigerated bulk tank, were northeastern farmers able to concentrate on dairying. Prior to these inventions, dairy farms were limited to herds of less than thirty cows, even in a day when hired men were common. The overwhelming tendency in the twentieth century has favored monoculture at ever larger scales of production made possible by the supposed miracles of technology.

The gains in quantity have come at a price. I've already discussed the price being paid in the Midwest and California. Here in the Northeast, the result has been the near total death of farming as a way of life. The overwhelming majority of farms have gone into dairy in the past seventy years. Grain growing was the exclusive domain of the Midwest, California and Florida supplied cheap fruits and vegetables, so dairying made sense here.

For a period of time—let's say between 1910 and 1970—it was the most rational thing that a New York farmer could do with his land. Every large and small city was served by several companies that turned milk into "value added" products like cheese and sour cream. Any town of consequence had its own creameries, its bottling plant.

Since 1970 that has changed. The local milkman is now just another article of folklore. The small dairy farmers were the first to go, then the local processing plants and distributors. Today even the largest dairying operations in the Northeast, selling to statewide cooperatives, have trouble competing with dairy products from the Midwest and lately California. Meanwhile, with fruits and vegetables pouring into supermarket bins from distant places (including other countries), there is little incentive for struggling dairymen to get into crops with which they have absolutely no experience. Many of them are elderly. Many have children who have seen their parents struggle and who decided some time ago to get into another line of work.

Today the rural landscape in upstate New York is one of dereliction and desolation. Every year, for the past fifteen years, one thousand farms have gone out of business. These days, farmers consider the land to be their retirement fund. They hope to attract buyers who will pay a price commensurate with its presumed "development value"—that is, as a cul-de-sac housing subdivision or strip mall. Most farmers don't hit the jackpot, of course, and so many corners of New York State that used to be primarily agricultural are returning to forest. This is not the worst thing that could happen to farmland, but in terms of history and culture it represents a tragic waste of investment, since most of this land was originally cleared with great effort. I believe that we are going to need the farmland that remains around our towns and cities. Right now, much of New York farmland that is not close to a major highway or a tourist town is undervalued. The barns may be collapsing and the fields may be overgrown with sumacs and poplars, but the land is there waiting to be reused.

These are some of the forces in our culture that prompted an educated man like Steve Gilman to take up vegetable farming in upstate New York as an honorable and plausible way of life. My idea was to follow Steve through a growing season, to gain a broader understanding of what he was doing in contrast to the conventional farming model.

SPRINGTIME

I went out to his Ruckytucks Farm for the first time on May 3, 1995. The farm lies tucked into a pocket between gentle hills 10 miles east of Saratoga Springs, about 3 miles shy of the Hudson River. Ruckytucks is apparently an idiomatic corruption of *rocky tucks,* which refers to outcroppings up to 10 feet high that snake down these wooded hills, vanishing and reappearing into the ground. Ruckytucks Road is winding and narrow. Though it was paved after Steve bought the place in 1989, the state Department of Transportation has refrained from "improving" it further. A handful of commuter homesteads have popped up in abandoned farm fields along the way since then, too. They're typical suburbanoid bunkers, parodies of imitations of tidewater plantation houses or center hall colonials, dressed up in the pathetic pastel vinyl claddings that have become standard among homebuilders these days. Steve and Sherrie's red-roofed house is an obvious contrast, since it's handmade and self-designed. Otherwise the house has the rough, unfinished look of something built during hours stolen from more pressing chores. The south-facing back of the house is occupied entirely by a solar greenhouse.

About 100 yards from the house stands a 30-by-100-foot "solar fieldhouse," an ingenious device raked on its hillside to achieve an optimum solar *angle of incidence.* On a 20-degree winter day, the temperature inside will go up to 90. Without ventilation, Steve explained as we walked the farm together, the fieldhouse could "cook" a crop in half an hour. So, the north wall of the structure is a plywood ventilator of his own design, kind of a stack of wooden ducts topped by three small wind-powered turbines that suck the hot air out as required. He was able to build it with the help of a small grant from the U.S. Department of Agriculture's Sustainable Agriculture Research and Education program (SARE).* When he erected the fieldhouse, Steve got into a hassle with the town officials. They wanted to classify it as a "building," so they could tax it and collect a permitting fee. Steve insisted that, lacking a foundation, it was merely "a piece of equipment," as grain silos are classified. Being the son and grandson of lawyers, he was happy to take the matter to the town board, where it was decided in his favor.

---

*The entire SARE program, nationwide, represents only three-quarters of one percent of the USDA's research budget. The rest goes to agribusiness projects.

The old camping trailer where he and Sherrie lived the first year is now a toolshed moored among a weedy stand of sumacs and last summer's goldenrod stalks. Parked near the solar fieldhouse are Steve's two tractors. The smaller one is his beloved 1949 Allis-Chalmers "G" model named *Geena*, with the motor mounted in the rear so the driver has a direct view of the crop rows moving under the till bars in front. A more recent acquisition is a 1962 International Model 340, named *Tractorius*. It is rigged with a front-end loader and is used more for turning and hauling compost. Nowadays, tractors this size are no longer manufactured in the United States. Steve scrounges parts through the newsletter networks, and even fabricates some parts of his own.

The spring of 1995 was unusually chilly, with few days registering past the 55-degree mark. It was also ominously dry—after a winter with only one major snowfall. That May afternoon I went out to the farm was probably the first really nice warm day of the year, close to 70 degrees. Dandelions and marsh marigolds bloomed along the roadside. The woods were suddenly filled with trillium, bloodroot, and trout lilies. As I approached the farm, the scrim of woods behind the old night pasture stood like a mauve-gray wall. A bluebird family had taken up residence in a birdhouse Steve had crafted out of a section of hollow log. Altogether, it was one of those perfect spring days when all the griefs and vicissitudes of winter dissolve in sunshine.

My impression of the farm was that it looked like a huge garden. Steve is rather sensitive and emphatic on this point. He is *a farmer*, he insists, not a gardener, with all the frivolity that the word implies. His farm just happens to look different than most of the remaining farms, which are composed of cow pasture and corn fields. Steve grows his crops in raised beds 52 inches wide and in lengths ranging from 100, to 250, to 500 feet. While to the casual observer they look like garden beds, they are designed for intensive commercial food production.

Ruckytucks Farm is a CSA operation. That is, *community supported agriculture*, a kind of co-op. Memberships are paid to the farmer in late winter to help get the year's operation going. The total sum is much less than a conventional farmer would normally borrow from a bank. There were sixty-three members of the Ruckytucks Farm CSA in 1995, and two ranks of memberships. One rank entitled each member to a large bag of mixed produce delivered to the home twice a week from June to October with no other obligations—just cash for food. The other rank cost less in cash and obliged the member to put in ten hours of labor during the season. Members who choose to work on the farm are invariably people who love tending plants and who receive a great deal of spiritual satisfaction from growing their own food. Steve also does a brisk trade supplying restaurants and retail food shops with fresh vegetables throughout the season.

Organic farming differs from conventional farming in a number of ways. It is not based on an industrial input/output formula. Steve and Sherrie do not have to mortgage their farm every year to pay for immense amounts of fertilizer, herbicides, pesticides, and enormous pieces of equipment. It's not uncommon for a conventional farmer to borrow in six figures every spring. The nutrients for Steve and Sherrie's crops come from the soil itself, and thoughtful farming methods keep the bugs off.

As soon as he finished the grading and drainage work on his land in 1989, Steve set about preparing the soil, a campaign that he expected would take several years. He designated six different zones of growing beds that presented differing degrees of soil conditions and difficulty in preparation, naming them, poetically, the Early field, the Mid field, the Far field, the Far-out field, the Moon field, and the Horsetail field. To date, he has gotten about half of the total on line.

The soil itself must be understood as an ecosystem, a community of organisms and the habitat they flourish in. Since the 15-acre night pasture had never been bombed with chemicals, the soil was alive. But it was a dense clay-based soil that had to be lightened up with organic material, the decaying plant matter that combines with sand and clay to make loam.

"The basic premise in organic farming is to feed the soil, not the plant," Steve said as we entered the Early field with its tender green rows of newly planted lettuce, beet, and rutabaga seedlings. "We don't buy fertilizer. Fertilizers are soluble chemicals that are in themselves toxic to soil life. Pesticides commit biocide in the soil. They 'target' one pest and kill everything else around it. We buy *soil amendments* because we're feeding soil life. We use soybean meal, which is manufactured as a feed for hogs and cattle. It's 47 percent protein. You literally have billions of microscopic animals and bacteria in one handful of soil. Those microorganisms actually eat that soybean meal, which is a flaky yellow powder. They have to digest it, break it down, and liberate the nutrients into the soil. Now, what happens is the populations of these microorganisms expand by billions. The protein of

RUCKYTUCKS FARM, 1995

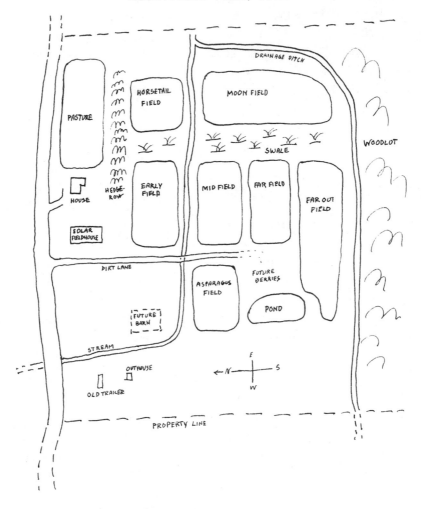

(J. H. KUNSTLER)

that soy meal grows into the protein of the new microorganisms. Then they start dying off, becoming food for other organisms, and that released protein becomes the organic forms of nitrogen, phosphorus, potassium, and micronutrients that the crops need. But it's in a biological, not industrial form.

"The conventional approach is to nail the crop plant with soluble chemicals," he continued. "The plant doesn't have a choice. So it gets hit with this stuff and it spurts. The problem is that this kind of abnormal, fast, fleshy growth is also a sign of weakness in plants. It attracts insects. Then the grower has to come in with insecticides to keep the bugs off and fungicides to keep the disease away. The minute you start down the path of chemical fertilizers, you have to use the rest of these things. The same company that sold you the fertilizer will be happy to sell you the other stuff. Those farms are now 100 percent dependent. If they don't use chemicals, they won't get a crop. They've killed off the natural fertility of their soil."

Steve's crops attract insects, but he manages them without chemical poisons. The year before, Steve had brought an entomologist out to the farm. He found sixteen different species of insects living in the lettuce alone, but only one was an agricultural pest, the tarnish plant bug. Among the rest were several beneficial insects, including ladybugs and lacewings, prodigious eaters of other bugs. He said the immature ladybugs looked just like little alligators. Steve referred to these beneficial insects as "his legions," and said that spraying chemical pesticides was "like killing your own troops with friendly fire."

One organic weapon for dealing with obdurate pests is a form of bacteria (*Bacillus thuringiensis*), BT, an insect disease agent which has been bred to attack particular species, leaving the others alone. BT works by dissolving the stomach lining of its victim. It has no persistent aftereffects in the soil. There are strains of BT specifically designed to infect mosquitoes, blackflies, cornworm, and cabbage worm, and, one of Steve's more determined adversaries, the Colorado potato bug. In a normal year he will spray the potato plants with a BT solution three or four times. He also shakes them off the plants with a pass of *Geena*, the Allis-Chalmers "G."

"I've hooked up these mechanical shakers on my tractor. It bends the plant over. Then as you drive along, it vibrates the plant a couple of times. Potato bugs don't have good feet. They drop into these Volkswagen fenders attached to the "G" so mechanically they're just removed."

Weeding is done both by hand and mechanically. It takes a crew of CSA workers ten minutes to weed a 250-foot-long crop bed. Steve has cobbled together a hiller-weeder implement to hang on *Geena* for potatoes. It was made out of an old one-row cultivator and some miscellaneous scraps of iron. However, he likes to encourage rows of wildflowers to grow between the crop rows as a habitat for beneficial insects.

Lightening the soil is a laborious process based on the repeated cultivation of cover crops, which are plowed back into the beds, adding organic body to the clay. Steve's cover crops of choice are oats and vetch. When they die off in the fall, the oats form a thick mat over the beds that act as a kind of protective mulch against early weeds in the spring. Vetch—a member of the pea family—is a nitrogen-fixer. Nodules on the roots capture nitrogen from the atmosphere, which, when plowed back under, act as an organic fertilizer. This year he intends to experiment with a type of cover crop called sorghum/sudan grass out in the Moon field and the Horsetail field. These fields lie on the lowest part of the property, have the wettest, heaviest clay soil, and need an additional year of preparation before they can be planted. He expects the sorghum/sudan to provide a great quantity of organic matter, and also a weedproof mat for the following spring.

This fine May afternoon, Steve was filled with enthusiasm, eager to move around outside on his plot of earth like a horse that had been cooped up in the barn too long. He'd spent the dark days of winter working as the Interstate Council President of the Northeast Organic Farming Association (NOFA). He'd written articles about a garlic growing research experiment they'd done in partnership with Cornell University. He'd worked on his computer crop-charting program, which plots the use of his planting beds across the season in bar graphs so there's always some productive activity going on in them. He'd done some carpentry for cash. He'd produced a few crops straight through the winter, too. Spinach from the previous fall had wintered over and was still growing in the solar fieldhouse.

THE OMINOUS BLUE SKY

I returned to the farm again the last week of June. Daisies, blue chicory, and black-eyed Susans bloomed along the roadside, along with the summer's first orange day lilies. The bluebirds had been evicted from their house by swallows and hadn't been seen around the farm for a while. It was hot and the deerflies were out in force. They don't suck your blood the way mosquitoes do, with a discreet syringelike proboscis. Rather, deerflies descend like tiny razor-wielding ninjas, their mouth-parts whirring. They literally slice you up, and slurp whatever blood leaks out. Before they do that, however, they go into orbit around your head for a while and drive you crazy. The satisfaction in swatting one doesn't last long, because the nearby woods furnish an inexhaustible supply of deerflies.

We had barely said hello when a large, slinky, rufous-colored animal appeared for a few seconds at the margin of the woods beyond the Moon field. Meka Moose, the younger of Steve and Sherrie's two black Labrador mixes shot off after it, but the creature skulked back into the trees like a wraith long before the dog crossed the central drainage stream. I thought it was a large cat, a very large cat. Steve was sure it was a coyote. Not a so-called *coy-dog*, which is a coyote-dog mix, but a purebred. True coyotes were low-slung and supple in the back end, like cats, he said, and the light color wasn't so unusual, either.

Lately, lots of wildlife has been returning to the populous Northeast, despite all the highways, malls, lube joints, and parking lots. Suburban sprawl is arguably a better habitat for some scavenging animals than it is for people. Raccoons love suburbia and coyotes have even appeared lately on the fringes of the Bronx. In Saratoga County, we've averaged at least one moose a summer popping up among the housing subdivisions and the outlet malls. They are moving down from Maine. Wild turkeys, exterminated here before the Civil War, were reintroduced by the state wildlife department twenty years ago and have succeeded so well that I see them often when I am out biking the countryside. Red fox have recovered from a devastating mange epidemic in the 1970s. Ospreys and eagles have returned in the Hudson Valley. The deer herds are said to be greater than they were in colonial days.

Steve has been fortunate where deer are concerned. Down in the lower Hudson Valley and southern Connecticut, suburbanites can barely grow vegetables. The deer will whip through a backyard garden like motorized string trimmers. Steve has not yet suffered much crop loss to deer. He believes that the two dogs keep them away—especially the smell of dog droppings. The fifteen acres of planting beds are not fenced, but whitetails can easily spring over an ordinary eight-foot fence, anyway. If a problem develops in the years ahead, Steve is considering a laser trip-switch system around the perimeter that would set off music, say, thrash metal, if an animal interrupted the light beam.

He's had a real battle, though, with crows. Crows like to pull out young corn sprouts just when they're breaking through the soil in spring. This year they'd already trashed two rows of gourmet sweet corn. The usual remedy around here is a device called a "crow-banger" which is a kind of small stationary cannon that automatically fires blank shells at timed intervals. Living anywhere near one is maddening. As an alternative, Steve spoke of buying "scare-eye balloons" invented by another farmer. They've got a couple of Mylar disk eyes and reflective flash-tape that flickers in the wind and makes crows insecure. For now, whatever corn had survived the crows' spring offensive had grown beyond the sprout stage.

Otherwise, Steve likes to cultivate a good relationship with the wild animals around the place. Though he allows the grassy rows beneath the planting beds to go into wildflowers for the bees, they eventually get mowed before they can go to seed, and he has noticed a particular red-tailed hawk hanging out in the nearby treetops whenever he mows. Mowing sends mice and voles skittering for cover, and in the hawk's world this is the equivalent of an all-you-can-eat buffet. Steve and Sherrie also grow two 75-foot rows of sunflowers specifically to feed wild songbirds.

The big story the past month and a half had been the nearly complete absence of rain—on top of a nearly snowless winter and a cool, dry spring. They'd had two meager rainfalls since my May visit, both under half an inch. So far, this had been the third-driest spring in the region since official record-keeping began in the 1890s. Neighboring Washington and Rensselaer counties had already been declared agricultural emergency zones by the state government.

Steve had been soaking the Early and Mid fields with water pumped out of the irrigation pond. Those fields, totaling four of the fifteen acres, were planted largely in salad crops, which need lots of water. The pond still looked full. It was fed by underground springs. The system he had rigged up is powered by a $200 pump and uses about $500 worth of PVC plastic pipe and vinyl hose. The pump will run six sprinklers at a time. They're called *rainbirds*, and they're about as cheap a sprinkler as you can buy.

"I still have rainbirds from ten years ago that work fine," he said. "I could have spent $30,000 irrigating this farm, but the concept here is to use small systems." Unlike other parts of the nation that absolutely depend on irrigation, upstate New York only resorts to it under extraordinary conditions, so the soil problems associated with constant irrigation are negligible.

That week, Steve had sent away to North Carolina for another $200 pump, and was getting ready to outfit the Far field and the Far-out field with pipe and hose. They amounted to five acres. The vegetables in those fields were already hurting. The young broccoli had prematurely turned a deep blue-green, which he said was a sign of stress. Garlic from the experiment with Cornell, which includes twelve varieties, was putting out *scapes,* or false seedheads, and was undersized. They'd been planted back in the fall and the soil around them had become hard as concrete. His winter squash was "set way back and might run into some frost," he said. The peppers and eggplants weren't visibly suffering—they originated in much hotter, drier climates—but he said they needed water "to take off." Same for the ten varieties of tomatoes. The sweet corn that had survived the crows was "set back." The old saying goes, *Fourth of July, knee high,* and though the Fourth was a week away, this corn was shin high.

Potatoes are also closely related to tomatoes, peppers, and eggplants. A lot of this year's potatoes were fancy blues for sales to the gourmet shops and restaurants. They'd been picked twice for Colorado potato bugs, but not yet sprayed with BT. Steve was growing a separate, smaller "trap crop" of potatoes in the Mid field as a tactic to keep the bugs off the blues in the Far field. He was also concerned about a late-season blight reported the previous year from different areas around the country. The blight, he said, was a fungus genetically the same as the disease that caused the Irish potato famine of the 1840s.

The Moon and Horsetail fields were in weeds, so they could do without sprinklers for now. When the sorghum/sedan grass hybrid seed that Steve had hoped to use as a cover crop arrived from the supplier in May, he discovered that it had been chemically treated with pesticides, and figured it would probably kill many of the beneficial microbes in the soil, so he sent it back—the use of chemical pesticides is also not allowable under organic certification standards. He now intended to use a "two-story" combination of soybeans and buckwheat, but so far the drought had kept him from tilling and seeding.

Steve was up at six in the morning and this time of year worked until ten at night. Around the solstice this far north, the sun goes down after eight-thirty and twilight lingers a good hour afterward. He would knock off field work during the hottest two hours of the day, three to five, and do less strenuous things, like showing me around. It was about five this particular June day when his daughter Maeve, nearing her fifth birthday, came back from town and ran out to where we stood in the Early field.

"We're thinning beets, now, so the shareholders will get some baby beets with the greens on, and later on they'll get big beets," Steve said, as he scooped the girl into his arms. They'd already shipped one lettuce crop and seedlings for a succession crop were sprouting in the beds. Six varieties of basil were going, including anise and hyssop basil. Flea beetles had left little pinholes in the kohlrabi leaves, but hadn't damaged the big edible roots, and that crop had also gone to shareholders and stores.

Maeve screamed, "Papa, papa, papa, papa, papa, papa!" apparently wound up from being in town. She wanted some attention, so we all went over to examine her "fairy garden." Steve had erected a tepee of bean poles for her, and the scarlet runner beans she had planted were already climbing. Inside the base of the tepee, they'd planted a cushion of thyme so Maeve could sit inside and contemplate her beans in a little cloud of thyme scent. She also had purple bush beans growing in a separate row, and a bizarre ornamental called elephant amaranth that had put out their funny trunk-like seedheads between broad earlike leaves. Maeve insisted we all go over to her swing, which hung from the limb of a 200-year-old oak tree behind the house. There was some wailing when Steve said, "In a minute, I'm talking to somebody," but she kept it up, and we went over there.

"This weather has been a shot across our bow," Steve summarized the past six weeks, while Maeve shrieked with happiness and her blond pigtails flew out behind her. "It gets on your consciousness after a while. You know you're in trouble when you start to take the weather personally."

The ropes of the swing creaked and Maeve cried, "Papa! Papa! I felt a raindrop!" But the afternoon sun burned down from a flawlessly blue sky.

High Summer

August 2 at Ruckytucks Farm and there had been no significant rainfall since the half-inch way back on June 2. All summer, gray-brown clouds had oppressed the area for days at a time, producing no rain, and holding the heat against the land like a layer of insulation. Other days, big, frightening thunderheads had sailed by to the north and south, never quite hitting Ruckytucks Farm. One storm in northern Saratoga County dropped three inches of rain in a half hour. Albany County had been nailed, and there had been damaging flash floods in the lower Hudson Valley. But

Steve had seen nothing but "sky sweat." Meanwhile, New York State was going for a record of continuous days over 90 degrees.

He'd gotten his new pump from North Carolina, but he'd had to steal extra hours each day to install it and a hundred-odd yards of PVC pipe with "stand-up" hose valves at intervals. Altogether it took fifteen hours of assembly and on July 15 he was able to soak the Far field and the Far-out field for the first time. The new equipment cost about $1,000 with all its accessories, which was more than the $700 he'd expected. He had been watering seven days a week, twice each evening. (Previous years he had averaged twelve waterings per season.) The pumps were gasoline powered. He would fill each tank after supper and it would take about an hour and a half of watering to run all the gas through. The rainbirds had to be moved around a bit, and sometimes they would fall over. At 11:00 P.M. he would refill the tanks and water for another hour and a half. He was going through a five-gallon can of gasoline every three days.

The pond itself was in surprisingly good shape. Other farmers in the area, especially dairymen who depended on ponds for their livestock, had resorted to heavy equipment to dig their parched ponds deeper. Steve's was down perhaps sixteen inches from the normal level, but it was fed by many springs. One spring ran down a little clay bed off the hillside, and even after months of drought was still producing a visible trickle above the ground.

Steve and Sherrie had sustained considerable crop damage. The main cash crop, lettuce, was down 15 percent. "I get upset if our lettuce losses are over 10 percent," he said. He'd plowed under two successions of sweet corn. Sweet corn was not a major market crop for him. It was grown for the shareholders rather than the stores and restaurants. A stand of late silver queen, a white variety, was coming along all right, and was now under the rainbirds.

The rainbirds, he said, had initially saved some of his crops from complete destruction. Now the plants had stabilized and were finally fruiting. Broccoli had made it through and he was still cutting the last of the side shoots. The sweet peppers should have been three times bushier, but they were putting out fruit. Steve laughed as he recalled the shareholder's pleas of the previous season, when peppers were bountiful: *"No more peppers! Please! No more peppers!"* The eggplants were also smaller and had sustained an invasion of flea beetles that left pinholes on the leaves. Maeve's scarlet runner beans were not doing very well on their tepee.

Up in the Far-out field, the garlic from the Cornell experiment had just been harvested. Earlier in the year, after such a mild winter and good "top growth" in March, they'd hoped for a bountiful crop. With the drought, the heads had come out about a half-inch smaller than normal. A patty pan variety of summer squash had been rescued from destruction but was only now putting out blossoms. By this time in a relatively normal season Steve would have been harvesting twenty pounds a day and selling it at three squashes for a dollar. The winter squash was still dangerously set back, and one row of the butternut variety was 90 percent wiped out.

For all that, Steve did not seem discouraged. "It's always a good year for some things and a bad year for something else," he said. The shareholders had paid their cash shares in February. The previous year they had received 412 pounds of produce in all, delivered to their homes twice a week. Over the season, it worked out to 88 cents a pound for fresh vegetables. This year, they'd gotten smaller deliveries. "But," Steve said, "we haven't heard a mournful word out of anybody. The weights will come back up. Part of the shareholders' agreement is to share in the vicissitudes of farming, and this is one with a capital V. They've been great. We have tremendous support from our shareholders and our chefs."

The thoroughbred racing season in Saratoga runs about six weeks, and the restaurants in town had been jammed with tourists. Steve would wake up at 6:00 A.M. to the blinks of the telephone answering machine, where the chefs in town had called in their orders—"sometimes semi-coherently"— late after the dinner rush. He'd had a bunch of them out for the annual chefs' tour in July, "to give them a more solid idea of where their food comes from," he said, "but this year they got the drought tour." He delivered to the restaurants and markets on Monday, Wednesday, Friday, and Saturdays in high summer. On Tuesdays and Thursdays he delivered bags to the shareholders.

Through the season of travail, the family had taken one Saturday off completely, but not together. Sherrie went down to New York City to see Ralph Fiennes in *Hamlet*, Steve drove out to western New York to check in with some other farmers, and Maeve visited her grandparents over in Bennington.

Because of the drought, Steve never did plant the "two-story" cover crop on the Moon and Horsetail fields, which would have been out of reach of the watering system in any case. He left it in weeds, which were hardier and could withstand the stressful conditions of the drought. He now had a crop of Queen Anne's lace there, an excellent habitat for beneficial insects. The ladybugs were in such good supply this year that he had to shake every harvested head of lettuce to get them off. Later on, Steve said, he would sow a winter cover crop of oats in the two fields. The oats he used were the kind used for horse feed. At four dollars per 50-pound bag, they were cheap. It would take four bags to cover the Moon field.

One of the Ruckytucks Farm shareholders was a board member of the Saratoga Lake Protection district. Saratoga Lake is unusually shallow and puts out huge amounts of a weed called milfoil. The milfoil grows so explosively that each summer the organization has to deploy machines that, in effect, mow the lake. They collect these immense mats of milfoil and distribute them to local farmers for mulch. Steve got a few tons of the stuff in July and a heap of it was now drying in the sun beside the lettuce beds in the early field. All kinds of crap emerges from the milfoil as it decomposes: bunji cords, plastic oil containers, and lots of monofilament fishing line. Fishing lures sometimes turned up when he tilled the crop rows.

The grass strips between the planting beds had proven to be a successful experiment. "We've noticed that crops do better in a plant community," he said. The longer roots of the grass and the wildflowers bring water up from deeper underground and assist the shallower crop roots in a process called transpiration. This turned out to be very helpful under such abnormal conditions as the drought presented.

There were no signs at all of any imminent break in the weather. Ninety-degree temperatures were expected as far ahead as the forecasts went in the newspapers. Even while we inspected the crop rows, a mat of hazy clouds hung suffocatingly low overhead, but the sky had looked threatening like that for half the summer without producing any rain. Steve had been up at the pond a few evenings earlier, gassing up the pump engines, when a hawk feather floated out of the sky and touched lightly down on the water right beside him, held there by the surface tension.

"The hawk is kind of a guardian around here," he said. "I stuck the feather in my hair and went around feeling like a warrior, able to handle all this stress for one evening."

KING HARVEST HAS SURELY COME

When I returned to Ruckytucks Farm on September 20 the drought had been punctuated by a couple of "rain events," as Steve put it with intentional irony. The most notable was a cloudburst in mid-August that had dumped two inches in one hour. Unfortunately, the ground was baked so hard, and the rain came down so fast, that most of it just ran down into the swale and off toward the Hudson River. A longer and more penetrating rain came at the end of August, leaving .8 of an inch. So far, September had brought only two inconsequential drizzles of .1 and .2 of an inch.

Meanwhile, two minor frosts had also hit the farm. So at five o'clock in the morning, Steve was now watering not just to hydrate the crops but also to prevent frost damage. Frost itself doesn't kill the plant—it's the *unfreezing* that bursts the plant cell. Running rainbirds accomplished two things. First, the presence of water vapor around the crops has a moderating effect. It tends to raise the temperature in the immediate vicinity a degree or two as a thermodynamic effect of condensation, which can make a big difference on a night when the thermometer hovers around 30 degrees Fahrenheit. And secondly, the spray "melts" frost off leaves, bringing them out of a frozen state in a gentle way that protects the cells from bursting.

The racing season was over in Saratoga, but the restaurant orders were still strong as the fall foliage season approached. Because of the drought, the trees were turning early, shutting down their food production systems for the year. Already the roadside sumacs and Virginia creepers were blazing scarlet. To make up for a difficult season, Steve and Sherrie planted a lot of late fall crops for the shareholders. "We got as much into the ground as we could," he said. They had two varieties of arugula going in beds where the blue potatoes had lately been harvested. The winter squash—called that because it stores well over winter—came out at about 75 percent of a normal crop, which Steve called "real decent, considering." The small melon crop failed. Some of the peppers and eggplants were still blooming in late September, as though it were July, which was yet another symptom of sustained stress. The cabbage, brussels sprouts, leeks, celeriac, and rutabaga did well.

Steve was waiting for a new computer to arrive by UPS. It was due any moment. One project he had in mind was a manual for the shareholders explaining what to do with vegetables they may never have seen before, like celeriac and kohlrabi. The average grocery store carries twenty to thirty varieties of all vegetables; Ruckytucks shareholders get about 150 varieties over the season. "I like to give them seven different kinds of baby summer squash rather than one big log of zucchini," Steve remarked as we made our way around the Far-out field. "I'm amazed we got as much out as we did. We're still getting those cobalt-blue days, like Colorado, except if you've ever lived in Colorado you know how dry it gets. I'd call it a challenging year."

It was far from over. The harvest and delivery of shareholders' produce would continue through Thanksgiving. Lettuce sprouting in the greenhouse would be moved into the solar fieldhouse and harvested until January. Seven cords of hardwood had to be cut and carted out of the woodlot. The night before I came out, Steve disked the Moon field in the dark and sowed that winter cover crop of oats. This night he intended to disk and sow the Horsetail field. Neither of these fields got formal cover crops of buckwheat and soybeans after all because of the drought. Instead, Steve left them in wildflowers, mowing them before they could go to seed. The total pesticide bill for the season came to $5.35 for one application of *Bacillus thuringiensis*, which went on the broccoli, cabbage, and cauliflower.

The family took one day off together back on August 6, Maeve's fifth birthday. She is very interested in horses, so they went to the races in Saratoga. They also made an expedition to Amherst, Massachusetts, the following weekend to attend the annual meeting of NOFA, where Steve gave a speech.

This winter would be different from past winters. Maeve would go off to kindergarten, a whole day at school, initiating a new pattern in her life that will continue for years to come. Steve got another grant from the U.S. Department of Agriculture to create a manual for running an organic farm. His grant runs three years. He would be able to forgo most of the usual midwinter carpentry—"except for a few jobs I promised some people before the grant."

This was Steve Gilman's twentieth year as a professional farmer. He characterized it as the most difficult one he'd been through. But after six years at Ruckytucks Farm, he could stand among the cold frames on the hillside behind the house and survey a piece of land carefully shaped by his own hands with thought and care. He had a right to feel proud of what he had accomplished. The farm looked especially lovely that September afternoon, two days before the equinox, with the long orderly beds of new lettuce glowing translucent green in late, low-angled sunlight, and the beds of cutting annuals blooming vividly behind them, and the dark, freshly disked Moon field in the distance, with sumacs blazing behind it at the margin of the woods. Steve has a long list of projects to look forward to in the years ahead. He intends to build a barn near the solar fieldhouse. The Moon and Horsetail fields will be planted in food crops for the first time next season. The asparagus beds come into production next year for the first time. He wants to grow berries in a field between the asparagus beds and the Far-out field, and he's thought out a system for doing it that involves stand-up pipes and wire to support raspberry canes. One imagines that it must be hard for Steve to stop thinking about systems for doing a thousand things, and the dreaming part of this enterprise would seem to be engrossing and very satisfying. In my own experience, it's hard to overestimate the spiritual rewards of successfully using your own ingenuity in a very direct way.

The thought and care evident in these forty-seven acres stands as a striking contrast to the air of dereliction that surrounds so many other farms in this part of the country, not to mention the fields and meadows surrendered to the beast of *development*. To most ordinary citizens serving the industrial economy, farming must seem a bygone way of life, of no particular importance except as history. But the idea that we can somehow do without local agriculture strikes me as crazy.

"If we could somehow dial up the Mayans and ask them what they did wrong," Steve Gilman said as we walked his well-tended fields together, "they'd surely say it was their food supply—and they lived a lot closer to the land than we do."

MY HOMETOWN: A RECONSIDERATION

I was born and raised in New York City—with a three-year intermezzo in the Long Island suburbs. My mother was born and raised in the city, and her mother before, and her mother's mother. My mother's great-grandfather was a successful Tammany Hall politician in the days of the heroic grafters. My father was born in New York City, and raised there with some intervals in Europe and Africa, since his father was a merchant in the international diamond trade. If I have a hometown, it is New York. My roots, such as they are, and the bones of my immediate ancestors, lie there.

I was yanked out of the city and replanted on Long Island at six, a cru-cial stage when children begin to reason for themselves and draw conclu-sions about the world. On the whole, I liked suburbia. Suburbia is well suited to children in the single-digit phase of development, when their needs are basic and minimal, mainly the availability of playmates and safe, *accessible* places to play games of their own invention. These things I had in spades. I had two little cohorts, one right across the street, the other down the block. We had spacious houses with vast (to a small child) base-ments, equipped in my case with a big Lionel train layout built by Dad, a junior woodworking bench, and a Ping-Pong table. We had backyards commodious enough for hardball games. We had bikes and all the streets of our "development" to roam in. For two of the three years I lived in sub-urbia, we had woods of several hundred acres adjoining our development. It served as a wilderness whose allure for a boy of six I have elaborated on in my previous book. (The third year it became a vast construction site for more suburban homes, with a different but equal allure.)

During these suburban years, therefore, I was exquisitely happy. The things we lacked were exactly those establishments and institutions that children of six and seven do not need to socialize successfully with their peers: shops, restaurants, sports facilities, theaters, museums, and libraries. Had I remained in suburbia I'm quite sure I would have eventually felt the lack of these things and the connections with a larger world that they rep-resent, as indeed my cohorts did who remained behind—which is why, I suppose, their teenage years centered on the artificial stimulation of mari-juana and rock and roll.

Anyway, at age eight I was uprooted a second time and transplanted back to Manhattan. This was the fall of 1957. My mother and I moved to an apartment on 93rd Street and Lexington Avenue. It was a so-so neigh-borhood, a little too close to the huge old Jacob Ruppert brewery (which exuded a miasma of hops on certain days of the brewing cycle) and also rather close to Spanish Harlem, which literally began at 96th Street, the Rio Grande of Manhattan. Gone for me was all the insulation of suburban development life, with its secure sameness and reassuring greenery. Instead of the front lawn, I now had a lobby, and a rather sinister elevator man named Roy, who rarely spoke, and who whistled a melancholy tune with a creepy tremolo effect that suggested he'd failed at professional whistling somewhere along the line, and who whistled his execrable tune exactly the same way every time I rode the elevator so that it became the score to a movie I thought of as *Whistling Roy the Child Murderer*, and who was miss-ing his right thumb. I was fascinated by the stump that remained, and couldn't help staring at the shiny scar as his hand rested on the elevator's throttle lever. The harder I stared, the harder Roy whistled, as though he were plotting his latest thrill-killing. By and by, there was some murky in-cident in which Roy came to our apartment door late one night, perhaps under the influence, and was prevented from entering only by the security chain. As a result of this escapade he was cashiered and vanished from the scene. I'm sure I assumed that he was coming after me that night, though more likely the incident was inspired by my mom, a good-looking divorcee in her thirties. For a few months I worried about meeting him on some dark, deserted street, and then I began to wonder if he might turn up whistling on the Ed Sullivan show with the harmonica-playing midgets and the rest of the oddball vaudevillians.

In suburbia, money had meant nothing to me. I never had any, and there was nowhere to spend it. One of the first features of city life that came to my notice was the proximity of shops and other places that purveyed goods and services. A mastery of America's simple currency system followed this discovery, and I was soon happily buying ten-cent comic books, Mars bars, vampire magazines, joy buzzers, and disappearing ink at the newsstand that operated around the corner on Lexington.

I enrolled at Public School Number Six—P.S. 6 in New York argot—at Madison and 82nd Street, and here I first learned about restaurants. The school had the very liberal policy of releasing its inmates to the streets at noon recess. The dismal cuisine of the cafeteria was optional. I doubt that I sampled it more than twice. Instead, we little cosmopolites frequented the local bistros where a charbroiled burger, french fries and a cherry Coke came to a dollar even, plus a fifteen cent tip for the counterman. My personal favorite was Prexy's on 86th Street, featuring "the hamburger with a college education," where each item was delivered from the grill on the flatbed car of an electric train. Of course, I was not always so flush, and on leaner days visited the pushcart of the resident hot-dog man, a tragi-comic figure bundled in rags who spoke only one barely comprehensible English phrase: "*Moostroonokraut?*" meaning did the customer want mustard, onions, sauerkraut, or some combo? There was no guesswork as to price because the menu was printed boldly on his umbrella: "Hot dogs—15 cents, sodas—10 cents," and it was a very limited menu.

The mind-boggling array of amusements available in New York to a child of eight made suburbia seem like a sensory deprivation tank. The Metropolitan Museum of Art stood a block away from P.S. 6. We went there constantly, especially to the galleries of arms and armor, and by Thanksgiving of my first year in the city I had become an expert in bodkins, poniards, krises, dirks, daggers, halberds, maces, and broadswords.

The Met housed the mummy's tomb, a kind of holy sepulcher to someone growing up in the golden age of horror movies. I also liked the reconstructed colonial kitchens and eighteenth century parlors in the remote American wing, with their weird lighting effects and sense of transporting the casual visitor back in time, as though any moment Mrs. Alexander Hamilton might step through the doorway and be horrified to see a boy in a polo coat staring at her furniture. In those days the Met did without the shakedown artists who now guard the entrance demanding "donations." It was unabashedly free, as was the Museum of the City of New York up on 104th Street and Fifth Avenue, with its fabulous collection of model ships and its magical dioramas of historical vignettes like the Blizzard of '88 and Peter Minuet conning the Indians.

It was a more complicated journey, with a crosstown bus transfer, to the Museum of Natural History, but well worth it because the dinosaurs were there, along with the shrunken heads, the blue whale, a live tarantula and scorpion exhibit, and a stuffed specimen of the world's most perverse creature: a deep-sea-dwelling anglerfish with its male mate *growing out of a stalk on its forehead!* This, too, was gloriously free, though the attached planetarium charged a whopping 35 cents for the show about the wise men and the Christmas star.

For the same amount of money I could get into triple features in the more run-down movie theaters on 86th Street, which occupied me from lunchtime clear to supper on drizzly Saturdays. The selections usually lacked any unifying theme. A typical bill featured *Samson and Delilah* with Victor Mature, *Little Abner,* with Stubby Kaye—both in color—and some grim adult film noir "B" thriller in black-and-white starring Richard Conte. To be exposed to such a sheer volume and variety of Hollywood rubbish surely had some broad educational value.

Over the years I discovered the city's other attractions on my own, or with my new city cohorts. There was, of course, Central Park with its rowboats for hire, Cherry Hill for sledding in winter, and the zoo (also free of charge then), which in those days actually boasted live lions, tigers, bears, gorillas, monkeys, and elephants—though not very happy ones, given the Death Row ambience of their quarters. The Staten Island ferry cost a laughable five cents and seemed, to a boy of nine, like an Atlantic crossing. Yankee Stadium was a fifteen-minute IRT ride from the Upper East Side, and children were treated just like any other paying customers there.

A choice after-school entertainment venue was the first-floor game empo-
rium of Abercrombie and Fitch, on 45th and Madison, where all the beautifully made English parlor games were out on display to be tried by
shoppers, and any reasonably well-dressed boy could play skittles or Brain-
teaser for hours without interference. (When you got bored nudging ball-
bearings into little slots and pockets, there was the gun department
upstairs.) Along similar lines was the Fascination arcade on Seventh Avenue off Times Square, where the basement was crammed with obsolete
game machines of pre-World War One vintage that actually operated for a
penny or two. What they lacked in electronic pizzazz and sound effects,
they made up for in mechanical elegance, with the little painted metal figure of Christy Mathewson hurling steel baseballs at the swinging figure
(chipped with age) of Honus Wagner.

Perhaps the most subtle entertainment I discovered was the pleasure of
sitting in hotel lobbies, watching adults come and go, among them the occasional celebrity like ZsaZsa Gabor or Harry Truman. The huge Waldorf
and stately Plaza were my hangouts of choice. Whenever approached by
some unctuous bell captain as to my reason for occupying a chair for such
a long time, I would reply in an all-purpose "foreign" accent (part Bela Lu-
gosi, part Charlie Chan) "Merry Chreestmas. America it is a wonderfool
country," and then they generally left me alone.

The important point in all this is that I was very much at liberty in the
great city. A child could move about in relative safety most anywhere in
town, even Times Square. Bus and subway fare ran to fifteen cents in those
days, and, in fact, was free to schoolchildren, who were issued monthly
transit passes. It was not necessary, and hardly desirable, to be accompanied by a parent to any of the places I frequented.

My old chums back in suburbia, whom I visited now and again, began to
show sure signs of social retardation as we slouched toward puberty. A trip
to the Coke machine at the nearest gas station was high adventure to
them. Their moms had to bring them to suburban department stores for
school clothes; I simply borrowed my mom's Bloomingdale's charge card
and shopped for my own button-down shirts and chinos. My suburban
chums wouldn't have had the slightest idea how to order in an Indian
restaurant, or even how to act. If pressed they might guess that a Van Gogh
was a kind of Chevrolet. Their experience of major league baseball was
limited to the 19-inch black-and-white screen. They had no regular ses-

sions, as I did, gazing into the eyes of a 400-pound gorilla sucking on an or-ange rind. I certainly never told them about the pleasures of hotel lobby sitting—it would've been like explaining life on Mars.

Though I acquired a stepfather who was a very nice man in the maga-zine business, and we eventually moved to a larger, nicer, apartment on 68th Street, my double-digit years growing up in the city turned rather grim. School was the problem. I finished at P.S. 6 and moved up to junior high. The gerrymandered district of the Senator Robert F. Wagner Inter-mediate School ran up the East Side in a slender ribbon and mushroomed in Harlem. I found myself in the sudden strange predicament of being overwhelmingly in the racial minority, and subject to routine persecutions because of it. This was the era before children brought firearms to school, but other means of intimidation and extortion existed, and I was often per-suaded to part with my pocket money. Fistfights erupted at each change of classes. Unprovoked attacks happened all the time. Visiting the lavatory was a form of suicide, so one developed supernatural powers of bladder control, and I learned to eschew the drinking fountains (where one's face was apt to be shoved into the basin anyway by passing pranksters). The building itself, a Modernist box designed to absorb abuse rather than exalt young spirits, had the steel-trap feel of a county penitentiary. I was miser-able there.

What followed was an improvement from the personal security stand-point, but a disaster otherwise. I applied to, and was accepted by, the renowned High school of Music and Art, a public school for "gifted" youngsters, who came to it from every far-flung corner of the five boroughs. This was the essence of the problem. Most of my schoolmates, including the ones I was disposed to be pals with, lived in the nether reaches of the Bronx, Brooklyn, and Queens, meaning they might as well have lived in Czechoslovakia. I never saw them after school. Later on, this made dating rather difficult. Our days were extraordinarily long, for on top of a regular academic load, we endured two extra hours of music rehearsal or, in my case, studio art instruction. And except for the semiannual concert and art show, there was no such thing as extracurricular activities—no sports teams, no proms. The school happened to be located in the center of the City College Campus in Harlem, an hour-long bus ride up a torturous route from 68th Street—and I lived relatively close compared to many other kids. One beleaguered boy in my home room, a clarinet genius with a prematurely heavy beard that gave him the look of a fifteen-year-old Richard Nixon, actually lived illicitly over the Nassau County line on Long Island (which would have disqualified him from attending M & A if it were known), and his combined journey by bus, commuter train, and subway took two hours each way in good weather.

Altogether these circumstances made me a solitary teenager, despite a sociable nature, and in time I began to pine for another way of life. I'd outgrown many of my childhood haunts, like the game department at Abercrombies. I'd long lost the price advantage that juvenile status confers on moviegoers. I knew all the museums so well that I could have given guided tours with a Bloomingdale's bag over my head. I was completely jaded with cosmopolis and its vaunted wonders. What I really longed to do at this stage was fish for bass, ride motorcycles, and go to teen dances with girls named Alice—none of which were available in my world. So I grew to loathe, detest and resent New York, and starting at about sixteen took to hanging out in bars, cadging drinks in exchange for being clever, and at seventeen, heading to college far, far upstate on a Greyhound bus, I departed my hometown as a permanent resident forever.

THE QUINTESSENTIAL PEDESTRIAN TOWN

Now I am forty-seven and have managed to live all my adult life outside of New York City. I spent my twenties and thirties fishing, riding motorcycles, and carrying on with females who could have been named Alice, and have pretty much got all that out of my system. The emotional gales of youth have blown out to sea, and with them my old grievances and resentments about city life. I no longer indulge in self-psychoanalysis, trying to figure out how Mom and Dad deformed me. Indeed, both are still alive in Manhattan (in separate apartments), and I rather enjoy visiting them from time to time.

My feelings about my old hometown have also changed in light of my professional interest in the issues of landscape and townscape. Though I have lived in a classic Main Street town nearly two decades now, I am always impressed at how much better Manhattan actually functions as a pedestrian village. Except for a few parts of a few cities, America is now thoroughly suburbanized, and one is forever getting in and out of cars, searching for a parking space, frittering life away in traffic. One can't help going to the mall, because that's where the necessities of life are—Main Street having become a permanent flea market.

I go to New York City perhaps six times a year, and what I like to do best is walk around Manhattan. For all its problems, New York has managed to do one thing that so many other towns and cities have fatally failed to do: preserve its basic pattern. The street grid is essentially the same as it was in 1930, or, indeed, 1900. No heroic utopian postwar redevelopment scheme was imposed over Manhattan; it *was* the original Radiant City quite on its own terms. How sad that Charles Edouard Jeanneret, *Le Corbusier,* the godfather of Modernist urban theory, saw only the dazzling towers, failing to notice what was going on at street level, where the action truly was. (Corb *hated* "filthy" city streets, especially the ones in Paris. He hated rubbing elbows with strangers, looking into the faces of the passing throng with all those inquisitive, penetrating eyes drilling into him. He seemed to hate the essence of the city. Apparently what he liked was riding in elevators by himself.)

No limited access highways were imposed over the face of Manhattan, as they were in absolutely every other U.S. city, though expressways ring the island's perimeter, spoiling the waterfront. A major portion of this system, the elevated West Side Highway, has disintegrated and was simply shut down a generation ago. Today ailanthus trees sprout on its derelict trestles and it begins to take on the ruined grandeur of a Roman aqueduct. Robert Moses wanted to build an eight-lane crosstown freeway at Houston Street in the 1950s and was repulsed by a public uproar—one of his rare defeats. The basic armature of the city endures.

Above Astor Place, it is a mechanistic grid of numbered streets running relentlessly to the points of the compass. Discounting obvious landmarks, like the Frick Museum, or the Empire State Building, the blocks within a neighborhood can seem identical; only the neighborhoods or districts change in character. The garment district looks much different than the upper East Side, which looks different than the upper West Side. A lifelong resident—my mom, for instance—blindfolded and plunked down at mid-block, say, on 73rd Street between Madison and Fifth, might be hard pressed to state exactly where she was within a quarter-mile.

Yet orientation is much simpler here than in Paris or Florence, as the streets all meet at right angles and the street corners all have signs, and any corner is, at most, a minute's walk from where you happen to be. The numbered streets go north and the numbered avenues march west. The anomalies of Lexington, Park and Madison avenues are easier to understand, within the general scheme, than the irregularities of English grammar. What New Yorkers lack in geometric variety, they get back in navigability. I daresay a ten-year-old Kentuckian of median intelligence could figure out how to get from Grand Central Station to Carnegie Hall faster than a French bumpkin could figure out how to get from Notre Dame to the Place Vendome.

Driving to New York City—as I must do occasionally when transporting bulky things, or my dog, who is not permitted to ride the train—is not such a nightmare as it might seem. Understand, I don't recommend it. I prefer the train and take it most of the time. I merely state that driving to town poses no extraordinary hazards or hardships. The old grid of streets works because the rich network of interconnecting streets provides a tremendous choice of routes to any particular destination. Even the old soot-blackened Central Park transverses, built for horsedrawn vehicles in the 1850s, retain their original dimensions yet convey motorized traffic with something that resembles efficiency. Of course, upon arrival you must stash your vehicle in a garage for the duration of your stay.

New York remains the quintessential pedestrian town—at least by American standards. Once at large on the sidewalks, a pedestrian has the firm sense of belonging there, of being in a place intentionally designed to the scale of the individual human being, however high the skyscrapers soar. Cars are present, but they do not have sole occupancy rights to the public realm. In the rest of America the pedestrian is irrelevant at best, and more usually a public nuisance. Where I live, you are enjoined by law from walking (or bicycling) on the main artery to the shopping mall district at the edge of town, and once there, no sidewalks connect the sprawling malls and hulking superstores to one another. It turns out that the cold, cruel Big Apple is designed as though people matter, while more and more in small-town America the individual is made to feel that he doesn't count. Small-town America has also been willingly colonized by corporate giants, who kill off the local merchant class, while it is New York City that fosters and nourishes small-scale business.

This class of local, small entrepreneurs makes walking around New York so rewarding. The vast majority of street-level shops and eating places are owned by people on the premises who care about what they do, and, in some cases, do what they do supremely well. The American outlands, in contrast, having surrendered completely to the national chain stores, must make do with the lowest common denominator merchandise mass-produced by third world factory slaves, and sold by $4.50-an-hour teenagers who have no personal stake in the operation, little to no knowledge about the product, and couldn't care less either about the customer or the company's long-term prospects. You can drive for an hour up the immense Route 441 commercial strip between Kissimmee and Orlando, Florida, and pass dozens of franchise fry pits, not a single one worth eating in. The blocks between 50th and 60th streets between Park and Fifth avenues contain more good restaurants than all the kudzu-infested counties between Atlanta and New Orleans.

In the city, every possible commercial niche is occupied, sometimes by products for which one might never have conceived a purpose. One store in the garment district sells nothing but satin tassels (at up to $500 each) for tying back draperies. A shop two blocks east of Penn Station (or the underground bunker that remains of it) sells stuffed water buffalo heads and mounted freeze-dried Mexican tarantulas. There is a fountain pen hospital in the financial district. In Chinatown you can buy duck feet and fish heads in sidewalk stalls. You can buy marijuana, crack cocaine, and sex up on Times Square. You can buy a Vermeer on Madison and 75th. There's a market for everything, including quite a few good things, and the city is a market entire, and the pedestrian has easy access to all of it. And whether one is buying or not, the trip itself is rich with sensations. You can't walk ten blocks in any direction without encountering shopfront extravaganzas of roasted meats, hand-made pastries, iced fishes, marzipans, pizzas, calzones, knishes, cannoli, kirschtortes, and a thousand other edible wonders. It's another irony that mainstream suburban America is full of diet-crazed fat people traveling about in cars, while New Yorkers walk off so many calories on a daily basis that they can eat great things with a clear conscience.

Manhattan is exciting because so many people live over the store. Scores of apartments with hundreds of denizens soar to occupy the airspace over the shops and markets. This density keeps the streets supplied with live bodies after sunset and gives the city its touted vitality. Living close to where you shop and do business is another essential of urban life generally extirpated elsewhere. New York City never surrendered to the absurdity of single-use zoning. It remains resolutely *mixed use* in character. Within 300 yards of my mom's building on 68th Street, there are five food markets, a U.S. post office, two liquor stores, three Chinese, two Italian, and one Afghani restaurants, five saloons, four newsstands, three flower shops, a bike shop, a video store, a catering establishment, a locksmith, a picture framer, lamp, shoe, book, furniture, and electronics shops, two dry cleaners, three branch banks, four movie theaters, one legitimate theater, three public parking garages, a high school, a major hospital, and more freelance psychiatrists, dentists, chiropractors, haircutters and dog-walkers than you could shake a stick at.

Many of these operations deliver. My mom can phone up the market with a list at noon and later that day a carton full of groceries will magically appear at her door on the twelfth floor. The cleaners, the liquor store and the Chinese restaurants also deliver. New Yorkers are pampered and catered to and they are fussy. They complain when they don't like the service or the merchandise, and guess what: it improves because the guy on the receiving end owns the business and he has to be concerned about what his customers think. This kind of behavior, and the assumptions about human nature that go with it, is what makes New Yorkers seem so bizarre to other Americans (and vice versa), who live out of their cars these days and rarely have face-to-face encounters with retail personnel older than nineteen. My mom's reaction to the suburban voids of Florida was unalloyed horror, and the Floridians' view of her world is similar.

There is a cost to all this human variety, richness of trade, and easy access to good things. It is expensive to live in Manhattan, especially in a nice building in a good neighborhood. For most young people lacking trust funds, it is unaffordable, unless they double or triple up, or find lodgings in worse neighborhoods. I know people in honorable vocations who live in places akin to roach motels. They persevere because the city itself is their living room, dining room, and entertainment center, and all they require of their apartments is a place to sleep and change outfits. If they are entering the matrimonial zone, with any notions of offspring, then there is the school question, nowadays a Hieronymus Bosch vision of the blackboard jungle. My raucous junior high school of thirty years ago seems like a Jesuit academy compared to today's chaotic free-fire zones. For civilized children public school is really out of the question, and so you can ratchet up the cost-of-living another twenty grand per year per child.

There naturally follows the public safety issue for people of all ages. My dad was mugged several times when in his sixties and seventies. He gives up his loot without a peep and lives. He's probably lucky. Other equally accommodating victims end up with their wallets lifted *and* their brains splattered on the sidewalk. You never know when the angel of death, dressed in high top sneakers and a sideways hat, will descend from the express platform and stop your celestial clock. The suspense arising out of this prospect is one of the excitements of urban life that people could happily do without. Yet it would be an error to think that murder and robbery are modern novelties unique to postwar America. Urban violence is something that seems to come and go in cycles and the great cities in history have all been beset at one time or another. Bandits owned the streets in the Rome of Diocletian. Venice in Casanova's time was a human sewer after dark. Gainsborough's London was infested with footpads, pickpockets, gin-fiends, baby-snatchers, cutthroats, and whores. New York City a hundred years ago spawned homicidal gangs like the Dead Rabbits. Today's violence seems to stand out for two reasons: first, it poses a stark contrast to the relatively calm period between 1920 and 1960—the years when, as is so often remarked by my parents' cohorts, people could sleep in Central Park on hot summer nights—and secondly, because the kind of firepower in the hands of boys nowadays would make an old-fashioned public enemy like John Dillinger turn green with envy.

Finally, there are the subsidiary woes of city life: the noise, the crowds, the pushing, the smells, the sirens ululating at all hours, the soul-sapping heat of summer, the decrepitating subway stations, the inevitable lines outside the movie theaters, the days when garbage overflows the sidewalks, the blithering crack-heads in the ATM vestibules, the cockroach climbing out of your moo shu pork, the cab drivers who don't know where Lincoln Center is, the people who look so much better than you ever will, the vagrant moments when the size and scale and roar and flash of the city are all too much, and one longs for peace.

RELIEF

When the idea to create a large, romantically picturesque landscaped park percolated into public consciousness in the 1850s, the logical spot for it seemed to be the 150-acre tract known as Jones Woods. The building that I grew up in from age eleven on, at 68th Street, stands well within its old boundaries. New York was booming in 1850. Since 1800 the population had quintupled to half a million. Development had reached 30th Street with no prospect for stopping there. The city's unique character as an island posed special problems: the downtown inhabitants were surrounded on three sides by water. Open countryside, once an easy walk, became increasingly inaccessible. The relentless grid of blocks made speculation and development easy, but the awesome monotony of the pattern began to distress even the ruling mercantile elite, who recognized the need for some kind of relief in the way of civic art. A handful of small park-like squares already existed, but some, like Gramercy Park, were private fenced-and-locked preserves belonging to the surrounding homeowners, and others, like City Hall Park, were untended scraps of public land without formal walks, benches, or plantings.

All manner of new industrial concerns were springing up over lower Manhattan at mid-century, many of them smelly and obnoxious: distilleries, slaughterhouses, soap, paint, and bone-boiling factories. Coal dust and dried horse manure dust hung in the streets. The city suffered the nation's highest mortality rate. A cholera epidemic carried away five thousand in 1849. Medical opinion of that day held that disease was caused by "bad air" and that infusions of fresh air would provide general prophylactic relief. Public parks, the thinking went, would act as the city's "lungs." They would also provide a venue for "manly and moral sports" to replace degenerate pastimes such as drinking, gambling, and cockfighting, popular among the swelling ranks of workingmen.

Jones Wood occupied a square parcel between what is now 66th and 76th streets and Third Avenue and the East River. It was the landscaped private country estate of a tavern keeper, John Jones, whose daughter had married into the wealthy Schermerhorn family. The estate was noted for its lawns, orchards, secluded lanes, blackberry patches, and its views up and down the river. In 1850 the common council resolved to seek state authorization to acquire the land. It happened that the Joneses and Schermerhorns didn't want to sell. So, one of their neighbors, State Senator James Beekman, introduced a bill at Albany to permit the city to take Jones Woods through eminent domain. Eventually the courts struck down the 1851 Jones Wood authorization bill.

Other park proposals were aired over the next two years, and the one that caught the public's imagination was for an enormous rectangular tract running roughly from the present-day 58th Street to 106th Street between Fifth and Seventh avenues. It would incorporate a new city reservoir that had to be built anyway and thus give the city the benefit of two major public works in one package. This is substantially the Central Park that exists today, though its boundaries are marginally different.

The uptown wards were well along in the process of losing their rural character by 1852. They contained half a dozen village centers, like Yorkville, Harlem, and Bloomingdale (the upper West Side), while the landscape between these was dotted by a motley assortment of old estates, small farms, cabins, factories, as well as orphanages, hospitals, and insane asylums. The site for the future Central Park was a rugged area of swamp, ravine, and copse, with bedrock jutting clear out of the ground in many places. About 1,500 people lived there, many of them in a settlement called Seneca Village located at what today is the mid-80s off Central Park West. Its population was about two-thirds free Africans and one-third Irish. It boasted three churches and a school. The park area residents were often lumped together as "squatters" in the press, but many of them either owned the land they lived on or paid rent. A Commission of Estimate took several years to assess thousands of parcels, and in 1855 $5 million was paid to compensate property owners for the public taking of parkland. It took another two years to clear the park of buildings and inhabitants. In 1858, Frederick Law Olmsted and Calvert Vaux won the design competition over thirty-two other entries with their "Greensward Plan." With Olmsted serving as Superintendent and Vaux as Chief Architect, the great work of building Central Park commenced.

A SUPREME ARTIFACT

Around noon on Thanksgiving Day, 1993, on a visit to town for the holiday, I went over to Central Park to clear my head before the traditional ritual of gluttony. The park entrance at Fifth Avenue and 69th Street is a modest cleft in the wall leading to a paved footpath. Not two steps down the path, I encountered the kind of weird and beguiling mystery that only seems possible in our post-modern age. There on a bench sat a pile of clothes: a blouse and what looked like a skirt lay carefully folded. On top of them, neatly side by side, stood two gold-flecked high-heeled women's party pumps. Underneath the bench, strewn rather than folded, lay a pair of women's underpants and a brassiere.

One's first impulse was to search the vicinity for a body—except there were no clumps of bushes around, only a few scraggly azaleas, nor any other landscape features or structures where a naked body might be stashed. Did I say naked? Well, the clothes *were* there. The mental leap was natural. Of course, one had to ask why either a victim or a murderer/rapist would take the trouble to fold a bunch of clothing *just so* in the commission of some monstrous crime. And, having taken so much care, then what was the meaning of the underwear strewn below? Altogether it suggested something more along the lines of an impulsive skinny-dipping by a carefree sophomore—except this spot was a quarter of a mile in either direction from the Conservatory Pond or the lake, and it was late November, less than fifty degrees, Fahrenheit. Was this perhaps some kind of alfresco art installation, a "statement" about homelessness or the exploitation of women or the wickedness of synthetic fibers? If so, had the display simply been left there by the artist, to be disassembled by the needy, or blown about in the weather? Or was somebody up in a Fifth Avenue penthouse a hundred yards away recording the reactions of perplexed passersby such as myself on videotape through a telephoto lens, while nibbling perfect little ingots of sushi?

As I stood there racking my brain, several other people entered the park: an elderly man with a dog, a middle-aged female jogger dressed in the latest spandex gear, a young man on rollerblades. I was positioned so that anyone coming in would have to see the mysterious pile of clothes. But none of them paid the slightest attention. This perplexed me further. Might this be the essence of the post-modern condition: that such displays *had no* inherent meaning, that in the process of *deconstructing* the *text* (i.e., the pile of clothes), I was assigning meaning where none had been intended? And what about the random chemical activity in my own brain? Had I eaten, say, a banana before leaving my mom's apartment, would I have reacted differently? Finally I gave up and continued on my way. But the incident was instructive, I soon realized, because such a fatuous intellectual struggle as the one I was engaged in would have been inimical to the sort of nineteenth century minds that created Central Park.

Theirs was a world of clear intent, and the clear intent of Olmsted and Vaux was to create an idealized romantic landscape that stood as a monument to what human beings were leaving behind in the evolutionary rush to industrialize and urbanize. They were well aware that the whole of Manhattan eventually would be paved over and built upon (this feat was accomplished in their lifetimes), that the island city would be more cut off from the rest of America than ever before, and that the 843 acres of Central Park would be the only rural landscape some city dwellers might get to for months at a time, perhaps ever in their lives. It is fair to say that the *central* experience of nineteenth century western culture was the mass movement of individuals away from land and landscape into the urban machine future. And so there always has been about Central Park a bittersweet aura of yearning for that which is gone forever. The park was a metaphor that everybody in that age could get at some level.

Central Park is not only a monument to a bygone phase of human evolution, it was also built *in the mode* of that earlier phase: entirely by hand, so we must recognize it as a gigantic handmade antique. The kinds of machines eventually developed for moving vast quantities of earth hadn't been invented by 1858. At the peak of construction, the summers of 1858–59, Olmsted superintended 3,600 workers. Common laborers were paid between 90 cents and $1.25 a day. The scale rose and fell according to the park commission's cash on hand. Foremen received $1.50 a day. The 160 stonecutters got $2.25. Stonebreakers were paid nine cents per cubic yard. Pavers received ten cents a day more than common laborers and blasting foremen got an extra 25 cents for hazardous duty. (Five workers were killed altogether.) The standard workday ran ten hours. The workers were organized into four great divisions subdivided into specialty teams and gangs: grubbers, graders, blasters, carters, wheelbarrow-men, blacksmiths, carpenters, masons and gardeners. The majority of the common laborers were Irish—"a small army of Hibernians"—while most of the gardeners were Germans. All of them were easily exploited because the financial panic of 1857 and the depression that followed it made jobs scarce.

While the task presented all kinds of engineering and construction problems—often solved impromptu—it was in essence a work of art, conceived as an artistic vision by men who considered themselves artists. This artistry is the most manifest element about the park today, and more than ever a contrast to the electrified urban colossus that surrounds it. The park's landscape flows at a scale and rhythm that is quite absent even in the rural landscapes of our own time, which we most often experience at fifty miles per hour, sealed inside our cars. It was designed in an era when human beings moved at a walk and very few wheeled vehicles or mounted equestrians sped about in a sustained fashion. So the handmade quality of the park's landscape and the artifacts in it—the bridges, the belvederes, the mall and its terrace—with all their careful embellishments, were matched to a rate of human locomotion that allowed a person to take it all in. This is what makes a walk in Central Park such a different (and more satisfying) experience than a drive in a Chevrolet along any state highway in Vermont.

That Thanksgiving Day, 1993, I proceeded on foot from the mystery clothing pile toward the Mall, through glades and dells little changed since my childhood. The scenic roadways—built originally for rich folk to enjoy recreational carriage rides—were closed to auto traffic but thronged instead with joggers, race-walkers, skaters, and cyclists working off big-calorie deficits for the holiday feast to follow. A hundred and thirty years ago ice-skating became a mania practically overnight when the park's lake was first filled, and it was a shockingly big deal for female skaters to inadvertently expose their hosieried ankles. Today the women marathon-runners-in-training whiz by in skintight body suits, their breasts shifting liquidly beneath the Lycra at every stride, and one is supposed to not notice. I am a runner myself back home, and enjoy an endorphin blast as much as the next guy, yet there seemed something both comic and pathetic about this mob of striving aerobicists. The spectacle of them panting along in what might be various orders of underwear surely would have horrified Victorians of any age, sex, or class. What seems normal today may be a laughable or frightful snapshot one hundred years from now.

The word *mall* has undergone an unfortunate mutation in our time. The Mall in Central Park bears no resemblance to the vast shopping bunkers that sprawl at every freeway interchange in America. This Mall is really the common street idealized, a long straight, formal, outdoor public room, sheltered under towering sycamore trees. Cars are wonderfully absent. Strollers, roller skaters, and various vaudevillian exhibitionists animate the central corridor. Benches line the Mall's edge from end to end, and even on this November day they were full of people doing what human beings seem to have an insatiable appetite for: watching other people. In its rich simplicity of design, this Mall underscores the current extraordinary impoverishment of civic art and civic life elsewhere in our everyday world.

The Mall terminates in the Bethesda Terrace, which was undoubtedly the park's heart in the minds of its creators. The terrace, with its large central fountain, a wonderful public space on its own terms, serves as a viewing platform for the lake and the high rocky outcroppings on the far shore. On this November day, the rowboats lay overturned and stacked for winter storage. The scene, with its picturesque backdrop, was serene, lovely, and specific, the antithesis of the grinding anonymous highway crudscape where so much of our national life takes place today. Far behind the lake loomed the distant towers of the great city, forming a massive, continuous wall enclosing the whole park.

A young woman in earth-colored casuals worked three lumbering retrievers where the terrace met the water's edge in a set of steps, tossing a stick for them over and over. It was hard to imagine the sort of city apartment that might accommodate such a pack of beasts, and then one recalled those amazing rambling duplexes in the prewar buildings on Park Avenue—you've glimpsed them in the Woody Allen movies—which can be as spacious as Connecticut country houses, and even look like them inside. In fact, I'd begun to notice semiconsciously that the park was full of a particular class of people that one rarely encounters in numbers anymore: rich WASPs. There were whole golden-haired, square-jawed, tweed-covered families of them—families being another oddity these days—strolling arm in arm, laughing and gabbing as if, for a few hours, they might be forgiven for racism, poverty, homelessness, pollution, corporate misfeasance and all the other ills of society. Taking the path around the boathouse at the east end of the lake, I followed not far behind just such a family, which included three loose-limbed collegiate offspring, when the distant cry, "Stop! Thief!" resounded from the rocky area known as the Ramble in the near distance. The family stopped, as I did, and we all pricked up our ears. No one properly identifiable as a thief ran into view. The father cocked his head toward the dark mass of rock and foliage and gravely pronounced the word "mayhem," as though he had just cracked some code explaining the entire premillennial zeitgeist. Then he laughed, exposing a brilliant set of Teddy Rooseveltean horse teeth, and the happy brood continued onward to turkey, cranberry sauce, and pumpkin pie in—one supposed—their magnificent chintz-bedizened prewar apartment.

My own family has a historical connection with the city's legacy of mayhem. I learned some years ago that my great-grandmother was one of the victims in a double murder/suicide in 1909. Her name was Dorothy Koff. She was the daughter of the city water commissioner and she had eloped some years earlier with my great-grandfather David Harburger, a young, poetically minded lawyer, who was the son of city Excise Commissioner Julius Harburger. The young couple had two daughters, one of them my grandmother. By and by Dorothy and David divorced—a scandalous thing in those days, but no more scandalous than the elopement had been. David drank himself to death in 1905. Dorothy remarried a violinist. One day this violinist came home and found Dorothy with an encyclopedia salesman—in each other's arms, or not, remains unclear. The violinist drew his pocket pistol, shot the salesman dead, shot Dorothy dead, and shot himself dead. My grandmother and her little sister witnessed the shooting. My great-great-grandfather, Julius Harburger, outlived his son and daughter-in-law. He had changed positions in the Tammany machine and was serving as county coroner at the time of the murders. We can only imagine what it was like the night that those particular bodies came into his place of business. As coroner, he managed to keep the sordid story out of the newspapers, though the event plainly unhinged him. *The New York Times* reported later that year that he had departed the city for a Lake George vacation "Railing at Police," as the headline said, and calling "police investigation of capital crime a farce." Two years later Julius Harburger was elected Sheriff of New York County, which is to say, Manhattan. He tried to appoint women as deputies but the courts overruled him. His 1914 obituary says that "as Sheriff he made it a custom to attend boxing bouts and often saw fit to interfere when they were not conducted according to his idea of sport and fair play." He drew his last breath in a brownstone that still stands on St. Mark's Place.

MY CITY IN HISTORY

When I boarded the Greyhound bus that took me from New York City to college thirty years ago, it was with the firm sense, even then, that I would never return on a full-time basis. For the last twenty years, I've lived in a classic Main Street town 175 miles upstate. It has suited me pretty well, though the town has made great strides toward utterly destroying its essential character in an absurd quest for "growth." I have a life here and I will probably remain for some time. Yet it is easy for me to come down to the city and I find more to admire about it all the time.

For all its present difficulties I believe that New York will endure even when other American cities like Los Angeles and Phoenix implode, because New York's physical armature is so sturdy, and because it depends so little on cars. The nation might run out of gasoline tomorrow and New York City would be one of the few places that could carry on business. Arguably, it might carry on better without ninety percent of the motor vehicles that currently infest its streets (including mine, when I'm there). The city's urbanism is adaptable because it is ageless. The many blocks and their buildings are endlessly recyclable, and in small enough pieces so that the cycle of birth-death-rebirth takes place continuously as in the cells of a gigantic coral reef.

Industrialism spurred New York's most robust phase of development, and in the technology-mad twentieth century the city grew into a bloated, soaring colossus. I personally believe that the city's scale can and will be reduced. It was probably necessary for mankind's collective ego to prove that such tall buildings as the Empire State and World Trade Center towers could be built, but it seems to me that the distortions of population density these monsters produce aren't worth it. They overload neighborhoods and strain the infrastructure. It is hard to say what an optimum building size might be there—Paris produces a very agreeable metropolitan density at about six stories. Perhaps New York would thrive at twelve stories. I don't have an exact figure and I don't suppose anyone else does. We have not yet seen any really big buildings taken down, but I believe the time will come in the next century when such demolitions will become routine. The grid could use some artistic modification and there's no reason to think it won't happen. New York's equivalent of Baron Haussmann may be a six-year-old kid in Chinatown today.

America was never mad for city life. The first two hundred years our thrust for settlement took the form of pioneering the wilderness. Everything about the rise of big cities in America was a kind of industrial nightmare, and everything about that nightmare only made Americans yearn more dreamily for its supposed antidote: a homestead in the natural landscape. Combine that yearning with some of the more absurd features of democracy, like the mortgage interest deduction and zoning, toss in the most pernicious devices of consumer capitalism, and you have the present alternative to city life in America, which is the mature auto suburb in all its ghastliness.

That this auto suburb is doomed as any sort of plausible habitat should not be doubted. Suburbia is set to tank out. Its laughably flimsy components were meant to be thrown away. Its very formlessness promotes its disposability. It was the negation of everything that makes places worth caring about, and we shall run shrieking from it to a better world.

There is an urbanism in America's future—or else we are not going to have much of a civilization—but it will take a physical form not yet recognizable to us: maybe something about halfway between a modern European city and an American small town. Overblown as it currently is, New York is still one of the best working models out of our own history. Its lessons are not apt to be found in the formless precincts of Orlando, Atlanta, or Houston. It is America's biggest small town. Its battered heart still beats with life.

CHAPTER 12

CODA: WHAT I LIVE FOR

THERE are times I feel so fortunate that I wonder if I am making up this life as it traces its mysterious arc through time. Solipsism is not a very attractive philosophy—especially in others—but such good fortune as I've known seems improbable to one who otherwise doesn't believe in dumb luck. Were I beset by catastrophe tomorrow, I could still say that I lived forty-seven pretty good years. In terms of sheer bulk chronology, I've outlasted George Gershwin, Jesse James, Lord Byron, Wolfgang Mozart, Martin Luther King, Jesus Christ, Huey Long, Lou Gehrig, Stonewall Jackson, Fats Waller, John F. Kennedy, F. Scott Fitzgerald, and one of the Beatles—and a few of these characters were far more beset by troubles in their short lives than I have been so far.

The world is full of terrible places where life is everything Thomas Hobbes said and worse.* For all the shortcomings I perceive about my

*"[In a state of nature] No arts; no letters; no society; and which is worst of all, continual fear and danger of violent death; and the life of man, solitary, poor, nasty, brutish, and short." From *Leviathan*, by Thomas Hobbes, 1651.

homeland these days, I must admit it has allowed me to function freely in my vocation, which is saying a lot. The only conditions I value more are loving relations with friends and kin and a more generalized gratitude for being born in the first place. I am not religious, but I am aware of a spiritual dimension to this mysterious world. As Ludwig Wittgenstein remarked, it is astonishing that anything exists. I believe we pass this way but once, and that this is the source of man's essentially tragic condition. Yet I believe simultaneously, perhaps incongruously, even obdurately and foolishly, that each of us is an offspring of the intelligent and benevolent organism that is the universe—though this model leaves a lot unaccounted for, from war to root canal therapy—and that we remain part of it, in some fashion, everlastingly.

My ancestors were mostly Jewish—the exception being my great-grandmother, a German Christian—but my parents observed none of the Jewish rituals or holidays. They prayed to the *Sunday Times* crossword puzzle. In our house (or apartment, following their divorce and subsequent remarriages) there was always a Christmas tree, and up to the age of six, I received chocolaty visits from the Easter Bunny, with no idea that he died in anguish on a cross for me. For all that, my parents are not the kind of Jews who pretend that they belong to the Swindon Hunt Club. They are cultural Jews, emphatically of the New York persuasion. A lot of Yiddish slang is flung around, mostly for comic effect. "That *farbissener* face!" "What a *farkokteh* idea!" Anyway, Judaism is more about human conduct than eschatology. I was therefore raised in what might be described as a religion-free household. Strange to relate, as a result of my travels around the United States the past seven years, I begin to come to the disquieting conclusion that we Americans are these days a wicked people who deserve to be punished. The idea embarrasses me, but I nevertheless stand by it. I suppose this is what comes of a vocation that places one, for instance, in a New Jersey gambling casino full of overweight slobs pissing away their kids' college tuition in pursuit of "excitement." I therefore also believe in the existence of genuine evil, as embodied, in the Hannah Arendt sense, by the behavior of many well-known American corporations, especially those that prey on the aspirations of children.

Perhaps in consequence of my singular theology, I have rather robust notions about right and wrong. They proceed also from the issue of personal honor, which I define as meaning what one says and vice versa. To

my way of thinking there are few personal virtues more important than being reliable in this sense. As for kindness and generosity, I suspect they derive as much from disposition as culture, and all it takes is a glance at the
Saturday morning TV shows to see how these matters are treated at the
cultural end these days. Experience has disposed me to be kind in my personal dealings and severe in my professional ones. For instance, the culture
of business, including the literature racket, has decayed in step with other
things in America, and the common decencies are seldom observed nowadays. Phone calls are not returned, letters not answered, checks not sent,
agreements not kept, and I get rather irked by all this. I squawk about it to
the amazement of my associates and representatives. The idea that business relations might be regulated by standards of decency makes them
howl with laughter. I believe that standards rise and fall in cycles and that
the time will come again when personal honor means something. I hope I
live to see it. Luckily, that is not all I live for.

I live in a little gray 1820s cottage with Jennifer Armstrong, an author
of children's books. By the time this book is in print, we will be married.
We have two dogs, a cat, and a canoe. Our house is about a two-minute walk
from the town's main street, with all its wonderful attractions. My daily life
is shapely and pleasing. I shape it by observing some self-discipline and am
pleased by the results. I'm not a nut about it, but self-employment does
call for a certain rigor. I believe Flaubert's dictum that *if you want to be
wild in your art, you must be bourgeois in your life*. I keep regular hours. I
commute twenty-seven seconds by bicycle up the street and across a square
to my office, which is a ground-floor apartment in an 1850s building that
was once a hotel. I usually get in before 8:30, depending on the traffic, har
har.

I enjoy writing. I don't suffer from blocks. I have enough ideas for books
to keep me busy for the rest of my life. Yet writing is not easy. I struggle to
produce three decent pages a day. It's like making bratwurst under an elec-
tron microscope. Nevertheless, I amuse myself. The operations of my own
mind entertain me hugely. To avoid overindulgence in that dubious realm,
therefore, I get out around noon, rain or shine, summer or winter, and run
three miles with the dogs. I eat a miserable, abstemious lunch of an apple
and a banana as a weight-control measure—since, in middle age, one develops the metabolism of garden slug. I compose sentences and paragraphs
all afternoon, sipping green tea. At five o'clock I bike over to the YMCA

and swim a mile in the pool to sweep all the bratwurst scraps out of my skull. I am fortunate once again in not having to spend any portion of my day sitting in a car, commuting, as tens of millions of my countrymen do, including many of my friends.

I own a 1992 Toyota pickup truck, but it sits in its parking space on the street for days at a time because most of what I need is within a one-minute bike ride of both my home and office. I exercise a lot because I like to cook and eat. My idea of bigtime fun is to make dinner for eight of my friends and get a little looped on cheap champagne in the process. I almost never work on weekends or evenings.

I never made more than $15,000 in any one year until well after I turned forty. I arrived in this town twenty years ago on a motorcycle from San Francisco after dropping out of the journalism business to write books. I settled here because, before California, I'd worked for a year on the nearby Albany newspaper, and gotten to know Saratoga, and it seemed like a good place to be a starving writer of books nobody had asked to be written. Through the seventies and eighties I worked a lot of odd jobs, from orderly in the psychiatric wing of the hospital, to digging holes for percolation tests in housing subdivisions. I lived on brown rice and onions for months on end. It was a stringent existence but there were many compensations. I had that motorcycle (and two successors) and a fly rod and beautiful coun-tryside to ramble about in, and I made lots of friends in town.

Over the years I pounded out eight novels. All of them were published and all of them were commercial flops in any meaningful sense, apart from their literary merit. I picked up some Hollywood option money on most of them. My first novel was optioned thirteen times. The options amounted to a couple of thousand dollars each, spread out over two decades: chump change. None of my books were made into movies. These old novels still turn up now and again in the discontinued merchandise bin at the Kmart. It's like finding a beloved relative in the gutter clutching a bottle in a pa-per bag.

In 1987, I took a badly needed sabbatical from fiction-writing and re-turned to journalism with a series of stories for the *Sunday New York Times Magazine* about land development issues. These led to a proposal for a book that would become *The Geography of Nowhere*. I had no particular creden-tials for the job, which proved to be an advantage, since so many problems with our everyday environment are caused by the *over*-specialization of trained specialists unwilling to look at the bigger picture beyond the narrow purview of their specialty. It was a worthy task for a generalist.

The Geography of Nowhere was moderately successful. It seemed to help people understand their feelings about a subject that had long bewildered them. I became something of a low-grade guru. I received many invitations to speak to civic groups, professional organizations, and colleges around the country. My initial reaction was panic that people were looking to me for illumination. What could be more natural than to feel unworthy of other people's esteem? I am aware that many successful figures secretly feel like frauds, including people far more knowledgeable and accomplished than myself. This is apparently a universal neurosis. Everybody feels inadequate. I've since formulated a social principle called Kunstler's Law, which states that *in any room containing 100 people, 99 of them each think that they are the only one who doesn't have his or her act together.*

In the face of this I decided to take my role seriously and do my best to be helpful, accepting the risk of the public arena that some people will see me as an imposter, a blowhard, or a fool. I think I give a good lecture. I speak with conviction. I believe it is a sin to bore an audience. It happens that I majored in the dramatic arts in college and my training as an actor helps. I understand the nature of a performance. An audience doesn't hunger for *the truth* so much as for authenticity. They know the truth can be slippery. Their hopes and dreams are something else.

I believe that rhetoric is undervalued these days. My own generation had much to do with devaluing it back in the sixties, when all public talk seemed mendacious. Part of what I do these days is an attempt to resuscitate rhetoric as an honorable and worthy feature of public life in this country. I am sensible that rhetoric sometimes changes the world. It frightens me to be in possession of it.

As a writer, though, I see myself primarily as a prose artist, not as a retailer of Big Ideas. I think the success of *The Geography of Nowhere* was due as much to the shapeliness of its prose as to any ideas it contained. Sooner or later, I intend to leave this subject behind. I have other fish to fry.

It is mid-September as I write, one of the last days before summer's end, a time of year that feels analogous to the position of my little life in its orbit around a greater wheel of time. In a while, I will gather up my French easel and a newly stretched canvas and head over to the Hudson River in my pickup truck with the canoe on the rack. The state is rebuilding the highway bridge at Schuylerville and there are several bright red work barges with cranes moored under it. I want to record the scene while all that equipment is still there. I spend most of my free time painting out in the open air. It is very important to me and I am very serious about it. When I am outside painting, I feel most in love with this world. I have a notion that writers burn out in their sixties but painters keep going to ninety or more. I love the idea of Monet pottering around the garden in his old age.

I feel an obligation to paint the landscape of my time, so I often paint highways with cars on them and even roadside monstrosities like McDonald's and Kmart. I especially like the contrast between the artificial light of their electric signs and the natural twilight in the background. The result on canvas is oddly beautiful, but of course what's left out is the roaring traffic and the smell of exhaust fumes. A few years ago I was painting a McDonald's with my easel set in the bark mulch bed of a Burger King parking lot across the highway. I was well under way when the manager bustled out and barked, "That ain't allowed here!" I dared him to call the police. I would have loved nothing better than to be arrested for painting. I assured him that the ensuing court case would be great publicity for Burger King, too. Eventually he skulked back inside to his Fry-o-laters, and that was the end of it. Today, I'll happily forgo that kind of amusement. I'm after tranquillity, solitude, and fresh air. So it's off to the river on the most beautiful day of the year. Yippee!

This is the essence of my private life. This is what I live for. I want to paint some more pictures and write some more books. I want to make my girl happy. I want to throw more Christmas parties and put on more Saturday night feeds. I want to learn how to read sheet music. I want to keep running with the dogs. I want to live in a nice town in a civilized country. I want to remain grateful for having been born.

INDEX

Page numbers in *italics* refer to illustrations.

ABOUT THE AUTHOR

James Howard Kunstler is the author of *The Geography of Nowhere*, eight novels, and several books for children. He has worked as a newspaper reporter and an editor for *Rolling Stone* and . is a frequent contributor to *The New York Times Magazine*. He lives in a classic Main Street town in upstate New York.